MW01627827
النادي العربي

THE DĪWĀN OF IMAM AL-SHĀFI'Ī رحمه الله

A TRANSLATION OF THE ILLUSTRIOUS IMAM'S ANTHOLOGY OF POETRY

بسم الله الرحمن الرحيم

THE DĪWĀN OF IMAM AL-SHĀFI'Ī رحمه الله

A TRANSLATION OF THE ILLUSTRIOUS IMAM'S ANTHOLOGY OF POETRY

Translated By

AKHTAR ALY
MUHAMMAD SALOOJEE
SYED AHAZ BIN ATIF

REVISED SECOND EDITION:

ISBN: 978-0-7961-2129-5

TITLE:
The Diwan of Imam al-Shafi'i ﷺ

AUTHOR:
Imam al-Shafi'i ﷺ

TRANSLATORS:
Akhtar Aly, Muhammad Saloojee & Syed Ahaz bin Atif

EDITION:
Revised Second Edition October 2023

DESIGNED BY:
Muhammad Sift Elahi (Art Director)
V3 STUDIO - Lahore
+92 301 84 27 281

PUBLISHED BY:
An-Nadi Al-Arabi
Darul Uloom Zakariyya

Plot 8, 9, 10, Stand 52 Golden Highway,
Zakariyya Park Johannesburg, 1813
South Africa

Mobile / Whatsapp: **(+27) 81-327-5665**

Email: **nadi.duz@gmail.com**

DISTRIBUTORS FOR INDIA:

Darul Ma'arif
Deoband, Saharanpur (India)
Mobile: **+91-9634 460 409**
WhatsApp: **+91-9760 312 986**

Transliteration Key

أ ؤ ئ	ʾ
ا	a
ب	b
ت	t
ث	th
ج	j
ح	ḥ
خ	kh
د	d
ذ	dh
ر	r
ز	z
س	s
ش	sh
ص	ṣ

ض	ḍ
ط	ṭ
ظ	ẓ
ع	ʿ
غ	gh
ف	f
ق	q
ك	k
ل	l
م	m
ن	n
هـ	h
و	w
ي	y

Extended Vowels:

ā: ا (*alif* with a *fatḥah* before it)

ī: ي (*yā* with a *kasrah* before it)

ū: و (*wāw* with a *ḍammah* before it)

Salutations:

ﷻ: *Subḥānahu wa ta'ālā*—used following the mention of Allah, translated as: "Glorified and exalted be He."

ﷺ: *Ṣallallāhu 'alayhi wa sallam*—used following the mention of the Prophet Muhammad, translated as: "May Allah bless him and grant him peace."

رحمه الله: *Raḥimahullāh*—used following the mention of a deceased Muslim, translated as: "May Allah have mercy on him."

Contents

Foreword to the First Edition

By the respected Mawlānā Shabbir Ahmad Saloojee
(May Allah preserve him)
(Principal of Darul Uloom Zakariyya)

Indeed, poetry that is free of misleading exaggeration is encouraged in Islam. It has been reported that Rasūlullāh would occasionally ask some of his Companions to recite poetry, such as the monotheistic poetry of Umayyah b. Ṣalt, for instance. In fact, Rasūlullāh himself recited the following couplet of Umayyah:

O Allah! If You forgive [then it is not astonishing for indeed] Your forgiveness is all encompassing. Which of Your slaves does not sin?

Imam Bukhārī has quoted in his *al-Adab al-Mufrad* as well as Imam Tirmidhī in his *Sunan* the narration of Miqdān b. Shurayḥ that Shurayḥ had asked 'Āishah: "Did Rasūlullāh ever recite poetry?" 'Āishah replied in the affirmative and mentioned that Rasūlullāh used to recite the following couplet of Ṭarafah b. al-Ba'd:

The passing of the days will make apparent for you
that which you are unaware of
And that person will convey information to you
whom you had not granted anything

Similarly, Rasūlullāh ﷺ has stated in a narration mentioned in Ṣaḥīḥ Muslim that of all the pre-Islamic poetical literature, Labīd's poetry has the most truth in it, such as the following couplet:

Indeed! Everything besides Allah is worthless
And every bounty will surely perish

Though Rasūlullāh ﷺ was not a poet himself, his blessed tongue would occasionally utter rhythmical sentences that resembled poetry. Such words encapsulated the message of the prophetic mission, which proved effective in provoking the enthusiastic spirit of the Ṣaḥābah ﷺ due to their timely utterance. A classic example of this is the following words recited by Rasūlullāh ﷺ during the Battle of Hunayn:

There is no falsehood in the fact that I am a Prophet
I am the son of 'Abd al-Muṭṭalib

Similarly, on the occasion of the Battle of Khandaq, Rasūlullāh ﷺ —himself covered in dust—carried a handful of sand and uttered the words:

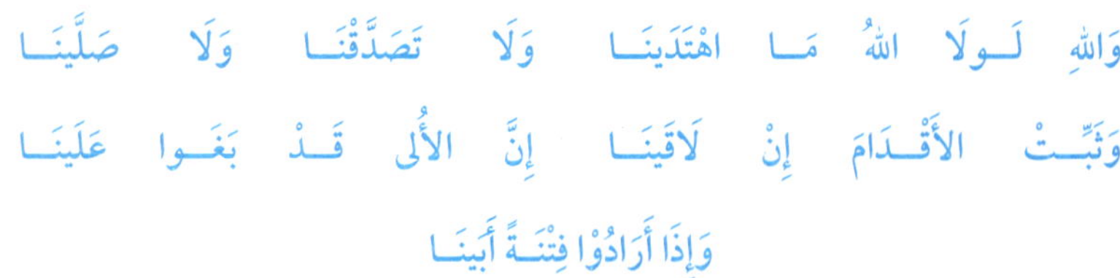

By Allah, had it not been for [the grace of] Allah, we would not have been guided
Nor would we have given charity nor performed salah

Keep us steadfast in the heat of battle
For indeed these people have oppressed us

When they intend [to afflict us with] a tribulation, we will certainly reject it

The blessed statements of Rasūlullāh ﷺ were characterized by refined diction, unique style, concision, perfect word choice, and the potential to touch hearts. Hence, they are considered the most perfect and eloquent speech after the Holy Qur'an. Testament to this fact is how his blessed invocations and sermons never failed to captivate even the hardest of hearts.

It should be borne in mind that the type of poets who have been condemned in the verse of the Holy Qur'an "As for the poets, they are followed by the straying people," (26:224) are those who, having polluted their poetry with falsehood, transgressed the limits in exaggerations and assimilations. They utilized their poetic talents for personal gain and ulterior motives, which, at times, were for the sinister purpose of condemning Islam and deriding Rasūlullāh ﷺ. As mentioned in *al-Tafsīr al-Maẓharī*, most commentators are of the view that those very poets are implied who composed inappropriate and disrespectful verses regarding Rasūlullāh ﷺ. Combating such poetry was of paramount importance to defend

Islam from sacrilegious propaganda. It is for this reason that Rasūlullāh ﷺ commanded Ḥassān b. Thābit to respond to them in poetic form. This form of rhetorical defense was considered a fundamental duty and a form of jihad.

It has been narrated that when the aforementioned verse was revealed, the poets of Islam: Ḥassān b. Thābit, ʻAbdullāh b. Rawāhah, and Kaʻb b. Mālik came crying to Rasūlullāh ﷺ ar said, "O Rasūlullāh ﷺ! We are doomed as this verse refers to poe and we compose poetry." Rasūlullāh ﷺ consoled them, sayin "You are indeed from the class of poets whom Allah has excluded from the admonition at the end of the verse" (i.e., those poets who believe, do righteous deeds, and remember Allah abundantly.)

Furthermore, those poets whose poetry does not contain the mentioned negative elements and instead is filled with eloquent meanings, wisdom, and life experiences are excluded from those poets whom the Holy Qur'an condemns. Moreover, if that poetry contains religious elements, then it actually constitutes an act of worship. In fact, there are *aḥādīth* and statements of Ṣaḥābah which encourage the learning of poetry and deriving benefit from it.

As for Imam al-Shāfiʻī, he is one of those outstanding personalities whom Allah had chosen for colossal and perpetuating services to this great *Dīn*. He had dedicated his entire life, firstly, to understand the divine directives of the pristine Shariah, and secondly, to impart that understanding to the Ummah at large.

Amongst his distinguishable characteristics was his strong grasp and mastery of the Arabic language. He spent a considerable period of time residing amongst the most eloquent of Arab tribes—the Banū Ḥudhayl—to master linguistics, dialectology, and rhetoric and to immerse himself in the study of Arab culture and history. His retention was so phenomenal that he committed countless poems and odes of the most famed Arab poets to memory, including ten thousand couplets of the Banū Hudhayl alone. This memorization was coupled with a complete comprehension of each poem's meaning and grammatical connotations. In this manner, he had developed a deep-rooted affinity with the Arabic language as a whole.

Despite his unparalleled aptitude in the Arabic language, Allah ﷻ had selected Imam al-Shāfiʿī ﵀ for the service of jurisprudence, and thus, he served in his capacity as a *mujtahid* and a *faqīh*. As a result, he could not dedicate himself completely to the field of poetry. Had he allotted all his efforts toward poetry, he would undoubtedly have become one of the most celebrated and accomplished poets the world had ever seen. Imam al-Shāfiʿī ﵀ himself states:

فَلَـولَا الشِّـعْرُ بِالعُلَـمَاءِ يُـزْرِي لَكُنْـتُ اليَـوْمَ أَشْـعَرَ مِـنْ لَبِيـدِ

If [devoting oneself to] poetry did not bring disgrace to the 'Ulamā'
Today I would have been a better poet than Labīd

Due to his commitment to the field of Islamic jurisprudence, we find that the poetry of Imam al-Shāfiʿī ﵀ consists primarily of concise couplets rather than prolonged lyrical odes. In fact, he deemed overindulgence in poetry unbefitting an Islamic scholar. He once remarked: "I acquired the knowledge of Arabic grammar, literary skills, and poetry as a means of assisting me in understanding Islam rather than making it my [sole] objective."

Even though Imam al-Shāfiʿī ﵀ did not pride himself on poetry being his specialty, his poetical talent was celebrated even among scholarly circles. His poetry is generally characterized by simple diction, lucid style, and comprehensive parables. His couplets do not present flowery exaggerations and imaginary scenarios but rather touch on conditions encountered in daily life and discuss basic concepts of Islam and human character. It is for this reason that his words cannot be included amongst the ornate fields of poetry in which flowers normally bloom. Instead, Imam al-Shāfiʿī's ﷺ proficiency and expertise in literary skills can be likened to growing beautiful roses and flowers in an entirely dry and barren land in a manner that pales the general style and standard of poetry into insignificance.

Throughout his life, Imam al-Shāfiʿī ﷺ had many experiences that significantly impacted him and shaped his worldview and perspective. Though he had many well-wishers who admired him and his work, he also had enemies who harbored resentment toward him. As a result, various accusations were leveled at him, which even resulted, on one occasion, in him being taken to the king of the time like a criminal in chains and fetters. He tolerated all of this for the sake of Islam. On the other hand, he was honored with such acceptance that thousands of people thronged around him just to have the honor of meeting him, while his contemporaries amongst the scholars were restless to have the honor of sitting at his feet as students with the utmost humility. He was not merely a secluded scholar but well-informed and aware of the individual and collective evils rampant in society. He had a sincere desire to eradicate these evils, which is evident in his poetry. Therefore, his poetry, as opposed to merely containing literary proficiency, was motivated by a desire to revive Islamic character. The subject matter of his poetry was composed out of concern, foresight, and a desire to advise. Each poem is capable of

being a topic of discussion on its own. It is advisable for students, both junior and senior alike, to commit the distinguished Imam's poetry to memory as any sensible individual will acknowledge that a few couplets that contain a comprehensive message are far more effective in effectuating change in the hearts of the reader and listener than lengthy, inundating expositions.

It gives me great joy and pleasure to witness the fruition of the efforts of the members An-Nadi Al-Arabi—the academic platform of our respected colleague Mawlānā Abdul Quddoos Qasmi Nayranwi (may Allah ﷻ preserve him), who is the student of the great scholar of Islam, Mawlānā Waḥīd al-Zamān Qāsmī Kayrānwī ﷺ.

It was Mawlānā Abdul Quddoos who had assigned the momentous task of translating the Dīwān of Imam al-Shāfi'ī ﷺ into English to the members of his An-Nadi Al-Arabi, namely Mawlānā Muhammad Saloojee and Mawlānā Akhtar Aly. The responsibility of translating this academic treasure into English with the necessary background in literary skills is the first attempt at translation by these young scholars and, therefore should be greatly commended. I, therefore, congratulate them both from the bottom of my heart for rendering this difficult and sensitive task with the greatest zeal, enthusiasm, and diligence. In completing this endeavor, they have exposed the English reader to the benefits of the valuable poetry, academic aptitude, wisdom, advice, and admonitions of Imam al-Shāfi'ī ﷺ.

We hope that the respectable scholarly class will look at this work with an eye of acceptance and that enthusiasts will derive maximum benefit from it. The present generation of students in Islamic madrasahs should especially utilize it as a means of beautifying their speeches and writings, as well as broadening their horizons in thought and reflection.

Finally, we beseech Allah ﷻ to bless the translators in their knowledge, practical acts of worship, research, and translations, and may He grant them success therein. May Allah ﷻ always accept them for the sincere and effective service of this great and pristine *Dīn* and bestow His pleasure and guidance upon them. May Allah ﷻ accept this noble effort, reward Imam al-Shāfi'ī ﵀, the two translators, their assistants, and their respectable teachers abundantly, and accept the works of An-Nadi Al-Arabi and grant them special guidance. *Āmīn*.

Foreword to the Second Edition

By the respected Mawlānā Abdul Quddoos Qasmi Nayranwi
(May Allah preserve him)
(Director of An-Nadi Al-Arabi)

Before the reader is the second edition of the English translation of the Dīwān of Imam al-Shafiʿī. This edition is distinctive from the previous edition in that it includes additional poems attributed to the Imam, along with a revised and improved translation of the previously included poems.

About 13 years ago, the thought came to my mind that there was a need for students to benefit from the exceptional Dīwān of Imam al-Shafiʿī. I assigned this project to two students affiliated with An-Nadi Al-Arabi—who are now distinguished graduates of Darul Uloom Zakariyya—namely Mawlānā Akhtar Aly and Mawlānā Muhammad Saloojee. They completed this project with admirable fervor and exceptional skill despite the limited amount of time they had at their disposal.

Despite their appreciative efforts, from that time, I felt that the numerous editions of the Dīwān could be collected, and all the additional poems found in them could then be added to the original book. It would also be an opportune time to revise the original translation and make necessary improvements. For this purpose, I endeavored to collect all the various editions of the Dīwān I could find. Over the years, many students at the Darul Uloom involved in An-Nadi Al-Arabi were suitable candidates to take on this task. Yet, due to other projects that required assistance, I was unable to assign it to any of them. Thus, the project remained unattended for many years until Mawlānā Ahaz Bin Atif arrived at Darul Uloom Zakariyya. In our first meeting, he did not hesitate to express his desire and enthusiasm to become involved in An-Nadi Al-Arabi, and he explained that his teacher, Mawlānā Asadullah Khan, had counseled him to do so upon his arrival at the Darul Uloom. Upon hearing Mawlānā Asadullah's name, I immediately felt a sense of approval as I knew that a student who studied under Mawlānā Asadullah and was reared by him would undoubtedly possess the necessary skills and discipline to undertake any task assigned to him. That is because, during his own time studying at the Darul Uloom, Mawlānā Asadullah was an extremely dedicated and capable student and was actively involved in An-Nadi Al-Arabi. During that time, he worked with a Mawlānā Abdullah Jaber on translating *al-Tarāwīḥ Akthar min Alf 'Ām fī Masjid al-Nabī* (Tarāwīḥ As Performed for Over One Thousand Years in Al-Masjid Al-Nabawī) from Arabic into English which was published shortly thereafter.

As time went on, my presumptions regarding Mawlānā Ahaz were proven correct—he spent his time in academic pursuits with diligence and vigor, and alongside that, he assisted those involved in translation at An-Nadi Al-Arabi. Thus, I specifically assigned him the project of the Dīwān, and so he went through the various editions I had with me and collected those poems of the Imam which were authentically narrated from him and then translated them. He also took the effort to carefully go over and revise the translations of the original poems. All throughout, he had the assistance of Mawlānā Saad Abdul Quddoos Qasmi, who expressed his satisfaction with the work upon its completion. Thus, it is hoped that the honorable readers will be appreciative of this work and that students, in particular, may derive benefit from it.

May Allah ﷻ accept the efforts of these students, and may He grant them the ability to continue to pursue religious and academic endeavors in the future. May He grant them ease in all their matters, and may He grant them the success of this world and the Hereafter. *Āmīn.*

Translators' Preface to the First Edition

By Mawlānā Akhtar Aly and Mawlānā Muhammad Saloojee

The book before you is the English translation of the respected Imam al-Shafi'ī's ﷺ collection of poetry. The respected Imam holds a dignified position amongst the scholars of his time for his jurisprudential knowledge and *ijtihād*, intelligence and perception, understanding and discernment, eloquence and rhetoric, self-sufficiency and generosity, and especially his asceticism and worship.

The brief yet comprehensive foreword included here by the respected principal of Darul Uloom Zakariyya, Mawlānā Shabbir Ahmad Saloojee, highlights the personality, qualities, and perfection of the respected Imam. Therefore, there remains no need further elaborate on the topic.

About five years ago, the respected Mawlānā Shabbir, through his God-given insight, while keeping in mind the intellectual, religious, literary, and Islamic proselyting needs of the present time, established in Darul Uloom Zakariyya a department known as An-Nadi Al-Arabi, so that students may associate themselves with it and bring to life their natural oratory, writing, and translation skills. He handed the reigns of this department over to the respected Mawlānā Abdul Quddoos, which resulted in many translations and other works being produced, some of which were included in the syllabus and earned acclaim from many Arab and Subcontinent scholars. In light of this, the respected Mawlānā Abdul Quddoos selected the Dīwān (poetic anthology) of Imam al-Shafi'ī ﷺ to be translated into English and also provided the necessary guidance in this regard. After the completion of the translation, the task of editing the translation was handed over to one of the lecturers in this institute, who painstakingly and with full dedication completed this task and also provided many important guidelines. May Allah ﷻ reward him and all the other respected teachers, increase them in the vastness of their knowledge, and bless them in their health and life. *Āmīn.*

It should be noted that this book is our first effort in the line of translation, and undoubtedly, if the grace of our Almighty Allah ﷻ and the guidance and encouragement of our respected teachers were not with us, we would never have been able to present this effort to our respected readers.

We beseech our almighty Allah ﷻ to grant unlimited blessings to our alma mater, Darul Uloom Zakariyya, and to keep our teachers, especially the respected Mawlānā Shabbir Ahmad, in our midst for many years to come and keep them safely in His protection with health and goodness. *Āmīn.*

Translator's Preface to the Second Edition

By Syed Ahaz B. Atif

In June of 2018, I came to Darul Uloom Zakariyya to enter the fifth year of its rigorous seven-year *'ālimiyyah* program. Despite having not stepped foot in the institute before, I did not feel estranged from the environment at all. This was largely due to the fact that my respected teacher Mawlānā Asadullah Khan—a graduate of the Darul Uloom and with whom I studied my initial four years—had time and again descriptively recounted to me his stay at the Darul Uloom when reminiscing over his student years there. After completing the initial four years of my *'ālimiyyah* studies with him, he expressed his desire that I take the opportunity to sit in the presence of the esteemed teachers at the same institute that he was fortunate to benefit from and encouraged me to pursue higher education at his alma mater. He had particularly advised that I join An-Nadi Al-Arabi, the Arabic department at the Darul Uloom, under the supervision of Mawlānā Abdul Quddoos Qasmi, a lecturer at the institute (May Allah ﷻ preserve him). In fact, Mawlānā Asadullah Khan himself had participated in the activities of An-Nadi Al-Arabi and had translated *al-Tarāwīḥ Akthar min Alf 'Ām fī Masjid al-Nabī* (Tarāwīḥ As Performed for Over One Thousand Years in

Al-Masjid Al-Nabawī) from Arabic into English. Thus, adhering to his sincere advice, from the beginning of my time at Darul Uloom Zakariyya till now, I have kept a close connection with An-Nadi Al-Arabi, and it is the fruit of that connection that I am now humbly presenting to the readers.

The Dīwān of Imam al-Shāfi'ī was originally translated by two graduates of Darul Uloom Zakariyya, Mawlānā Muhammad Saloojee and Mawlānā Akhtar Aly, in 2011. Their translation gained great acceptance, especially amongst the students of the Darul Uloom, who, since its original publication, have continued to use its poems and their respective translations to decorate their various speeches and writings.

Some years later, my dear and respected teacher Mawlānā Abdul Quddoos Qasmi (May Allah preserve him) felt that the value of the Dīwān could be increased by collecting the various editions of the Dīwān in Arabic and adding and translating poems attributed to the Imam that were not previously included. Additionally, he felt that it would serve as an opportunity to revise and beautify the original translation. He tasked me with this daunting project during my first year of study at the Darul Uloom. I did not possess such proficiency in Arabic nor the necessary skills and level of knowledge to take upon the nearly insurmountable task of translating the poetical masterpiece that is the Dīwān of Imam al-Shāfi'ī, but under the instruction and guidance of teachers and mentors who I am indebted to, I tirelessly worked to improve my Arabic in attempt to do justice to the translation. Although my progress was slow during the initial phases of the project—largely due to the daily coursework and regimented schedule—I would arduously spend my weekends and holidays and whatever free time I could find to work on the project until, by my seventh and final year of the program, the project had come to completion by the grace of Allah ﷻ.

Regarding my contribution to this work, I firstly correlated the Arabic text of the poems in the first edition with Dr. Mujāhid Muṣṭafā Bahjat's *Dīwān al-Shāfi'ī* published by Dar al-Qalam-Dimashq as well as with Dr. Imīl Badī' Ya'qūb's *Dīwān al-Imām al-Shāfi'ī* published by Dar al-Kitāb al-'Arabī-Beirut. I then edited the English of the first edition while referring to prior English and Urdu translations. I then added 53 poems authentically narrated from the Imam, which I came across in other editions of the Dīwān and then translated them.[1] Afterward, I confirmed all these translations with Mawlānā Saad Qasmi, and whichever doubts and questions we had, we had them resolved by my teacher Mawlānā Abdul Quddoos Qasmi and other professors in the language. Within the poems themselves, I placed in brackets words that are generally understood in Arabic but not so in English so that the translation could be read smoothly, as well as words that clarify the intended meanings of the verses. I also placed footnotes, wherever needed, to explain any nuances found in the poems. Then, I rearranged the poems to a more suitable arrangement based on length and topic, and I wrote short introductory paragraphs for each poem to facilitate understanding the message behind it as well as the lessons that can be derived from it. I compiled an index of the major themes and topics across the poems to facilitate finding a poem for a specific topic. Finally, I wrote a short biography of the Imam, referring to and referencing original sources as much as possible.

1 All the poems from the first edition were kept despite doubts in attribution so as to preserve the work of the original translators. It should be noted that Imam al-Shāfi'ī ﷺ did not compose all of the poems in this anthology. Rather, some of the poems were composed by others and Imam al-Shāfi'ī ﷺ quoted them in various situations. For details on the sourcing of the poems, I refer the respected reader to the two sources I mentioned above.

I did not attempt to render the Arabic, i.e., make the translation rhyme, and instead tried to keep true to the original Arabic as much as possible. This was so that beginner students of the Arabic language (who are the primary audience of this work) may be able to follow and appreciate the Arabic of the poetry through the medium of English.

I humbly present this work, knowing that others more adept in the Arabic language than I may find errors and faults in it. It is my hope that they will present their corrections and suggestions so that the translation can become one of a greater standard, *Inshā' Allah*.

I beseech Allah ﷻ to accept this work from me. I ask that He allows students and the general public alike to benefit from this work. I pray that He allows this work to be a means of elevating the status of Imam al-Shāfi'ī ﷺ in the hearts of believers. *Āmīn.*

Acknowledgments

I cannot begin except by praising and thanking my Lord and Creator, who granted me the strength and ability to take upon this project and who allowed it to come to fruition. Whatever gratitude I show to Him can never be equivalent to His many favors upon me. Thereafter, I am grateful to my loving parents and grandparents, who supported me in this endeavor with their supplications and encouragement.

My gratitude goes to my dear and respected teacher, Mawlānā Abdul Quddoos Qasmi, who took me under his wing and guided and nurtured me in my studies, especially in the Arabic language. I am grateful to him for accepting me in his An-Nadi Al-Arabi and for tasking me with this project and providing me with the necessary resources for it. I am indebted to my mentor and friend Mawlānā Saad Qasmi who extensively reviewed the work and provided me with valuable feedback and insight.

I thank all my family, friends, and colleagues who have contributed to the editing of this work. I also thank Mufti Mahmud ul Hasan for editing the Arabic text of the poems. I am grateful to my predecessors, Mawlānā Muhammad Saloojee and Mawlānā Akhtar Aly, for paving the way for me with their commendable original translation. May Allah reward the aforementioned individuals with the best of rewards in this life and the next. *Āmīn.*

A Brief Biography of Imam al-Shāfi'ī

Name and Lineage

His full name, with his lineage, is Abū 'Abdillāh, Muḥammad b. Idrīs b. al-'Abbās b. 'Uthmān b. Shāfi' b. al-Sā'ib b. 'Ubayd b. 'Abd Yazīd b. Hāshim b. al-Muṭṭalib b. 'Abd Manāf al-Qurashī al-Muṭṭalibī al-Hāshimī.[1] His lineage links with that of the Messenger of Allah at 'Abd Manāf.

Amongst the people in his lineage, his great great great grandfather Shāfi' met the Prophet in his youth and Shāfi's father al-Sāib took part in the battle of Badr on the side of the disbelievers. He was captured by the Muslims and was later freed for ransom. Upon being freed, he accepted Islam.[2]

Birth and Childhood

His mother was Fāṭimah bint 'Abdillāh—the great-granddaughter of Ḥusayn. In Rajab 150 A.H., she gave birth to a son whom she named Muḥammad. This was in Gaza, in present-day Palestine. Sadly, the Imam became an orphan at an early age, so his mother took him at the age of two from Gaza

1 al-Khaṭīb al-Baghdādī, *Tārīkh Baghdād* (Beirut: Dār al-Gharb al-Islāmī, 2002), 2:394.
2 Ibn Ḥajar al-'Asqalānī, *al-Iṣābah fī Tamyīz al-Ṣaḥābah* (Beirut: Dar al-Jīl, 1992), 3:23.

to Makkah so that his relatives could look after him. During his childhood in Makkah, his attention was divided into mainly two things: seeking knowledge and archery. He completely engrossed himself in acquiring knowledge, studying all day and night, and likewise, he became so skilled in archery that he was able to make perfect shots in ten out of ten rounds.[1]

Early Studies

When he was old enough, he began to attend a small class, b his mother did not have enough to pay the fees, so the teache. kindly accepted to teach him for free. In spite of his impoverished condition, he excelled in the class and became such that he would teach the other students in place of the teacher, thereby lessening the teacher's burden. It was with this zeal that he completed memorizing the Holy Qur'an at the early age of seven, and that too in such a way that he knew the meaning and intent of the verses.[2]

After this, he went to the desert to live amongst the various Arab tribes, such as the Banū Ḥudhayl, who were considered one of the most eloquent of the Arab tribes. He lived with them for about twenty years, gaining mastery in poetry, literature, and Arab history.[3] It was through this experience of his that authorities in the language would later attest to his proficiency and would even refer to him.

While still in Makkah, Imam al-Shāfiʿī ﷺ learned jurisprudence and hadith at the feet of the luminaries present in Makkah, such as the Mufti of Makkah Muslim b. Khālid al-Zanjī ﷺ (d. 181 A.H.), his

1 al-Baghdādī, *Tārīkh Baghdād*, 2:397.
2 Ibid., 2:401.
3 Ibid.

paternal uncle Muḥammad b. ʿAlī b. Shāfiʿ, the *muḥaddith* Sufyān b. ʿUyaynah (d. 198 A.H.), and others.[1] When he reached the age of 15, Muslim b. Khālid Zanjī gave him permission to issue legal verdicts in Makkah.[2]

With Imam Mālik

When Imam al-Shāfiʿī was around 20 years old, the fame of Imam Mālik b. Anas (d. 179 A.H.) and his *Muwatta*' had become widespread, and so Imam al-Shāfiʿī went to Madinah Munawwarah upon the advice of an elder to further his knowledge of hadith and jurisprudence from Imam Mālik. But before he left for Madinah, he borrowed someone's copy of the *Muwatta*' and memorized the whole thing in nine nights. Then, he arrived in Madinah and sought permission from Imam Mālik to sit in his lessons. Imam Mālik had great foresight and told Imam al-Shāfiʿī, "O Muḥammad, be conscious of Allah and avoid sin, as you will soon have a great status." After giving him permission to sit in his lessons, he told Imam al-Shāfiʿī to bring someone to recite the *Muwatta*' for him. Instead, he recited the book from memory, and his recitation pleased Imam Mālik. In just a few days, Imam al-Shāfiʿī had finished reciting the *Muwatta*', but in spite of that, he remained with Imam Mālik in Madinah until his demise in 179 A.H.[3]

With Imam Muhammad

After working for a brief time as an administrator for the Abbasid Caliphate in Yemen, Imam al-Shāfiʿī travelled to Baghdad around 185 A.H. to learn from Imam Muḥammad b.

1 Ibid., 2:393.
2 Ibid., 2:404.
3 Shihāb al-Dīn al-Ḥamawī, *Muʿjam al-Udabā'* (Beiruit: Dār al-Gharb al-Islāmī, 1993), 6:2395-2396.

Ḥasan al-Shaybānī (d. 189 A.H.), the illustrious student of Imam Abū Ḥanīfah (d. 150 A.H.). He bought all of Imam Muḥammad's books and learned them all with him. In spite of openly stating that he was a follower of Imam Mālik, Imam al-Shāfi'ī greatly praised and respected Imam Muḥammad, and he likewise loved him, honored him, and even financially supported him. Imam Muḥammad would cancel his appointments with the *khalīfah* just to sit with Imam al-Shāfi'ī, and they would often debate about their different jurisprudential approaches.[1]

Return To Baghdad

After returning to Makkah and teaching there for about nine years, Imam al-Shāfi'ī then returned to Baghdad in 195 A.H. The people there were greatly impressed by his knowledge such that when he arrived, there were around fifty circles of learning in the Jami' Masjid, and after he started teaching there, all of them slowly dwindled away until only his circle of learning was left.[2] It was during this time that his new jurisprudential methodology spread in Iraq. Also, during this time, Imam Aḥmad b. Ḥanbal (d. 241 A.H.) met the Imam and benefitted from his company. He was present for all of the Imam's lessons and would encourage others not to lose the chance to benefit from him.[3]

Leaving For Egypt

A little while into the Imam's stay in Baghdad, the Abbasid *khalīfah* Ma'mūn appointed al-'Abbās b. Mūsā as the governor of Egypt. Imam al-Shāfi'ī decided to go to Egypt with him. In 200 A.H., the Imam arrived in Egypt alongside the new

1 Muḥammad Abū Zuhrah, *al-Shāfi'ī: Ḥayātuhu wa 'Aṣruhu - Ārā'hu wa Fiqhuhu* (Cairo: Dār al-Fikr al-'Arabī, 1948), 23-25.

2 al-Baghdādī, *Tārīkh Baghdād*, 2:409.

3 Ibid., 406 and 409.

4 al-Ḥamawī, *Mu'jam al-Udabā'*, 6:2414-2415.

governor.[4] The Imam gained many more students here, and his jurisprudential methodology then spread across all of Egypt and the other nearby lands.

Demise

After a period of about four years spent dedicated to scholarly pursuits in Egypt, the Imam's previous ailment of piles became severe such that his blood kept flowing, and he became weak.[1] This continued for some time until the 29th of Rajab, 204 A.H., on the eve of Friday after 'Ishā' in which his soul departed for the hereafter at the age of 54.[2] He was buried near Mount al-Muqattam in Cairo, Egypt, and a mausoleum built on the site in 608 A.H. remains till today.

Legacy

His most famous students of Baghdad are: Ḥasan b. Muḥammad al-Zaʿfarānī ﷺ (d. 260 A.H.), Imam Aḥmad b. Ḥanbal al-Shaybānī ﷺ (d. 241 A.H.), Abū Thawr Ibrāhīm b. Khālid al-Kalbī ﷺ (d. 240 A.H.), and Ḥusayn b. 'Alī al-Karābīsī ﷺ (d. 256 A.H.).[3]

His most famous students of Egypt are: Ismāʿīl b. Yaḥyā al-Muzanī ﷺ (d. 264 A.H.), Rabīʿ b. Sulaymān al-Jīzī ﷺ (d. 256 A.H.), Rabīʿ b. Sulaymān al-Murādī ﷺ (d. 270 A.H.), Ḥarmalah b. Yaḥyā al-Tujaynī ﷺ (d. 266 A.H.), Muḥammad b. 'Abdillāh b. 'Abd al-Ḥakam ﷺ (d. 268 A.H.), and Yūsuf b. Yaḥyā al-Buwayṭī ﷺ (d. 231 A.H.).[4]

The Imam is said to have written over 100 hundred books, the

1 Ibn Ḥajar al-'Asqalānī, *Tawālī al-Ta'sīs li M'ālī Muḥammad Ibn Idrīs* (Beirut: Dār al-Kutub al-'Ilmiyyah, 1986) 177.

2 Ibn Abī Ḥātim al-Rāzī, *Ādāb al-Shāfiʿī wa Manāqibuhu* (Beirut: Dār al-Kutub al-'Ilmiyyah, 1993),74-75.

3 Abū Zuhrah, *al-Shāfiʿī: Ḥayātuhu wa 'Aṣruhu - Ārā'hu wa Fiqhuhu*,147-148.

4 Ibid., 149-152.

most famous of them being: *al-Risālah*, in which he laid down the principles of jurisprudence, and *al-Umm,* in which he expounded upon the details of his jurisprudential school.[1]

The Imam had two sons, one of them being Abū 'Uthmān Muḥammad, who served as the *qāḍī* of the Arabian Peninsula and later of the city of Ḥalab in Syria. He passed away in 240 A.H. and sadly, his progeny did not continue.[2] His other son was Abū al-Ḥasan Muḥammad, who passed away in 231 A.H. and whose progeny also did not continue.[3] The Imam also had one daughter by the name of Zaynab. She had a son by the name of Abū Muḥammad, who was said to have acquired the blessings of his grandfather.[4]

May Allah illuminate the grave of Imam al-Shāfi'ī, accept his unparalleled services for the service of *Dīn*, and allow people to continue to benefit from his works until the Last Day. *Āmīn.*

1 Ibid., 153.
2 Tāj al-Dīn al-Subkī, *Ṭabaqāt al-Shāfi'iyyah al-Kubrā* (Cairo: Dār Hajr li al-Ṭabā'ah wa al-Nashr wa al-Tawzī', 1992) 2:71-73.
3 Ibid.
4 Ibid., 2:186.

قافية الهمزة
The End-Rhyme of the Letter *Hamzah*

الرِّضَى بِقَضَاءِ اللّٰهِ ﷻ
Contentment with the Decree of Allah ﷻ

Although we face many hardships and trials in life, we must always remember that they are from Allah ﷻ and that they will soon come to pass. The worldly life is not meant to be one of ease and comfort for a Mu'min, as it is only a preparation for the Hereafter.

دَعِ الأَيَّامَ تَفْعَلُ مَاتَشَاءُ ١ وَطِبْ نَفْسًا إِذَا حَكَمَ القَضَاءُ
وَلَا تَجْزَعْ لِحَادِثَةِ اللَّيَالِي ٢ فَمَا لِحَوَادِثِ الدُّنْيَا بَقَاءُ
وَكُنْ رَجُلًا عَلَى الأَهْوَالِ جَلْدًا ٣ وَشِيمَتُكَ السَّمَاحَةُ وَالوَفَاءُ
وَإِنْ كَثُرَتْ عُيُوبُكَ فِي البَرَايَا ٤ وَسَرَّكَ أَن يَكُونَ لَهَا غِطَاءُ
تَسَتَّرْ بِالسَّخَاءِ فَكُلُّ عَيْبٍ ٥ يُغَطِّيهِ، كَمَا قِيلَ، السَّخَاءُ
وَلَا تُرِ لِلأَعَادِي قَطُّ ذُلًّا ٦ فَإِنَّ شَمَاتَةَ الأَعْدَا بَلَاءُ
وَلَا تَرْجُ السَّمَاحَةَ مِنْ بَخِيلٍ ٧ فَمَا فِي النَّارِ لِلظَّمْآنِ مَاءُ

وَرِزْقُـكَ لَيْـسَ يَنْقُصُـهُ التَّـأَنِّي ٨ وَلَيْـسَ يَزِيـدُ فِي الـرِّزْقِ العَنَـاءُ

وَلَا حُـزْنٌ يَـدُومُ وَلَا سُرُورٌ ٩ وَلَا بُـؤْسٌ عَلَيْـكَ وَلَا رَخَـاءُ

إِذَا مَـا كُنْـتَ ذَا قَلْـبٍ قَنُـوعٍ ١٠ فَأَنْـتَ وَمَالِـكُ الدُّنْيَـا سَـوَاءُ

وَمَـنْ نَزَلَـتْ بِسَـاحَتِهِ المَنَايَـا ١١ فَـلَا أَرْضٌ تَقِيـهِ وَلَا سَـمَاءُ

وَأَرْضُ اللهِ وَاسِـعَةٌ وَلَكِـنْ ١٢ إِذَا نَـزَلَ القَضَـا ضَـاقَ الفَضَـاءُ

دَعِ الأَيَّـامَ تَغْـدِرُ كُلَّ حِـينٍ ١٣ فَـمَا يُغْنِـي عَـنِ المَـوْتِ الـدَّوَاءُ

1. Let the [passing of the] days be, doing as it wishes, and be happy when the Divine Decree is passed.

2. Worry not about the calamities of the nights, as the calamities of the worldly life have no permanence.

3. Be strong and resilient in the face of hardships, and let your nature be that of generosity and loyalty.

4. If your faults are well-known amongst people and concealing them would please you,

5. Then conceal [them] with generosity, as generosity is said to cover all faults.

6. Never show [your] enemies any weakness, as the malicious joy of [one's] enemies is a calamity.

7. Do not expect generosity from a miser, as there is no water in the fire for the thirsty.

8. Deliberation [in acquiring provision] does not decrease your provision, nor does [enduring additional] hardship increase it.

9. Neither grief nor joy last forever, and [likewise] neither

suffering nor prosperity [last forever].

10. If you are one who has a content heart, then you and the king of the world are equal.

11. At whose courtyard death descends, neither the sky nor the earth can save him.

12. The land of Allah ﷻ is vast, but when the Divine Decree descends, the vastness constricts [and there is no escape].

13. Let the [passing of the] days [keep] deceiving, as no medicine is effective against death.

2

الصَّبْرُ عَلى فَقْدِ الأَحِبَّاءِ

Patience at the Loss of Loved Ones

Anyone granted a long life is bound to witness the loss of a beloved; patience is advised upon such a calamity, which is only worthy of one's enemies.

مَنْ يَتَمَنَّ العُمْرَ فَلْيَدَّرِعْ ١ صَبْرًا عَلَى فَقْدِ أَحِبَّائِهِ
وَمَنْ يُعَمَّرْ يَلْقَ فِي نَفْسِهِ ٢ مَا يَتَمَنَّاهُ لِأَعْدَائِهِ

1. One who wishes for a long life should don the armor of patience upon losing his loved ones.

2. One who is granted a long life will encounter that which he wishes for his enemies.[1]

1 Referring to the loss of loved ones.

قِيمَةُ الدُّعَاءِ

The Value of Supplication

Du'ā' is our private life-line to Allah ﷻ. Wherever, whenever, and however we are, we can supplicate to Allah ﷻ and He will hear us. But it is important to remember that He will fulfill that du'ā' whenever He wills; it is our duty to have patience and keep supplicating.

أَتَهْزَأُ بِالدُّعَاءِ وَ تَزْدَرِيهِ ١ وَمَا تَدْرِي بِمَا صَنَعَ الدُّعَاءُ

سِهَامُ اللَّيْلِ لَا تُخْطِي وَلَكِنْ ٢ لَهَا أَمَدٌ وَلِلْأَمَدِ انْقِضَاءُ

فَيُمْسِكُهَا إِذَا مَا شَاءَ رَبِّي ٣ وَيُرْسِلُهَا إِذَا نَفَذَ الْقَضَاءُ

1. Do you ridicule *du'ā'* and consider it to be insignificant? You are not aware of what *du'ā'* has achieved.

2. The arrow of [supplication at] night [1] does not miss, but rather it [is put on hold for] a [stipulated] time which will come to an end.

3. Then, my Lord withholds it [till] when He wishes, and He sends it forth when the Divine Decree is fulfilled.

جَهْدُ البَلَاءِ

An Arduous Trial

The difficulty of trials differs from person to person. One

1 Referring to the *du'ā'* made at *tahajjud* time.

should not consider the trial they are going through to be the most difficult trial possible.

أَكْثَرَ النَّاسُ فِي النِّسَاءِ وَقَالُوا ١ إِنَّ حُبَّ النِّسَاءِ جَهْدُ البَلَاءِ

لَيْسَ حُبُّ النِّسَاءِ جَهْدًا وَلَكِنْ ٢ قُرْبُ مَنْ لَا تُحِبُّ جَهْدُ البَلَاءِ

1. People crossed limits regarding women and said that love for women is a difficult trial.

2. Love for women is not difficult, but rather proximity with whom you despise is [truly] a difficult trial.

عُمْرُ الفَتَى

The Life of a Young Man

A very sensitive time during the life of man is when he is blossoming into adulthood. Thus, experiencing separation from his loved ones during this time is especially painful and heartbreaking.

وَاحَسْرَةً لِلْفَتَى سَاعَةً ١ يَعِيشُهَا بَعْدَ أَوِدَّائِهْ

عُمْرُ الفَتَى لَوْ كَانَ فِي كَفِّهِ ٢ رَمَى بِهِ بَعْدَ أَحِبَّائِهْ

1. How remorseful are those moments for a young man which he lives after [parting with] his loved ones!

2. If the life of a young man was completely in his control,[1] he would throw it away after [parting with] his loved ones.

[1] Literally: "in his palm."

قافية الباء
The End-Rhyme of the Letter *Bā'*

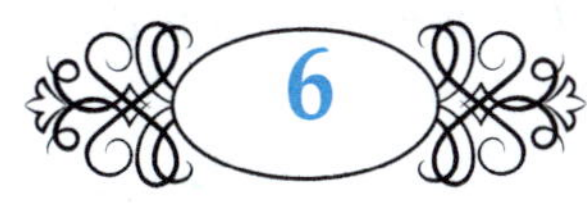

حُسْنُ الخُلُقِ وَالسَّعْيُ لِنَفْعِ الأَصْدِقَاءِ
Good Character and Striving to Benefit Friends

Responding to insults with insults only tarnishes one's character. Instead, one should beautify their character by putting the needs of others before their own.

إِذَا سَبَّنِي نَذْلٌ تَزَايَدْتُّ رِفْعَةً ١ وَمَا العَيْبُ إِلَّا أَنْ أَكُونَ مُسَابِبُهْ
وَلَوْ لَمْ تَكُنْ نَفْسِي عَلَيَّ عَزِيزَةً ٢ لَمَكَّنْتُهَا مِنْ كُلِّ نَذْلٍ تُحَارِبُهْ
وَلَوْ أَنَّنِي أَسْعَى لِنَفْعِي وَجَدْتَنِي ٣ كَثِيرَ التَّوَانِي لِلَّذِي أَنَا طَالِبُهْ
وَلَكِنَّنِي أَسْعَى لِأَنْفَعَ صَاحِبِي ٤ وَعَارٌ عَلَى الشَّبْعَانِ إِنْ جَاعَ صَاحِبُهْ

1. When a vile person insults me, I increase in rank. The only failing [on my part] would be that I insult him [back].

2. If my lower-self was not valuable to me, then I would have enabled it to fight against every vile person.

3. If I were to strive for my own benefit, you would find me exceedingly negligent in [acquiring] what I seek.

4. But rather, I strive to benefit my companion, and it is a disgrace for one who is full if his companion is hungry.

7

دُعَاءٌ طَيِّبٌ

A Nice Supplication

A supplication made for a brother in his absence as well as a supplication made for someone you do not know, are sincere supplications indeed.

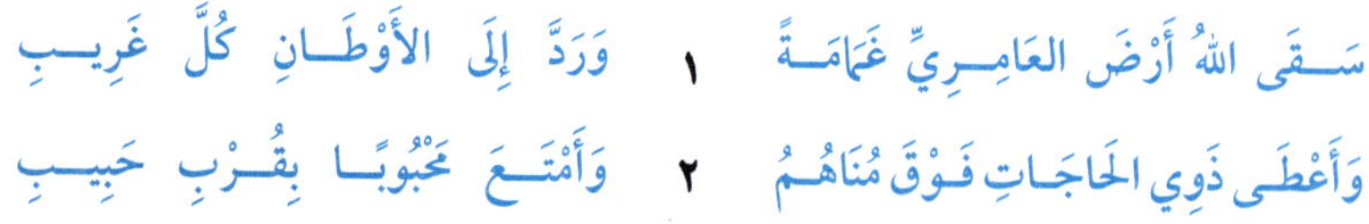

سَقَى اللهُ أَرْضَ العَامِرِيِّ غَمَامَةً ١ وَرَدَّ إِلَى الأَوْطَانِ كُلَّ غَرِيبِ

وَأَعْطَى ذَوِي الحَاجَاتِ فَوْقَ مُنَاهُمُ ٢ وَأَمْتَعَ مَحْبُوبًا بِقُرْبِ حَبِيبِ

1. May Allah water the land of al-'Āmirī with abundant rain and may He return every stranger to his [respective] homeland.

2. May He bestow upon those in need more than their desires and may He provide the lover with the closeness of the beloved.

8

الكُفْرُ بِالمُنَجِّمِينَ

Disbelieving in the Astrologers

Astrologers claim that the positions of the stars determine the fate of man, but as a Muslim believing in the divine decree of Allah ﷻ, accepting the predictions of astrologers would be tantamount to disbelief.

خَبِّرَا عَنِّي المُنَجِّمَ أَنِّي ١ كَافِرٌ بِالَّذِي قَضَتْهُ الكَوَاكِبْ

عَالِمًا أَنَّ مَا يَكُونُ وَمَا كَانَ ٢ قَضَاءٌ مِنَ المُهَيْمِنِ وَاجِبْ

1. Inform the astrologer on my behalf that I disbelieve in what the stars have decreed,

2. Knowing that what is to occur and what has already occurred is a definite decree from al-Muhaymin.[1]

9

حَقُّ الأديب

The Right of a Refined Person

One of the rights of people is that they are treated according to their status, as has been mentioned by the Prophet ﷺ. Doing so ensures that the structures of society are maintained and that there remains harmony between its individuals.

أَصْبَحْتُ مُطَّرَحًا فِي مَعْشَرٍ جَهِلُوا ١ حَقَّ الأَدِيبِ فَبَاعُوا الرَّأْسَ بِالذَّنَبِ

وَالنَّاسُ يَجْمَعُهُمْ شَمْلٌ، وَبَيْنَهُمُ ٢ فِي العَقْلِ فَرْقٌ وَفِي الآدَابِ وَالحَسَبِ

كَمِثْلِ مَا الذَّهَبِ الإِبْرِيزِ يَشْرَكُهُ ٣ فِي لَوْنِهِ الصُّفْرُ، وَالتَّفْضِيلُ لِلذَّهَبِ

وَالعُودُ لَوْ لَمْ تَطِبْ مِنْهُ رَوَائِحُهُ ٤ لَمْ يَفْرِقِ النَّاسُ بَيْنَ العُودِ وَالحَطَبِ

1. I have been thrown into a society ignorant of a refined person's right, for they have sold the head for the tail.[2]

2. The people are united, but there is a difference between them

[1] Name of Allah ﷻ meaning One who is ever-watchful and ever-protective.
[2] Meaning that they do not understand the value of anything.

in intellect, mannerisms, and noble descent.

3. Like how brass shares a color with pure gold, while preference belongs to gold.

4. And [similarly] agarwood[1], if its fragrances did not emanate from it, people would not have differentiated between it and firewood.

10

الغُرُورُ بِالقَوْلِ

Conceit of One's Speech

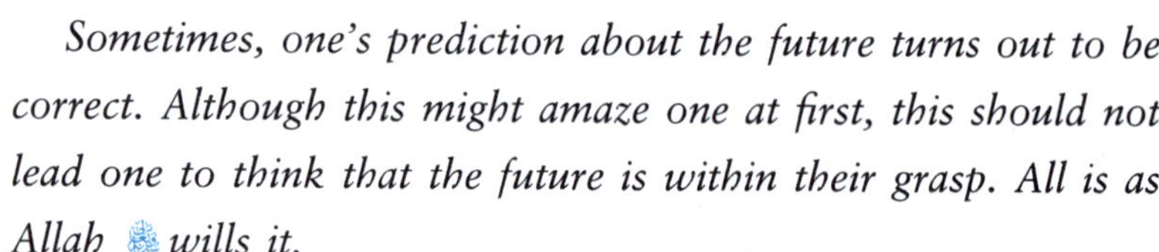

Sometimes, one's prediction about the future turns out to be correct. Although this might amaze one at first, this should not lead one to think that the future is within their grasp. All is as Allah ﷻ wills it.

إِذَا وَافَقَ التَّقْدِيرُ مَا هُوَ كَائِنٌ ١ تَحَيَّرَ عَقْلُ المَرْءِ وَهْوَ لَبِيبُ

فَيَنْطِقُ جَهْلًا بِالمُحَالِ لِسَانُهُ ٢ فَيُخْطِي بِهِ مِنْ حَيْثُ كَانَ يُصِيبُ

1. When [one's] estimation corresponds with what was to be, the intellect of man is bewildered even though he may be intelligent.

2. Thus [out of conceit], his tongue ignorantly speaks of impossibilities, and by it, he errs where he was correct.

[1] Agarwood is a special kind of wood known for its fragrance and is commonly used to make perfumes.

التَّرْحَالُ لِنَيْلِ المُرَادِ

Travelling for Accomplishing One’s Purpose

Travelling with the intention of earning ḥalāl provision, seeking knowledge, spreading the Dīn, or any other such intention is commendable in and itself, whether one returns successful or dies in the journey.

سَأَضْرِبُ فِي الآفَاقِ شَرْقًا وَمَغْرِبَا ١ أَنَالُ مُرَادِي أَوْ أَمُوتُ غَرِيبَا

فَإِنْ تَلِفَتْ نَفْسِي فَلِلَّهِ دَرُّهَا ٢ وَإِنْ سَلِمَتْ كَانَ الرُّجُوعُ قَرِيبَا

1. I will travel to the horizons of the East and West, accomplishing my purpose or dying a stranger.
2. If I lose my life, then how excellent is that! And if it remains safe, then return is near.

عَلَيَّ رَقِيبٌ

There is One Who is Watching Me

Being human, it is all too often that we forget that Allah ﷻ is watching us and our actions, and thus we fall into sin. We must remain aware of this reality and continuously repent and turn to Allah ﷻ.

إِذَا مَا خَلَوْتَ الدَّهْرَ يَوْمًا فَلَا تَقُلْ ١ خَلَوْتُ وَلَكِنْ قُلْ عَلَيَّ رَقِيبُ

وَلَا تَحْسَبَنَّ اللهَ يَغْفُلُ سَاعَةً ٢ وَلَا أَنَّ مَا يَخْفَى عَلَيْهِ يَغِيبُ

غَفَلْنَا لَعَمْرُ اللهِ حَتَّى تَرَاكَمَتْ ٣ عَلَيْنَا ذُنُوبٌ بَعْدَهُنَّ ذُنُوبُ

فَيَا لَيْتَ أَنَّ اللهَ يَغْفِرُ مَا مَضَى ٤ وَيَأْذَنُ فِي تَوْبَاتِنَا فَنَتُوبُ

1. If you are alone for some time one day, then do not say: "I am alone," but rather, say: "There is One who is watching me."

2. Do not think that Allah is oblivious for [even] a moment, nor that what is hidden is concealed from Him.

3. We are [so] heedless—by Allah—to the extent that sins after sins have accumulated upon us.

4. If only Allah would forgive what has passed and permit us to repent, [by which we may sincerely] repent.

13

جَوْرُ أَهْلِ الزَّمَانِ

The Oppression of Time's People

People blame time for the worsening conditions, but in reality, people have stooped so low in morals that they have become like dogs. Their promises cannot be relied upon, let alone anything lesser than that.

فَمَا جَارَ الزَّمَانُ وَمَا تَعَدَّى ١ وَلَكِنْ أَهْلُهُ مُسِخُوا كِلَابَا

مَوَاعِدُهُمْ مَوَاعِدُ كَاذِبَاتٍ ٢ إِذَا حَصَّلْتَهَا كَانَتْ سَرَابَا

1. Time did not wrong, nor did it transgress. Rather, its people have been transmuted into dogs.

2. Their promises are lies; if you were to obtain them, they would [turn out to] be a mirage.

14

غُرُورُ المَظْهَرِ

Deceiving Appearance

Excellent character and the lack thereof determine one's status amongst people, such that the young are granted respect and the old are treated with contempt.

أَرَى الغِرَّ فِي الدُّنْيَا إِذَا كَانَ فَاضِلًا ١ تَرَقَّى عَلَى رُوسِ الرِّجَالِ وَيَخْطُبُ

وَإِنْ كَانَ مِثْلِي لَا فَضِيلَةَ عِنْدَهُ ٢ يُقَاسُ بِطِفْلٍ فِي الشَّوَارِعِ يَلْعَبُ

1. I see that the [young man], inexperienced in the world, if he possesses excellence, rises above the heads of men and addresses [them].

2. And if he is [old] like me and devoid of excellence, he is equated to a child playing on the streets.

15

حَالُ النَّاسِ

The Condition of People

People are granted different qualities by Allah ﷻ and in different amounts. Those jealous of others ignore the many favors that Allah ﷻ granted them, and so they are ungrateful to Him and are at risk of losing those very favors.

أَصْبَحْتُ بَيْنَ أَدِيبٍ مَا لَهُ حَسَبٌ ١ يَسْمُو بِهِ وَحَسِيبٌ مَا لَهُ أَدَبُ

فَذَاكَ يَحْسُدُنِي إِذَا كُنْتُ ذَا حَسَبٍ ٢ عَالٍ وَيَحْسُدُنِي هَذَا عَلَى الأَدَبِ

1. I came to be between a refined man without noble descent—by which he may be exalted—and a man of noble descent without refinement.

2. The latter is jealous of me when I am of noble descent, while the former is jealous of me on the basis of [my] refinement.

أنتَ حَسْبِي

You Are Sufficient for Me

The essence of conviction in Allah ﷻ is to forgo any concerns of the worldly life, knowing that one has Allah ﷻ on their side.

أَنْـتَ حَسْـبِي وَفِيـكَ لِلْقَلْـبِ حُـبٌّ ١ وَلَحَسْـبِي إِنْ صَـحَّ لِي مِنْـكَ حُـبُّ

مَـا أُبَـالِي إِذَا وِدَادُكَ لِي صَـحَّ ٢ مَـدى الـدَّهْرِ مَـا تَعَـرَّضَ خَطْـبُ

1. You are sufficient for me, and for You the heart has love. And if Your love for me is true, then surely it is sufficient for me.

2. I am not worried—when Your love for me is genuine—about whatever calamities present themselves throughout time.

الحَثُّ عَلَى التَّرْحالِ

Encouragement to Travel

Although travelling builds one's character in ways unattainable by remaining at home, it is on the condition that the journey is for a commendable intention, such as spreading the Dīn, acquiring knowledge, or earning ḥalāl provision. On the way to noble intentions such as these, one gains the many benefits found in travelling.

مَا فِي الْمُقَامِ لِذِي عَقْلٍ وَذِي أَدَبٍ ١ مِنْ رَاحَةٍ فَدَعِ الْأَوْطَانَ واغْتَرِبِ

سَافِرْ تَجِدْ عِوَضًا عَمَّنْ تُفَارِقُهُ ٢ وَانْصَبْ فَإِنَّ لَذِيذَ الْعَيْشِ فِي النَّصَبِ

إِنِّي رَأَيْتُ وُقُوفَ الْمَاءِ يُفْسِدُهُ ٣ إِنْ سَاحَ طَابَ وَإِنْ لَمْ يَجْرِ لَمْ يَطِبِ

وَالْأُسْدُ لَوْلَا فِرَاقُ الْأَرْضِ مَا افْتَرَسَتْ ٤ والسَّهمُ لَوْلَا فِرَاقُ الْقَوْسِ لَمْ يُصِبِ

وَالشَّمْسُ لَوْ وَقَفَتْ فِي الْفُلْكِ دَائِمَةً ٥ لَمَلَّهَا النَّاسُ مِنْ عُجْمٍ وَمِنْ عَرَبِ

وَالْبَدْرُ لَوْلَا أُفُولٌ مِنْهُ مَا نَظَرَتْ ٦ إِلَيْهِ فِي كُلِّ حِينٍ عَيْنُ مُرْتَقِبِ

والتِّبْرُ كَالتُّرْبِ مُلْقًى فِي أَمَاكِنِهِ ٧ وَالْعُودُ فِي أَرْضِهِ نَوْعٌ مِنَ الْحَطَبِ

فَإِنْ تَغَرَّبَ هَذَا عَزَّ مَطْلَبُهُ ٨ وَإِنْ تَغَرَّبَ ذَاكَ عَزَّ كَالذَّهَبِ

1. [In staying] in one place—for one who possesses intellect and refinement—there is no rest, so leave the homelands and migrate.

2. Travel, you will find a [better] recompense for what you parted with, and endure hardships, as the enjoyment of life is in doing so.

3. I have seen that stagnation of water putrefies it, [whereas] if it flows, it becomes pure, and if it does not flow, then it will not become pure.

4. The lion cannot hunt without leaving the den, and the arrow cannot hit its target without leaving the bow.

5. If the Sun were to stop in its orbit forever, all people—non-Arabs and Arabs [alike]—would become weary of it.

6. If the Moon would not set, then the eyes of anticipation would not look towards it at all times.

7. Gold nuggets scattered in their source are like dirt, and agarwood in the ground is [merely] a type of wood.

8. If this [gold] separates [from its source], then it is sought after rarely [due to its high price], and if that [agarwood] separates [from its source], then it becomes precious like gold.

18

خالِفْ هَوَاكَ

Oppose Your Desires

The nature of the lower-self is to lead man away from pursuing praiseworthy actions. The remedy seems easy but requires great effort.

إِذَا حَارَ أَمْرُكَ فِي مَعْنَيَيْنِ ١ وَلَمْ تَدْرِ حَيْثُ الخَطَا وَالصَّوَابُ

فَخَالِفْ هَوَاكَ فَإِنَّ الهَوَى ٢ يَقُودُ النُّفُوسَ إِلَى مَا يُعَابُ

1. When you are confused between two matters and do not know which is correct and [which is] incorrect,

2. Then oppose your desires, as desires lead the souls to that which is blameworthy.

19

سُكُوتِي عَنِ اللَّئِيمِ جَوَابْ

My Silence is a Response for the Wicked

Responding to the comments of your critics is a futile endeavor, as their hate blinds them from accepting anything in your favor. Responding to them would rather add fuel to the fire of hatred in their hearts. Instead, adopt the simple approach of silence.

قُلْ بِمَا شِئْتَ فِي مَسَبَّةِ عِرْضِي ١ فَسُكُوتِي عَنِ اللَّئِيمِ جَوَابْ

مَا أَنَا عَادِمُ الجَوَابِ و لكِنْ ٢ مَا مِنَ الأُسْدِ أَنْ تُجِيبَ الكِلَابْ

1. Say what you wish in insulting my honor, as my silence is a response for the wicked.

2. It is not that I am lacking a response, but rather, it is not for a lion to respond to dogs.

20

الإِيفَاءُ بِالحُقُوقِ

Fulfilling Rights

Imam al-Shāfi'ī ﵀ was informed that a man had passed away, so he rose and asked his companions to accompany him to offer condolences. They told him that the house was far, so the Imam recited the following:

لَئِنْ بَعُدَتْ دَارُ الْمُعَزَّى وَنَابَهُ ١ مِنَ الدَّهْرِ يَوْمٌ وَالْخُطُوبُ تَنُوبُ

لَمَشْيٌ عَلَى بُعْدٍ عَلَى عِلَّةِ الوَجَا ٢ أَدِبٌّ وَمَنْ يَقْضِ الحُقُوقَ دَبُوبُ

أَلَــذُّ وَأَحْـلَى مِــنْ مَقَـالٍ وَ خَلْفَـهُ ٣ يُقَـالُ إِذَا مَـا قُمْـتَ: أَنْـتَ كَـذُوبُ

وَهَـلْ أَحَـدٌ يُصْغِي إِلَى عُـذْرِ كَاذِبٍ؟ ٤ إِذَا قَـالَ لَمْ تَـأْبَ المَقَـالَ قُلُـوبُ

1. If the abode of the one who is to be consoled is far while a day of Time afflicts him—and calamities afflict [everyone]—
2. My walking forward slowly for a distance despite an ailment on the foot—one who fulfills rights surely does so walking forward in any condition—
3. Is more pleasant and sweet than a [simple] speech after which it is said when you have risen: "You are a liar."
4. Does anyone incline [to accept] the excuse of a liar? When [such a person] speaks, hearts do not go towards such a statement [to accept it].

الحظوظ

Fates

This worldly life is not that of permanence; the conditions of the affluent can be switched with those of the destitute at a moment's notice. Therefore, be grateful to Allah ﷻ for whatever condition he has put you in.

تَمُـوتُ الأُسْـدُ فِي الغَابَـاتِ جُوعًـا ١ وَلَحْـمُ الضَّـأْنِ تَأْكُلُـهُ الـكِلَابُ

وَ عَبْـدٌ قَـدْ يَنَـامُ عَـلَى حَرِيـرٍ ٢ وَذُو نَسَـبٍ مَفَارِشُـهُ الـتُّرَابُ

1. Lions die starving in the jungles, while dogs feast on sheep meat.

2. A slave sometimes sleeps on silk, while a nobleman's bedding is dirt.

22

القَنَاعَةُ وَمَصِيرُ الظَّالِمِينَ

Contentment and the Outcome of Oppressors

Many people spend their whole lives greedily pursuing others to fulfill their desire for wealth, whereas true wealth is being content and self-sufficient. Like greed, another disease of the heart is pride, which leads some to oppress others. One should leave the haughty and arrogant oppressor to Allah ﷻ who will, in a short while, recompense him for his actions.

بَلَوْتُ بَنِي الدُّنْيَا فَلَمْ أَرَ فِيهِمُ	١	سِوَى مَنْ غَدَا وَالبُخْلُ مِلْءُ إِهَابِهِ
فَجَرَّدْتُ مِنْ غِمْدِ القَنَاعَةِ صَارِمًا	٢	قَطَعْتُ رَجَائِي مِنْهُمُ بِذُبَابِهِ
فَلَا ذَا يَرَانِي وَاقِفًا فِي طَرِيقِهِ	٣	وَلَا ذَا يَرَانِي قَاعِدًا عِنْدَ بَابِهِ
غَنِيٌّ بِلَا مَالٍ عَنِ النَّاسِ كُلِّهِمْ	٤	وَلَيْسَ الغِنَى إِلَّا عَنِ الشَّيْءِ لَا بِهِ
إِذَا ظَالِمٌ يَسْتَحْسِنُ الظُّلْمَ مَذْهَبًا	٥	وَلَجَّ عُتُوًّا فِي قَبِيحِ اكْتِسَابِهِ
فَكِلْهُ إِلَى صَرْفِ اللَّيَالِي فَإِنَّهَا	٦	سَتُبْدِي لَهُ مَا لَمْ يَكُنْ فِي حِسَابِهِ
فَكَمْ قَدْ رَأَيْنَا ظَالِمًا مُتَمَرِّدًا	٧	يَرَى النَّجْمَ تِيهًا تَحْتَ ظِلِّ رِكَابِهِ
فَعَمَّا قَلِيلٍ وَهْوَ فِي غَفَلَاتِهِ	٨	أَنَاخَتْ صُرُوفُ الحَادِثَاتِ بِبَابِهِ
فَأَصْبَحَ لَا مَالٌ وَلَا جَاهَ يُرْتَجَى	٩	وَلَا حَسَنَاتٌ تَلْتَقِي فِي كِتَابِهِ
وَجُوزِيَ بِالأَمْرِ الَّذِي كَانَ فَاعِلًا	١٠	وَصَبَّ عَلَيْهِ اللهُ سَوْطَ عَذَابِهِ

1. I tested the people of the world, and I only saw one who set out in the morning while full of greed.

2. So I drew, from the sheath of contentment, a sharp sword and I severed my hope in them with its blade.

3. Thus, this one does not see me standing in his path, nor does that one see me sitting at his doorstep.

4. [I am] in no need—without wealth—of all people; [true] wealth is only by not needing something, not by having that thing.

5. When an oppressor condones oppression as a doctrine and persists arrogantly in his evil deeds,

6. Then entrust him to the alternation of nights, as it will soon reveal to him what he never anticipated.

7. How many an insolent oppressor have we seen who considered the stars—out of arrogance—to be under the shadow of his stirrup.

8. Soon thereafter, while he was in his heedlessness, the calamities of Time alighted at his door.

9. Thus, he became one without wealth and honor to be hoped for and without good deeds to be found in his book [of deeds].

10. He was recompensed for the actions he used to commit, and upon him, Allah unleashed the scourge of punishment.

دُعَابَةٌ

Joking

Imam al-Shāfi'ī ﵀ once said, "I married a Qurayshī woman in Makkah, and I was joking with her and said:

وَمِـنَ البَلِيَّـةِ أَنْ تُحِـبَّ ١ وَلَا يُحِبَّـكَ مَـنْ تُحِبُّـهْ

1. It is a tribulation that you love [someone] and they do not love you [back].

She replied:

وَيَصُـدَّ عَنْـكَ بِوَجْهِـهِ ١ وَتُلِـحَّ أَنْـتَ فَـلَا تُغِبُّـهْ

1. And [likewise is a tribulation] that he turns his face away from you while you persist and remain present every day.

مَظَاهِرُ الشَّيْبِ ومَحَاسِنُ الأَعْمَالِ

The Effects of Old Age and Good Deeds

In a famous narration, the Prophet ﷺ said, "Make use of five before five," one of them being "youth before old age." Those still in their prime should take the advice of those who have tasted old age.

خَبَـتْ نَـارُ نَفْـسِي بِاشْـتِعَالِ مَفَارِقِـي ١ وَ أَظْلَـمَ لَيْـلِي إِذْ أَضَـاءَ شِـهَابُهَا

أَيَـا بُومَـةً قَـدْ عَشَّشَـتْ فَـوْقَ هَامَتِـي ٢ عَـلَى الرَّغْـمِ مِنِّـي حِينَ طَـارَ غُرَابُهَـا

رَأَيْـتِ خَـرَابَ العُمْـرِ مِنِّـي فَزُرْتِنِـي ٣ وَمَـأْوَاكِ مِـنْ كُلِّ الدِّيَـارِ خَرَابُهَـا

أَأَنْعَمُ عَيْشًا بَعْدَمَا حَلَّ عَارِضِي ٤ طَلَائِعُ شَيْبٍ لَيْسَ يُغْنِي خِضَابُهَا
وَعِزَّةُ عُمْرِ الْمَرْءِ قَبْلَ مَشِيبِهِ ٥ وَقَدْ فَنِيَتْ نَفْسٌ تَوَلَّى شَبَابُهَا
إِذَا اصْفَرَّ لَوْنُ الْمَرْءِ وَابْيَضَّ شَعْرُهُ ٦ تَنَغَّصَ مِنْ أَيَّامِهِ مُسْتَطَابُهَا
فَدَعْ عَنْكَ سَوْءَاتِ الأُمُورِ فَإِنَّهَا ٧ حَرَامٌ عَلَى نَفْسِ التَّقِيِّ ارْتِكَابُهَا
وَ أَدِّ زَكَاةَ الْجَاهِ وَاعْلَمْ بِأَنَّهَا ٨ كَمِثْلِ زَكَاةِ الْمَالِ تَمَّ نِصَابُهَا
وأَحْسِنْ إِلَى الأَحْرَارِ تَمْلِكْ رِقَابَهُمْ ٩ فَخَيْرُ تِجَارَاتِ الكِرَامِ اكْتِسَابُهَا
وَلَا تَمْشِيَنْ فِي مَنْكِبِ الأَرْضِ فَاخِرًا ١٠ فَعَمَّا قَلِيلٍ يَحْتَوِيكَ تُرَابُهَا
وَمَنْ يَذُقِ الدُّنْيَا فَإِنِّي طَعِمْتُهَا ١١ وَسِيقَ إِلَيْنَا عَذْبُهَا وَ عَذَابُهَا
فَلَمْ أَرَهَا إِلَّا غُرُورًا وَ بَاطِلًا ١٢ كَمَا لَاحَ فِي ظَهْرِ الفَلَاةِ سَرَابُهَا
وَمَا هِيَ إِلَّا جِيفَةٌ مُسْتَحِيلَةٌ ١٣ عَلَيْهَا كِلَابٌ هَمُّهُنَّ اجْتِذَابُهَا
فَإِنْ تَجْتَنِبْهَا كُنْتَ سِلْمًا لِأَهْلِهَا ١٤ وَإِنْ تَجْتَذِبْهَا نَازَعَتْكَ كِلَابُهَا
فَطُوبَى لِنَفْسٍ أُودِعَتْ قَعْرَ دَارِهَا ١٥ مُغَلَّقَةَ الأَبْوَابِ مُرْخًى حِجَابُهَا
فَلَنْ تَخْرَبَ الدُّنْيَا بِمَوْتِ شِرَارِهَا ١٦ وَلَكِنْ بِمَوْتِ الأَكْرَمِينَ خَرَابُهَا

1. The fire of my lower-self went out by my hair turning white; my night darkened while the flame [of my hair] glowed.

2. Oh, an owl has made a nest on my head, when its crow[1] had flown away, despite my [disapproval].

3. You saw the desolation of my age, so you visited me, as your abode, from amongst all abodes, is the desolate one.

4. Am I to enjoy life when the first indications of old age have alighted on my cheeks, such that even dying them does not help?

[1] Referring to black hair.

5. Dignity in the life of man is before his old age; the soul whose youth has passed has indeed passed away.

6. When a man's complexion yellows and his hair whitens then the pleasure of his days becomes spoiled.

7. So shun evil deeds from yourself, as committing them is unlawful for the God-conscious soul.

8. Give the alms of honor[1], and know that it is like the alms of wealth which has reached its minimum amount.

9. Be good to noble people, you will own them, as the best trade for honorable people is earning [their respect].

10. Do not walk on the shoulders of the Earth proudly, for in a little while, its dirt will encompass you.

11. Whoever [wants to] taste [the pleasures of] the worldly life, [then let him know] that I have [already] tasted it, and its sweetness and pain have been brought to us.

12. I saw it as only being delusions and falsehood, like how a mirage appears in the middle of a desert.

13. [This world] is only a useless corpse upon which are dogs whose [only] concern is its enticements.

14. If you abstain from it, then you will be safe from [the evil of] its dwellers. And if you [try to] snatch it, then its dogs will fight you [for it].

15. So glad tidings for the soul that has been placed in the depth of its house, with locked doors and drawn curtains.

1 Referring to all the good deeds one can do through one's honor for the benefit of others.

16. The world will not go into ruin with the death of its wicked people, but rather its ruination will be by the death of the noble people.

حَقِيقَةُ الدُّنْيَا

The Reality of the Worldly Life

The worldly life is worth far less than the wing of a mosquito for Allah whereas most of His slaves take it as the be-all and end-all. People are bound to quarrel with you regarding it, as it is open flesh for anyone and everyone to chew on.

هِيَ الدُّنْيَا فَلَا يُغْضِبْكَ مِنْهَا ١ وَلَا مِنْ أَهْلِهَا سَفَهٌ يُعَابُ

لِتَطْلُبَ جِيفَةً وَ تَنَالَ مِنْهَا ٢ وَتُنْكِرَ أَنْ تُهَارِشَكَ الكِلَابُ

1. It is only the worldly life, so do not let blameworthy foolishness make you angry about it and its people.

2. [How can it be that] you seek a corpse and [try to] get some [benefit] from it, and [then] you deny dogs from quarreling with you?

قافية التاء

The End-Rhyme of the Letter *Tā'*

الأَحْيَاءُ الخَالِدُونَ

The Eternally Alive

We spend our short lives doing good deeds to elevate our level in Paradise. After our deaths, the chance to do so is lost, except through what is known as ṣadaqah jāriyah, or "ongoing charity." This can take many forms and is not restricted to monetary acts; any act that has a lasting benefit counts as such. Doing so allows us to continue to accrue good deeds as if we are still alive.

١ النَّاسُ بِالنَّاسِ مَا دَامَ الحَيَاةُ بِهِمْ ... وَالسَّعْدُ لَا شَكَّ تَارَاتٌ وَهَبَّاتُ

٢ وَأَفْضَلُ النَّاسِ مَا بَيْنَ الوَرَى رَجُلٌ ... تُقْضَى عَلَى يَدِهِ لِلنَّاسِ حَاجَاتُ

٣ لَا تَمْنَعَنَّ يَدَ المَعْرُوفِ عَنْ أَحَدٍ ... مَا دُمْتَ مُقْتَدِرًا فَالسَّعْدُ تَارَاتُ

٤ وَاشْكُرْ فَضَائِلَ صُنْعِ اللهِ إِذْ جُعِلَتْ ... إِلَيْكَ لَا لَكَ عِنْدَ النَّاسِ حَاجَاتُ

٥ قَدْ مَاتَ قَوْمٌ وَمَا مَاتَتْ مَكَارِمُهُمْ ... وَعَاشَ قَوْمٌ وَهُمْ فِي النَّاسِ أَمْوَاتُ

1. People are dependent on each other as long as they are alive, and good fortune—no doubt—is of fleeting moments.
2. The best of people in existence is a man by whose hands the needs of people are fulfilled.
3. Do not ever prevent the hand of goodness from [reaching] someone so long as you are capable, as good fortune is fleeting.
4. Be grateful for the virtues of Allah's doing when [the needs of people] are entrusted to you, and not that [your] needs [are entrusted] to people.
5. People have died while their noble deeds have not, and [on the other hand] people live while they are dead amongst people.

27

طَلَبُ المَكَارِمِ

Seeking Goodness

There are many people who seem outwardly generous, but in reality, they have ulterior motives. To avoid them, there is a sign by which one may identify a sincere, generous person.

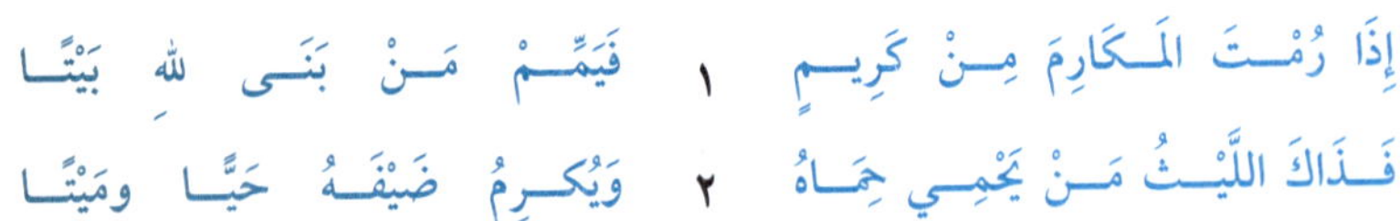

إِذَا رُمْتَ المَكَارِمَ مِنْ كَرِيمٍ ١ فَيَمِّمْ مَنْ بَنَى لِلهِ بَيْتًا
فَذَاكَ اللَّيْثُ مَنْ يَحْمِي حِمَاهُ ٢ وَيُكْرِمُ ضَيْفَهُ حَيًّا وَمَيْتًا

1. If you desire goodness from a generous person, then resort to one who built a house for Allah,
2. As that is the lion who protects his den and honors his guest [during his] life and [after his] death.

28

خِيرَةُ الإِخْوَانِ

The Best of Friends

A few characteristics, when found in a person, make him worthy of true friendship and companionship. Such people are so special that one would not mind even sharing one's own good deeds with them. But alas, such people are a rarity in our time.

أُحِبُّ مِنَ الإِخْوانِ كُلَّ مُوَاتِي ١ وَكُلَّ غَضِيضِ الطَّرْفِ عَنْ عَثَرَاتِي

يُوَافِقُنِي فِي كُلِّ أَمْرٍ أُرِيدُهُ ٢ وَيَحْفَظُنِي حَيًّا وَبَعْدَ مَمَاتِي

فَمَنْ لِي بِهَذَا؟! لَيْتَ أَنِّي أَصَبْتُهُ ٣ فَقَاسَمْتُهُ مَا لِي مِنَ الحَسَنَاتِ

تَصَفَّحْتُ إِخْوَانِي فَكَانَ أَقَلَّهُ ٤ عَلَى كَثْرَةِ الإِخْوَانِ أَهْلُ ثِقَاتِ

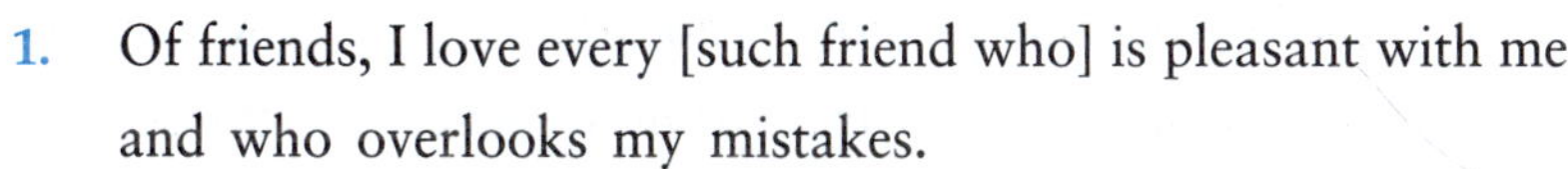

1. Of friends, I love every [such friend who] is pleasant with me and who overlooks my mistakes.

2. He agrees with me in every matter I wish, and he safeguards me in life and after my death.

3. So who will find me [someone] with these [characteristics]? If only I were to find him and then share with him all that I have of good deeds.

4. I have scrutinized my friends, but very few of them—despite their plentitude—are people of reliability.

مُنْتَهى الجُودِ

The Furthest Extent of Generosity

We sometimes imagine what we would do if we had a lot of wealth, but we tend to only think of spending on ourselves. And on the other hand, when we do have wealth, we tend to reject those who ask without even a second thought.

يَـا لَهْـفَ نَفْـسِي عَـلَى مَـالٍ أُفَرِّقُـهُ ١ عَـلَى المُقِلِّـينَ مِـنْ أَهْـلِ المُـرُوءَاتِ

إِنَّ اعْتِـذَارِي إِلَى مَـنْ جَـاءَ يَسْـأَلُنِي ٢ مَا لَيْسَ عِنْدِي لَـمِنْ إِحْدَى المُصِيبَاتِ

1. Oh, the sorrow of my soul over wealth [that had it been in my possession] I would distribute amongst the needy people of chivalry!
2. My presenting excuses to one who comes begging me for that which I do not have is surely from amongst afflictions.

النَّاسُ دَاءٌ

People are a Sickness

In life, it is not guaranteed that everyone will get along with you. Some might harbor feelings of animosity against you, but instead of reciprocating, you should save yourself from that burden and, as the English proverb goes, "Forgive and forget."

لَمَّا عَفَوْتُ وَلَمْ أَحْقِدْ عَلَى أَحَدٍ	١	أَرَحْتُ نَفْسِيَ مِنْ هَمِّ العَدَاوَاتِ
إِنِّي أُحَيِّي عَدُوِّي عِنْدَ رُؤْيَتِهِ	٢	لِأَدْفَعَ الشَّرَّ عَنِّي بِالتَّحِيَّاتِ
وأُظْهِرُ البِشْرَ لِلإِنْسَانِ أَبْغِضُهُ	٣	كَأَنَّهُ قَدْ حَشَى قَلْبِي مَحَبَّاتِ
وَلَسْتُ أَسْلَمُ مِنْ خِلٍّ يُخَالِطُنِي	٤	فَكَيْفَ أَسْلَمُ مِنْ أَهْلِ العَدَاوَاتِ
النَّاسُ دَاءٌ وَدَاءُ النَّاسِ قُرْبُهُمُ	٥	وَفِي اعْتِزَالِهِمُ قَطْعُ المَوَدَّاتِ

1. When I forgave and did not harbor hatred for anyone, I relieved my soul of the distress of enmity.

2. I greet my enemy upon seeing him to defend myself from harm by means of the greetings.

3. I display happiness to the person I am angry with, as if he has filled my heart with love.

4. I am not safe from friends mingling with me, so how can I be safe from the people of enmity?

5. People are a sickness, and this sickness is proximity with them, and in withdrawal from them is cutting ties of friendship [1].

31

الدَّرَاهِمُ تُنْطِقُ النَّاس

Dirhams Make People Speak

Although one positive quality of wealth is that it grants one the courage to speak, its negative quality is that it makes one forget one’s previous condition. When one is bestowed with wealth, they

[1] But since withdrawal from people is unbecoming, one should always forgive and overlook.

should strive to have compassion on those in a condition similar to their former one, and likewise, they should use their newfound courage to speak up for the rights of others.

وَأَنْطَقَتِ الدَّرَاهِمُ بَعْدَ صَمْتٍ ١ أُنَاسًا طَالَمَا كَانُوا سُكُوتَا

فَمَا عَطَفُوا عَلَى أَحَدٍ بِفَضْلٍ ٢ وَلَا عَرَفُوا لِمَكْرُمَةٍ ثُبُوتَا

كَذَاكَ المَالُ يُنْطِقُ كُلَّ عَيٍّ ٣ وَيَتْرُكُ كُلَّ ذِي حَسَبٍ صَمُوتَا

1. Dirhams made people—who were previously for a long time silent—speak[1].

2. [But due to arrogance and forgetting their days of hardship and poverty], they did not have compassion for anyone out of graciousness, nor did they recognize [any] basis for good deeds.

3. Likewise, [being granted] wealth makes every powerless one speak, and [being deprived of] wealth leaves every person of noble descent silent.

32

فَضِيلَةُ قِلَّةِ المَالِ

The Virtue of Having Less Wealth

During one's time as a student, having less wealth and no family to look after is, in fact, a blessing. This allows one to focus solely on acquiring knowledge. Only when one has completed this chapter in their life should they begin the next.

[1] Meaning that there were many who gained the courage to speak through the prestige they gained from wealth and affluence.

قَلِيلُ المَالِ لَا وَلَدٌ يَمُوتُ ١ وَلَا هَمٌّ يُبَادِرُ مَا يَفُوتُ

خَفِيفُ الظَّهْرِ لَيْسَ لَهُ عِيَالٌ ٢ خَلِيٌّ مِنْ حُرِمْتُ وَمِنْ دُهِيتُ

قَضَى وَطَرَ الصِّبَا وَأَفَادَ عِلْمًا ٣ هَمَّتُهُ التَّعَبُّدُ وَالسُّكُوتُ

1. [He is] less-of-means, and [he does not have] a child who would die, nor [does he have any] worry that would bring to mind that which he could lose.

2. [He is] light-weighted; he does not have dependents, [he is] free from [complaints such as:] "I have been deprived [from...]" and from "I have been struck [by...]".

3. He has fulfilled the need of youth and has acquired knowledge, and thus, [only] worship and silence preoccupy him.

33

آلُ النَّبِيِّ ﷺ ذَرِيعَتِي

The Noble Family of the Prophet ﷺ is My Medium

By loving those who the Prophet ﷺ loved, especially his noble family, it is hoped that nearness to him will be reached, thus gaining salvation in the Hereafter.

آلُ النَّبِيِّ ذَرِيعَتِي ١ وَهُمُ إِلَيْهِ وَسِيلَتِي

أَرْجُو بِأَنْ أُعْطَى غَدًا ٢ بِيَدِ اليَمِينِ صَحِيفَتِي

1. The noble family of the Prophet is my medium, and they are my means to him.

2. I hope that [through loving them], tomorrow[1] I will be given my book of deeds in my right hand.

اِعْتِبَارُ حَيَاةِ الفَتَى

Considering the Life of a Young Man

The path of acquiring knowledge is not an easy one. It is long, difficult, and bitter. But at the end of it, one is saved from the disgrace of ignorance, is truly alive, and gains worth in the sight of Allah.

تَصَبَّرْ عَلَى مُرِّ الجَفَا مِنْ مُعَلِّمٍ ١ فَإِنَّ رُسُوبَ العِلْمِ فِي نَفَرَاتِهِ
وَمَنْ لَمْ يَذُقْ مُرَّ التَّعَلُّمِ سَاعَةً ٢ تَجَرَّعَ ذُلَّ الجَهْلِ طُولَ حَيَاتِهِ
وَمَنْ فَاتَهُ التَّعْلِيمُ وَقْتَ شَبَابِهِ ٣ فَكَبِّرْ عَلَيْهِ أَرْبَعًا لِوَفَاتِهِ
حَيَاةُ الفَتَى وَاللهِ بِالعِلْمِ وَالتُّقَى ٤ إِذَا لَمْ يَكُونَا لَا اعْتِبَارَ لِذَاتِهِ

1. Be patient at the bitterness of harsh treatment from a teacher, for the consolidation of knowledge is in his reprimanding.

2. Whoever has not tasted the bitterness of learning for a short time will swallow the disgrace of ignorance his whole life.

3. Whoever missed learning during his youth, then proclaim upon him four *takbīr*[2] due to his death.

4. The life of a young man—by Allah—[acquires worth] through

[1] Referring to the Day of Judgement.

[2] Referring to the funeral prayer which consists of four *takbīr*.Because such a person does not possess knowledge, it is as if he has died.

knowledge and piety; if these two are not to be [found], then he is worthless.

القُضَاة

The Judges

A judge has great power over people. Those who abuse this power to acquire worldly benefits will only face damnation in the Hereafter. When vested with authority, especially over that which concerns the peoples' Hereafter, one should be extra vigilant about oneself.

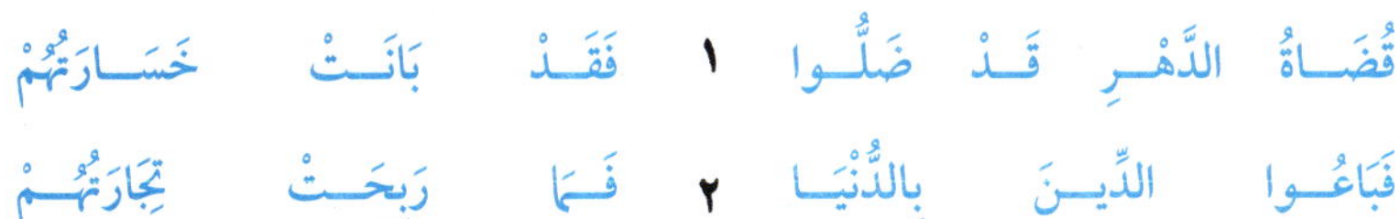

1. The judges of this era [whose aim is acquiring worldly benefits] have gone astray as their loss has become manifest.

2. They have sold the *Dīn* in exchange for the worldly life, and their trade reaped no profit[1].

العَفْوُ وَالصَّفْحُ

Forgiving and Overlooking

Although one can wait until the Day of Reckoning to see those who have harmed them receive the appropriate punishment, it is

[1] This is an adaptation (*iqtibās*) of verse 16 of Sūrah Baqarah.

always better to forgive them in this worldly life so that they may enter Paradise without difficulty. Just like you would want to be forgiven before that dreadful Day, do the same to others.

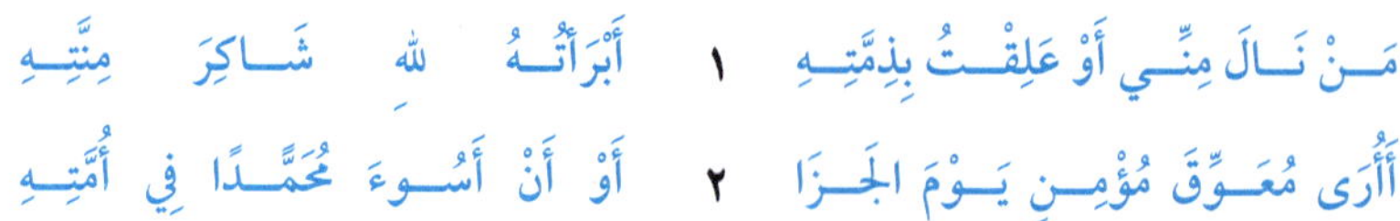

مَنْ نَالَ مِنِّي أَوْ عَلِقْتُ بِذِمَّتِهِ ١ أَبْرَأْتُهُ لِلّٰهِ شَاكِرَ مِنَّتِهِ

أَأُرَى مُعَوِّقَ مُؤْمِنٍ يَوْمَ الجَزَا ٢ أَوْ أَنْ أَسُوءَ مُحَمَّدًا فِي أُمَّتِهِ

1. Whoever harmed me or I hung in his conscience[1], I have forgiven him for Allah, grateful for His bestowal [of giving me the ability to forgive him].

2. Am I to be considered a hindrance for a believer on the Day of Recompense [from entering Paradise]? Or that I wrong Muhammad ﷺ [by not forgiving someone from] his Ummah?

1 Meaning that I am entitled to a right or claim against him.

قافية الجيم
The End-Rhyme of the Letter *Jīm*

الإيمانُ بِاللّٰهِ
Belief in Allah ﷻ

One who gains the realization of who Allah ﷻ truly is and thereafter builds his relationship with Him, will be free of all worries and concerns as he knows that Allah ﷻ will look after him.

صَبْرًا جَمِيلًا مَا أَقْرَبَ الفَرَجَا ١ مَنْ رَاقَبَ اللهَ فِي الأُمُورِ نَجَا

مَنْ صَدَّقَ اللهَ لَمْ يَنَلْهُ أَذَى ٢ وَمَنْ رَجَاهُ يَكُونُ حَيْثُ رَجَا

1. Adopt patience without complaint [and see] how near relief is. Whoever is cognizant of Allah in all matters will be successful.

2. One who is sincere with Allah, harm will not reach him. One who hopes in Allah, He will be as he hoped.

38

عَداوَةُ الشُّعَراءِ

The Enmity of the Poets

A few centuries ago, the poet was one of the central figures in society, such that even kings and nobles feared him and would ensure that they kept good relations with him. His poetry was given much emphasis and the entire society would memorize the verses he would utter. People who held high positions would often bribe the poet to earn his praise and be safe from his ridicule.

١ مَاذَا يُخَبِّرُ ضَيْفُ بَيْتِكَ أَهْلَهُ ... إِنْ سِيلَ كَيْفَ مَعَادُهُ وَمَعَاجُهُ

٢ أَيَقُولُ: جَاوَزْتُ الفُرَاتَ وَلَمْ أَنَلْ ... رَيًّا لَدَيْهِ، وَقَدْ طَغَتْ أَمْوَاجُهُ

٣ وَرَقَيْتُ فِي دَرَجِ العُلَا فَتَضَايَقَتْ ... عَمَّا أُرِيدُ شِعَابُهُ وفِجَاجُهُ

٤ وَلَتُخْبِرَنَّ خَصَاصَتِي بِتَمَلُّقِي ... وَالمَاءُ يُخْبِرُ عَنْ قَذَاهُ زُجَاجُهُ

٥ عِنْدِي يَوَاقِيتُ القَرِيضِ وَدُرُّهُ ... وَعَلَيَّ إِكْلِيلُ الكَلَامِ وَتَاجُهُ

٦ تُرْبِي عَلَى رَوْضِ الرُّبَا أَزْهَارُهُ ... وَيَرِفُّ فِي نَادِي النَّدَى دِيبَاجُهُ

٧ وَالشَّاعِرُ المِنْطِيقُ أَسْوَدُ سَالِخٌ ... وَالشِّعْرُ مِنْهُ لُعَابُهُ وَمُجَاجُهُ

٨ وَعَدَاوَةُ الشُّعَرَاءِ دَاءٌ مُعْضِلٌ ... وَلَقَدْ يَهُونُ عَلَى الكَرِيمِ عِلَاجُهُ

1. What will the guest of your house tell his family if he is asked how was [the hospitality at] his destination and his lodging?

2. Will he say: "I crossed the Euphrates, and I was not quenched by it," even though its waves overflow?

3. "I ascended the stairs of loftiness, but its mountain paths and roads became constricted from what I desired"

4. My destitution will surely inform of my flattery[1] [like how] glass tells of the filth of water.

5. I have the jewels of poetry and its pearls, and upon me is the diadem of speech and its crown.

6. [I am like] a meadow of spring whose flowers[2] increase [its beauty] and [I am like] a gathering of generosity whose silk brocade[3] glistens.

7. The eloquent poet is a black-skinned snake, and his poetry is its spit and saliva.

8. The enmity of poets is a difficult ailment, but treating it is easy for the generous one.

39

كُلَّمَا اشْتَدَّتْ فُرِجَتْ

Whenever There Was Hardship, Ease Came

Throughout the many trials and calamities of life, as Muslims, we should never lose hope in the help of Allah ﷻ. Even if we cannot imagine any possible solution for our problems, there is definitely one with Allah ﷻ.

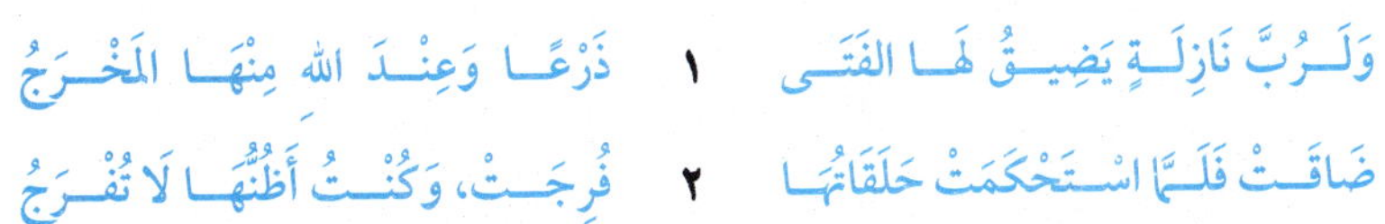

وَلَـرُبَّ نَازِلَـةٍ يَضِيـقُ لَهَـا الفَتَـى ١ ذَرْعًـا وَعِنْـدَ اللهِ مِنْهَـا المَخْـرَجُ

ضَاقَـتْ فَلَـمَّا اسْـتَحْكَمَتْ حَلَقَاتُهَـا ٢ فُرِجَـتْ، وَكُنْـتُ أَظُنُّهَـا لَا تُفْـرَجُ

1. Many a calamity becomes unbearable for a young man, while

1 Meaning that my poor condition will show that I am speaking flowery words only for some material gain.

2 Referring to his own poetry.

3 Once again referring to his own poetry.

deliverance from it is with Allah.

2. [My life] became constricted, then when the links of the calamity became firm, an opening was made, all the while I was thinking that it would never open.

قافية الحاء
The End-Rhyme of the Letter *Hā*

غَلَبَةُ القَضَاءِ
Dominance of Divine Decree

During times of grief, one way to find solace is by reminding oneself of predestination as by knowing that Allah ﷻ destined something to be so, one knows there must be wisdom behind it. One must also remember the āyah: "Do not become despondent of the mercy of Allah." (39:53)

اَلهَمُّ فَضْلٌ وَالقَضَا غَالِبٌ ١ وَكَائِنٌ مَا خُطَّ فِي اللَّوْحِ

أَنْتَظِرُ الرَّوْحَ وَأَسْبَابَه ٢ آيِسَ مَا كُنْتُ مِنَ الرَّوْحِ

1. Grief is subordinate while the Divine Decree is dominant, and what has been inscribed on the [Preserved] Tablet is to be.

2. I await mercy and its means, and I am not despondent of [His] mercy.

اَلصَّمْتُ شَرَفٌ

Silence is Honor

There are some people who argue simply for the sake of arguing. Observing silence and refraining from arguing is the best course of action with such ignorant people, which is in line with the āyah, "And when the ignorant address them, they say [words of] peace." (25:63)

قَالُوا سَكَتَّ وَقَدْ خُوصِمْتَ قُلْتُ لَهُمْ	١	إِنَّ الجَوَابَ لِبَابِ الشَّرِّ مِفْتَاحُ
وَالصَّمْتُ عَنْ جَاهِلٍ أَوْ أَحْمَقٍ شَرَفٌ	٢	وَفِيهِ أَيْضًا لِصَوْنِ العِرْضِ إِصْلَاحُ
إِنَّ الأُسُودَ لَتُخْشَى وَهْيَ صَامِتَةٌ	٣	وَالكَلْبُ يُخْسَى لَعَمْرِي وَهْوَ نَبَّاحُ

1. They said: "You remained silent while you were argued with?" I said to them: "Responding is surely the key to the door of evil.

2. And silence before an ignorant or foolish person is an honor, and in it also, one's dignity is completely preserved.

3. The lion is feared while it is silent and—I swear by my life—the dog is driven away while it is barking."

تَجَنُّبُ الحِرْصِ

Avoiding Greed

Greed is one of the diseases of the spiritual heart that

causes dissatisfaction and leads one toward sins. It can also eventually lead one toward continuously asking others for wealth and favors.

أُقْسِمُ بِاللهِ لَرَضْخُ النَّوَى ١ وَشُرْبُ مَاءِ القُلُبِ المَالِحَهْ

أَحْسَنُ بِالإنسانِ مِنْ حِرْصِهِ ٢ وَمِنْ سُؤَالِ الأَوْجُهِ الكَالِحَهْ

1. I swear by Allah that crushing date pits [and eating them] and drinking the water of salty wells,
2. Is better for man than his greed and asking those with scowling faces.

43

الفِقْهُ والتَّصَوُّفُ مُتَلازِمَانِ

Fiqh and *Taṣawwuf* Go Hand In Hand

All the Islamic sciences are such that they complement one another. Engrossing oneself in one and not delving into the other at all will lead to an imbalance. To become a well-rounded and developed scholar of Dīn, one should be acquainted to some extent with all the Islamic sciences.

فَقِيهًا وَصُوفِيًّا فَكُنْ لَيْسَ وَاحِدًا ١ فَإِنِّي وَحَقِّ اللهِ إِيَّاكَ أَنْصَحُ

فَذَلِكَ قَاسٍ، لَمْ يَذُقْ قَلْبُهُ تُقًى ٢ وَهَذَا جَهُولٌ، كَيْفَ ذُو الجَهْلِ يَصْلُحُ؟

1. A *faqīh* and a sufi, become [both] not one; indeed—by Allah's right—I advise you,
2. As that one [a *faqīh*] is hard-hearted, his heart has not tasted

God-consciousness, and this one [a sufi] is ignorant. How can an ignorant one reform [himself and others]?

فِرَاسَةُ المُفْتِي

The Foresight of a Mufti

Al-Rabī' b. Sulaymān [1] ﵀ said:

"One day, I was with al-Shāfi'ī, and a Bedouin went past the people with a piece of paper and handed it to al-Shāfi'ī. Al-Shāfi'ī looked into it, asked for ink, and wrote something in it. So I followed the Bedouin and asked him if I could have a look. In it was:

سَلِ الْمُفْتِيَ الْمَكِّيَّ هَلْ فِي تَزَاوُرٍ ١ وَضَمَّةِ مُشْتَاقِ الْفُؤَادِ جُنَاحُ

1. Ask the Meccan mufti: Is there any sin in meeting and embracing the beloved of [one's] heart [whilst fasting]?

And the response of al-Shāfi'ī therein was:

أَقُولُ: مَعَاذَ اللهِ أَنْ يُذْهِبَ التُّقَى ١ تَلَاصُقُ أَكْبَادٍ بِهِنَّ جِرَاحُ

1. I say: Allah forbid that the contact of two infatuated [2] hearts do away with piety.

I disapproved that al-Shāf'ī gave a legal ruling in such a manner, so he told me: 'O Abū Muhammad, this Hāshimī man had gotten married in this month [of Ramadan]. He is young and asked if he would get a sin for kissing or embracing without

1 Abū Muḥammad Rabī' b. Sulaymān al-Murādī al-Miṣrī (d. 270 A.H.) was one of the students of Imam al-Shāfi'ī ﵀ in Egypt and was the transmitter of most of his books.

2 Literally: "wounded"

intercourse, so I gave him this ruling.’ I then followed the young man and asked him his condition. He told me that he was as al-Shāfi‘ī had said. I have not seen foresight better than this.”

قافية الدال
The End-Rhyme of the Letter *Dāl*

أُطْلُبِ العِلْمَ
Seek Knowledge

The knowledge we seek in this worldly life is in reality in preparation for the Hereafter, as it guides us to act in the present in a manner that will bring success to us in the future.

مَـنْ طَلَـبَ العِلْـمَ لِلْمَعَـادِ ١ فَـازَ بِفَضْـلٍ مِـنَ الرَّشَـادِ

فَنَـالَ حُسْـنًا لِطَالِبِيـهِ ٢ بِفَضْـلِ نَيْـلٍ مِـنَ العِبَـادِ

1. One who seeks knowledge for the life to come has [indeed] acquired a large portion of guidance.
2. He has acquired what is good for its seekers by virtue of acquiring from the slaves [i.e., his teachers].

لَا تَقْنَطْ مِنْ رَحْمَةِ اللّٰهِ

Do Not Despair of the Mercy of Allah ﷻ

A man came to Imam al-Shāfiʿī ؒ complaining about his many sins. Imam al-Shāfiʿī ؒ mentioned to him the forgiveness of Allah ﷻ and recited the following couplet:

إِنْ كُنْتَ تَغْدُو فِي الذُّنُوبِ جَلِيدًا	١	وَتَخَافُ فِي يَوْمِ المَعَادِ وَعِيدَا
فَلَقَدْ أَتَاكَ مِنَ المُهَيْمِنِ عَفْوُهُ	٢	وَأَتَاحَ مِنْ نِعَمٍ عَلَيْكَ مَزِيدَا
لَا تَيْأَسَنْ مِنْ لُطْفِ رَبِّكَ فِي الحَشَا	٣	فِي بَطْنِ أُمِّكَ مُضْغَةً وَوَلِيدَا
لَوْ شَاءَ أَنْ تَصْلَى جَهَنَّمَ خَالِدًا	٤	مَا كَانَ أَلْهَمَ قَلْبَكَ التَّوْحِيدَا

1. If you are fixated on committing sins while fearing the warning of the Day of Judgement,
2. Then [know that] the forgiveness of al-Muhaymin[1] has [already] come to you and that He has granted you many more favors.
3. Do not despair of the [consistent] benevolence of your Lord [from the time you were] inside your mother's womb as an embryo and a baby.
4. Had He wished that you burn in Hell forever, He would not have inspired your heart with *tawḥīd*.

1 Name of Allah ﷻ meaning One who is ever watchful and ever protective.

الحُسَّادُ

The Jealous Ones

Imam al-Shāfi'ī ﷺ was told that someone was saying that he was not a jurist. He laughed and quoted the following:

إِنِّي نَشَأْتُ وَحُسَّادِي ذَوُو عَدَدٍ ١ رَبَّ المَعَارِجِ! لَا تُفْنِي لَهُمْ عَدَدَا

1. I have risen [in status] while those who are jealous of me are many. [O] the Lord of loftiness, do not destroy their number[1].

التَّسْلِيمُ الخَالِصُ

Pure Submission

The biggest worry and concern people have is about their sustenance for the day. Although working for a living is not blameworthy, worrying about it is not appropriate for a Mu'min. This is because a Mu'min believes that everything is in the control of Allah ﷻ, and that regardless of how much one works, one will only get what Allah ﷻ wills for him. By submitting to the will of Allah ﷻ, we will free ourselves from all worries.

إِذَا أَصْبَحْتُ عِنْدِي قُوتُ يَوْمِي ١ فَخَلِّ الهَمَّ عَنِّي يَا سَعِيدُ

وَلَا تَخْطُرْ هُمُومَ غَدٍ بِبَالِي ٢ فَإِنَّ غَدًا لَهُ رِزْقٌ جَدِيدُ

أُسَلِّمُ إِنْ أَرَادَ اللهُ أَمْرًا ٣ فَأَتْرُكُ مَا أُرِيدُ لِمَا يُرِيدُ

1 As being the target of jealousy means that one has been blessed with bounties from Allah ﷻ.

وَمَـا لِإِرَادَتِي وَجْـهٌ، إِذَا مَـا ٤ أَرَادَ اللهُ لِي مَـا لَا أُرِيـدُ

1. When I begin a new day having with me my sustenance for that day, then empty me of worry, O Sa'īd.
2. And do not let the worries of tomorrow come to my mind, as tomorrow has new sustenance [preordained for me].
3. If Allah wills a matter, I submit and I leave what I want for what He wills.
4. My intentions have no worth when Allah has willed for me what I do not want [which will surely be better for me].

49

عَدَاوَةُ الحَسَدِ

The Enmity of Jealousy

Jealousy is a disease that holds such a grip on the heart that it may never transform into love, but then again, Allah ﷻ is the One who turns the hearts.

كُلُّ العَـدَاوَاتِ قَـدْ تُرجَـى مَوَدَّتُهَـا ١ إِلَّا عَـدَاوَةَ مَـنْ عَـادَاكَ عَـنْ حَسَـدِ

1. The [transformation into] love of all types of enmity is hoped for, except for the enmity of one who harbors it out of jealousy.

حُقُوقُ النَّاسِ

The Rights of People

A man came to Imam al-Shāfiʿī ﵀ and told him that such-and-such friend of his was sick. Imam al-Shāfiʿī ﵀ then said, "By Allah, you have done me well and have alerted me to a good deed. You have saved me from making an excuse mixed with a lie." Thereafter, he asked his slave for his sandals and said, "Surely walking barefoot with a severe wound in the heat of the sun-baked ground in a state of hunger is easier than making an excuse to a friend mixed with a lie." He thereafter recited the following:

أَرَى رَاحَةً فِي الحَقِّ عِنْدَ قَضَائِهِ	١	وَيَثْقُلُ يَوْمًا إِنْ تَرَكْتَ عَلَى عَمْدِ
وَحَسْبُكَ عَارًا إِنْ تَقُلْ عُذْرَ كَاذِبٍ	٢	وَقَوْلُكَ لَمْ أَعْلَمْ وَذَاكَ مِنَ الجَهْدِ
وَمَنْ يَقْضِ حَقَّ النَّاسِ ثُمَّ ابْنِ عَمِّهِ	٣	وَصَاحِبِهِ الأَدْنَى عَلَى القُرْبِ وَالبُعْدِ
يَعِشْ سَيِّدًا يَسْتَعْذِبُ النَّاسُ ذِكْرَهُ	٤	وَإِنْ نَابَهُ خَطْبٌ أَتَوْهُ عَلَى قَصْدِ

1. I feel at ease when fulfilling a right, and it weighs heavy if you leave it for a day intentionally.

2. It will suffice as shame for you if [you state] a false excuse [when failing to fulfill a right], and your saying, "I did not know" [despite knowing] is a strain.

3. The one who fulfills the right of people, then his cousin, and his near and distant companions,

4. Will live with respect, people will enjoy mentioning him, and if a calamity bites him, they will come to him deliberately [for the sole purpose of assisting him].

أَمَانِي الإِنْسَانِ

The Wishes of Man

Whenever we desire something, we tend to see only the apparent and immediate benefit and do not consider the possible long-term harms. But whatever Allah ﷻ wills for us is better for us, both in this worldly life and in the Hereafter, although it might not seem that way. What we should focus on instead is striving to increase our God-consciousness.

يُرِيــدُ الْمَــرْءُ أَنْ يُعْطَــى مُنَــاهُ ١ وَيَأْبَــى اللهُ إِلَّا مَــا أَرَادَا

يَقُــولُ الْمَــرْءُ: فَائِـدَتِي وَمَــالِي ٢ وَتَقْــوَى اللهِ أَفْضَــلُ مَــا اسْــتَفَادَا

1. Man desires that he be granted [all] his wishes, and Allah rejects [all those wishes] besides that which He wills.

2. Man says [to himself]: "[How do I increase] my benefit and my wealth?" [He does not realize that] the consciousness of Allah is the best benefit that can be obtained.

الاَسْتِعْدَادُ لِلْمَوْتِ

Preparation for Death

One cannot know when exactly one's soul will leave one's body, so one should prepare for it as if it can happen within the next moment. It is not blameworthy to have high hopes and aspirations, but they should not make one heedless of the sudden appearance of the angel of death.

وَمُعْتِبِ العِيسِ مُرْتَاحٍ إِلَى بَلَدٍ ١ وَالمَوْتُ يَطْلُبُهُ فِي ذَلِكَ البَلَدِ
وَضَاحِكٍ وَالمَنَايَا فَوْقَ هَامَتِهِ ٢ لَوْ كَانَ يَعْلَمُ غَيْبًا مَاتَ مِنْ كَمَدِ
آمَالُهُ فَوْقَ ظَهْرِ النَّجْمِ سَابِحَةٌ ٣ وَالمَوْتُ مُنْتَظِرٌ مِنْهُ عَلَى الرَّصَدِ
مَنْ كَانَ لَمْ يُؤْتَ عِلْمًا فِي بَقَاءِ غَدٍ ٤ مَاذَا تَفَكُّرُهُ فِي رِزْقِ بَعْدِ غَدِ

1. Many a driver of camels of good stock happily goes to a land while death is seeking him in that land.
2. Many a person laughs while death is over his head; if he knew the unseen, he would have died from distress.
3. His hopes are floating above the backs of stars, while death is waiting for him on the path.
4. One who has not been given knowledge about tomorrow, how is he contemplating about provision for after tomorrow?

سِهَامُ الغَزَالِ

The Arrow of the Gazelle

An accidental gaze at the opposite gender, even though forgiven, can, at times, have far-reaching effects on one's lower-self. That is why scholars advise that one should limit one's gaze to those who are permissible to look at and that one should try one's best to avoid prolonging the first gaze, as that can potentially lead one down the path of sin.

خُذُوا بِدَمِي هَذَا الغَزَالَ فَإِنَّهُ ١ رَمَانِي بِسَهْمَي مُقْلَتَيْهِ عَلَى عَمْدِ

1. Seize, in retribution for my blood, this gazelle, as it has shot me with the two arrows of its eyes intentionally.

54

مَنْ يَجْحَدُ وُجُودَ اللهِ

One Who Denies the Existence of Allah ﷻ

Creation is known as "the Qur'an which is observed" as it guides one endowed with intellect towards the Oneness of Allah ﷻ. From the cells in our bodies to the stars in the sky, from the fish in the sea to the insects in the caves, from the particles in the air to the comets in orbit, everything points towards a Maker and a Sustainer.

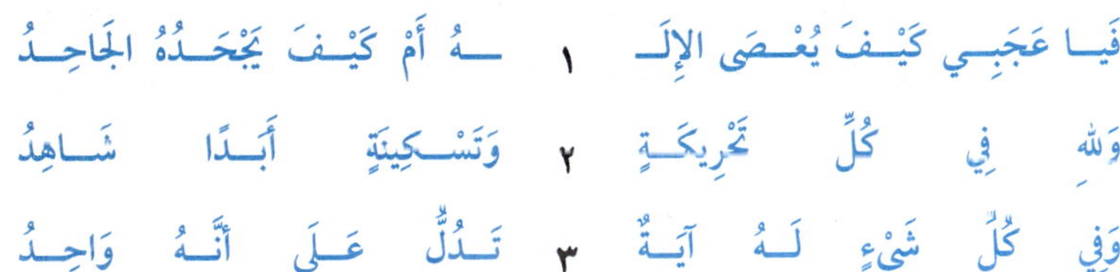

فَيَا عَجَبِي كَيْفَ يُعْصَى الإِلَـ ١ ـهُ أَمْ كَيْفَ يَجْحَدُهُ الجَاحِدُ

وَلِلهِ فِي كُلِّ تَحْرِيكَةٍ ٢ وَتَسْكِينَةٍ أَبَدًا شَاهِدُ

وَفِي كُلِّ شَيْءٍ لَهُ آيَةٌ ٣ تَدُلُّ عَلَى أَنَّهُ وَاحِدُ

1. How strange! How can Allah be disobeyed or how can one deny [His existence]?

2. As Allah has and forever will have, in every movement and stillness, a witness [to His existence].

3. And in everything of His [in existence] there is a sign indicating that He is One.

مِحَنُ الزَّمَانِ

The Trials of Time

Trials and tribulations afflict everyone, but especially so, they afflict the pious and the righteous. This is because Allah ﷻ loves such people and wants to see them turn to Him even more. Likewise, moments of true and lasting happiness are rare for them, as Allah ﷻ has saved that for them in the Hereafter.

مِحَنُ الزَّمَانِ كَثِيرَةٌ لَا تَنْقَضِي ١ وَسُرُورُهُ يَأْتِيكَ كَالأَعْيَادِ

مَلَكَ الأَكَابِرَ فَاسْتَرَقَّ رِقَابَهُمْ ٢ وَتَرَاهُ رِقًّا فِي يَدِ الأَوْغَادِ

1. The ordeals of time are many and unending and its [moments of] happiness come to you like the 'Eids[1].
2. [Time] has taken possession of and enslaved great people while you see it as a slave in the hands of the wretched.

قِلَّةُ الإِخْوَانِ عِنْدَ الشَّدَائِدِ

Shortage of Friends During Hardships

Finding a true friend is one of the hardest challenges in life, but when one does find such a person, one should cherish them and keep them close, as they will be the one shoulder to lean on during the most trying of times when all others will have gone.

[1] Meaning that they are infrequent as there are only two days of Eid in the year.

وَلَمَّا أَتَيْتُ النَّاسَ أَطْلُبُ عِنْدَهُمْ ١ أَخَا ثِقَةٍ عِنْدَ ابْتِلَاءِ الشَّدَائِدِ
تَقَلَّبْتُ فِي دَهْرِي رَخَاءً وشِدَّةً ٢ وَنَادَيْتُ فِي الأَحْيَاءِ هَلْ مِنْ مُسَاعِدِ؟
فَلَمْ أَرَ فِيمَا سَاءَنِي غَيْرَ شَامِتٍ ٣ وَلَمْ أَرَ فِيمَا سَرَّنِي غَيْرَ حاسِدِ

1. When I came to the people seeking among them a friend [I could] rely on when I am tried with hardships,
2. I moved about during my time [in both] ease and difficulty, and I called out in the quarters [of the city]: "Is there any helper?"
3. So I did not see in [the conditions] that hurt me [anyone] besides one who rejoices at [my] misfortunes, and I did not see in [the conditions that] delighted me [anyone] besides one who was jealous [of me].

57

الوَقارُ وَخَشْيَةُ الله

Dignity and Fear of Allah ﷻ

A man came to Imam al-Shāfi'ī ﷺ while he was lying on his back and said, "Verily the followers of Abū Ḥanīfah are the only eloquent ones." Upon hearing this, Imam al-Shāfi'ī ﷺ sat up and recited the following couplet:

فَلَوْلَا الشِّعْرُ بِالعُلَمَاءِ يُزْرِي ١ لَكُنْتُ اليَوْمَ أَشْعَرَ مِنْ لَبِيدِ
وَأَشْجَعَ فِي الوَغَى مِنْ كُلِّ لَيْثٍ ٢ وآلِ مُهَلَّبٍ وَأَبِي يَزِيدِ
وَلَوْلَا خَشْيَةُ الرَّحْمَنِ رَبِّي ٣ حَشَرْتُ النَّاسَ كُلَّهُمُ عَبِيدِي

1. If [devoting oneself to] poetry did not bring disgrace to the

scholars, today I would have been a better poet than Labīd[1],

2. And [I would have been] more courageous in battle than every lion and the family of Muhallab and Abū Yazīd[2].

3. If it were not for fear of al-Raḥmān my Lord, I would have gathered all of the people [and made them] to be my slaves.

مَا الرَّفْضُ دِينِي

Shiism is Not My Religion

A common method people would use to discredit scholars was to label them as being of a deviant sect. If one is made the target of such an accusation, they should try to clear their name in public and then leave the rest to Allah.

قَالُوا تَرَفَّضْتَ قُلْتُ: كَلَّا ١ مَا الرَّفْضُ دِينِي وَلَا اعْتِقَادِي
لَكِنْ تَوَلَّيْتُ غَيْرَ شَكٍّ ٢ خَيْرَ إِمَامٍ وَخَيْرَ هَادِي
إِنْ كَانَ حُبُّ الوَلِيِّ رَفْضًا ٣ فَإِنَّنِي أَرْفَضُ العِبَادِ

1. They said, "You have become a Shia." I said, "Certainly not! Shiism is not my religion nor my creed.

2. But rather, I have befriended, without a doubt, the best leader and the best guide."[3]

[1] Labīd bin Rabī'ah (d. 39 A.H) was one of the most eloquent poets in the Age of Ignorance and one of his poems was counted amongst the famous *Mu'allaqāt*. He accepted Islam and passed away during the *khilāfah* of 'Uthmān.

[2] These were two Arab tribes famous for their courage and bravery.

[3] Referring to 'Alī.

3. If loving a saint is [tantamount to] Shiism, then I am the most Shi'i slave [of Allah].

الأَخِلَّاءُ وَالغَدْرُ

Friends and Betrayal

Sometimes we might consider someone to be our friend, but they do not consider us the same. They may be two-faced—feigning friendship when with us and cursing us behind our backs. For this reason, it is important that we carefully choose who we take as a friend and confidant, lest we feel the pain of betrayal.

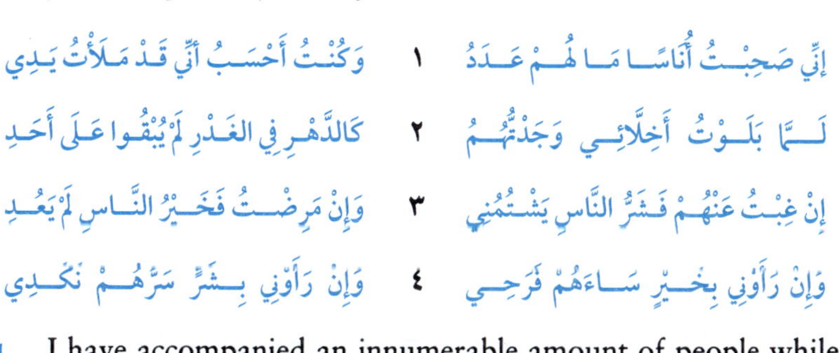

إِنِّي صَحِبْتُ أُنَاسًا مَا لَهُمْ عَدَدُ ١ وَكُنْتُ أَحْسَبُ أَنِّي قَدْ مَلَأْتُ يَدِي

لَمَّا بَلَوْتُ أَخِلَّائِي وَجَدْتُهُمُ ٢ كَالدَّهْرِ فِي الغَدْرِ لَمْ يُبْقُوا عَلَى أَحَدِ

إِنْ غِبْتُ عَنْهُمْ فَشَرُّ النَّاسِ يَشْتُمُنِي ٣ وَإِنْ مَرِضْتُ فَخَيْرُ النَّاسِ لَمْ يَعُدِ

وَإِنْ رَأَوْنِي بِخَيْرٍ سَاءَهُمْ فَرَحِي ٤ وَإِنْ رَأَوْنِي بِشَرٍّ سَرَّهُمْ نَكَدِي

1. I have accompanied an innumerable amount of people while thinking that I had filled my hand [with friends].

2. When I tested my friends, I found them to be like Time in betrayal—they did not spare anyone.

3. If I am absent from them, then the worst of [those] people reviles me. And if I am sick, then [even] the best of [those] people does not visit [me].

4. If they see me with ease, my happiness displeases them. And if they see me in hardship, my worry delights them.

60

لَوْمٌ وَعِتَابٌ

Rebuke And Reprimand

Once, Imam al-Shāfiʿī ﵀ went to Yemen and stayed with a relative of his who was a chief. When the Imam intended to return home, the chief offered excuses to him, fearing that he was the reason the Imam was returning home early, so Imam al-Shāfiʿī ﵀ wrote to him:

أَتَانِي عُذْرٌ مِنْكَ فِي غَيْرِ كُنْهِهِ	١	كَأَنَّكَ عَنْ بِرِّي بِذَاكَ تَحِيدُ
لِسَانُكَ هَشٌّ بِالنَّوَالِ وَلَا أَرَى	٢	يَمِينَكَ إِنْ جَادَ اللِّسَانُ تَجُودُ
فَإِنْ قُلْتَ: لِي بَيْتٌ وَسِيطٌ وَبَسْطَةٌ	٣	وَأَسْلَافُ صِدْقٍ قَدْ مَضَوْا وَجُدُودُ
صَدَقْتَ وَلَكِنْ أَنْتَ خَرَّبْتَ مَا بَنَوا	٤	بِكَفَّيْكَ عَمْدًا وَالبِنَاءُ جَدِيدُ
إِذَا كَانَ ذُو القُرْبَى لَدَيْكَ مُبَعَّدًا	٥	وَنَالَ الَّذِي يَهْوَى لَدَيْكَ، بَعِيدُ
تَفَرَّقَ عَنْكَ الأَقْرَبُونَ لِشَأْنِهِمْ	٦	وَأَشْفَقْتَ أَنْ تَبْقَى وَأَنْتَ وَحِيدُ
وَأَصْبَحْتَ بَيْنَ الحَمْدِ وَالذَّمِّ وَاقِفًا	٧	فَيَا لَيْتَ شِعْرِي أَيَّ ذَاكَ تُرِيدُ؟

1. Your apology came to me not in its true essence, as if by it you are desisting from treating me well.

2. Your tongue is quick [to give] gifts, and I do not think that if your tongue gave generously that your hands would do the same.

3. If you said: “I have an exquisite and spacious house, and [my]

truthful predecessors and ancestors have passed,"

4. You would have spoken the truth, but you have intentionally destroyed with your own two palms what they built [of respect], and [your] buildings are new [and are not like the previous].
5. When you have relatives that have been distanced [from you] and a stranger has acquired whatever he desires from you,
6. Relatives will separate themselves from you for their matters and you will fear that you will remain alone,
7. And you will come to be standing between praise and disparagement. So O, how I wish I knew which of those you want!

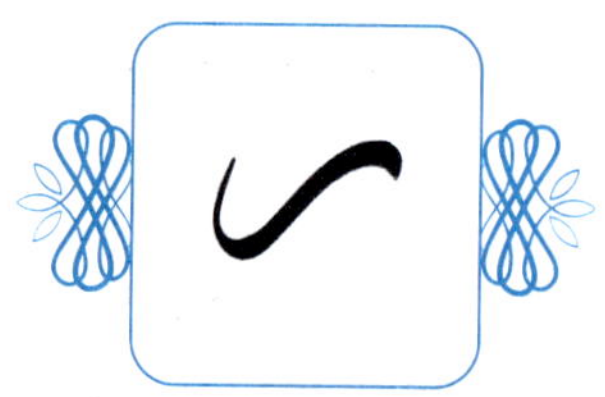

قافية الراء
The End-Rhyme of the Letter *Rā'*

طَلَبُ المَعَالِي
Seeking Loftiness

The path of seeking knowledge is bound to be full of hardships and difficulties. In reality, this path does not end with the completion of a course and receiving a certificate. Rather, this path is to continue till one's demise, as knowledge is to be sought from "the cradle to the grave."

وَنَاعِيَةٍ لِلْبَيْنِ قُلْتُ لَهَا: اقْصِرِي ١ فَمَا المَوْتُ أَحْلَى مِنْ مُعَالَجَةِ الفَقْرِ
سَأُنْفِقُ رَيْعَانَ الشَّبِيبَةِ كُلَّهَا ٢ عَلَى طَلَبِ العَلْيَاءِ أَوْ طَلَبِ الأَجْرِ
سَأَطْلُبُ عِلْمًا أَوْ أَمُوتَ بِبَلْدَةٍ ٣ يَقِلُّ بِهَا هَطْلُ الدُّمُوعِ عَلَى قَبْرِي
وَلَيْسَ اكْتِسَابُ العِلْمِ يَا نَفْسُ فَاعْلَمِي ٤ بِمِيرَاثِ آبَاءٍ كِرَامٍ وَلَا صِهْرِ
وَلَكِنْ فَتَى الفِتْيَانِ مَنْ رَاحَ وَاغْتَدَى ٥ لِيَطْلُبَ عِلْمًا بِالتَّجَلُّدِ وَالصَّبْرِ

فَـإِنْ نَـالَ عِلْمًا عَـاشَ فِي النَّـاسِ مَاجِدًا ٦ وَإِنْ مَـاتَ قَـالَ النَّـاسُ: بَالَـغَ فِي العُذْرِ

إِذَا هَجَـعَ النَّـوَّامُ أَسْـبَلْتُ عَـبْرَتِي ٧ وَأَنْشَدْتُ بَيْتًا وَهُوَ مِنْ أَلْطَفِ الشِّعْرِ

أَلَيْـسَ مِـنَ الْخُـسْرَانِ أَنَّ لَيَالِيًـا ٨ تَمُـرُّ بِـلَا عِلْـمٍ وَتُحْسَـبُ مِـنْ عُمْـرِي

1. I said to many of those who wail upon [my] separation [from home]: "Restrain yourself, as death is not sweeter than treating poverty."

2. I will spend the prime of [my] youth completely in seeking loftiness or seeking reward.

3. I will seek knowledge, or I will die in a land in which the torrent of tears on my grave will be less.

4. O the lower-self, know that earning knowledge is not through the inheritance of honorable forefathers nor through in-laws.

5. But a true youth is one who spends the mornings and evenings seeking knowledge with endurance and patience.

6. If he acquires knowledge, he will live glorified among the people. And if he dies, people will say: "[There's no blame on him] as he did whatever he could."

7. When the one given to sleep sleeps peacefully, I shed my tears and I recite a verse which is of the loveliest poetry:

8. "Is it not a loss that nights pass by without [acquiring] knowledge and they are counted as my life?"

62

التَّكَثُّر مِنَ الأَصْدِقَاءِ

Increasing Friends

The importance of having true friends cannot be overstated. Such people serve as lifelines in the face of difficulties. Maintaining relationships with such friends is far easier than dealing with just one enemy.

وَأَكْثِرْ مِنَ الإِخْوَانِ مَا اسْطَعْتَ إِنَّهُمْ ١ بُطُونٌ إِذَا اسْتَنْجَدْتَهُمْ وَظُهُورُ

وَلَيْسَ كَثِيرًا أَلْفُ خِلٍّ لِعَاقِلٍ ٢ وَإِنَّ عَدُوًّا وَاحِدًا لَكَثِيرُ

1. Increase friends as much as possible because when you seek their help, they will support you in every way possible.[1]
2. A thousand friends are not much for an intelligent person, but just one enemy is surely too much.

63

الرَّزِيَّةُ فَقْدُ الأَحْرَارِ

The True Calamity is the Loss of Noble People

Although everyone must die, the deaths of some leave a bigger void than those of others. Noble people, especially scholars and saints, possess wide spheres of positive influence in society, the extent of which is only felt after their deaths.

1 Literally: "They will be in front of you and behind you."

لَعَمْـرُكَ مَـا الرَّزِيَّـةُ فَقْـدُ دَارٍ ١ وَلَا شَـاةٌ تَمُـوتُ وَلَا بَعِـيرُ

وَلَكِـنَّ الرَّزِيَّـةَ فَقْـدُ حُـرٍّ ٢ يَمُـوتُ بِمَوْتِـهِ خَلْـقٌ كَثِـيرُ

1. By your life, a true calamity is not the loss of a house nor the death of a sheep or a camel.

2. Rather, a true calamity is the loss of a noble man; by his death, a great amount of people pass away.

أَدَبُ المُنَاظَرَةِ

Etiquettes of Debating

People who think they possess knowledge jump at opportunities to debate others and show off what they know. On the other hand, true seekers of knowledge know their true worth and refrain from such an act. But sometimes, the need arises, and in such a situation, one should keep the following points in mind.

إِذَا مَـا كُنْـتَ ذَا فَضْـلٍ وَعِلْـمٍ ١ بِـمَا اخْتَلَـفَ الأَوَائِـلُ وَالأَوَاخِـرْ

فَنَاظِـرْ مَـنْ تُنَاظِـرُ فِي سُـكُونٍ ٢ حَلِيـمًا لَا تَلَـجُّ وَلَا تُكَابِـرْ

يُفِيـدُكَ مَـا اسْـتَفَادَ بِـلَا امْتِنَـانٍ ٣ مِـنَ النُّكَـتِ اللَّطِيفَـةِ وَالنَّـوَادِرْ

وَإِيَّـاكَ اللَّجُـوجَ وَمَـنْ يُرَائِـي ٤ بِـأَنِّي قَـدْ غَلَبْـتُ وَمَـنْ يُفَاخِـرْ

فَـإِنَّ الـشَّرَّ فِي جَنَبَـاتِ هَـذَا ٥ فَمَيِّـزْ بِالتَّقَاطُـعِ وَالتَّدَابُـرْ

1. If you possess virtue and knowledge of what the earlier and later [scholars] differed on,

2. Then [when the need arises] debate who [you wish to] debate calmly and forbearingly. Do not be obstinate and insist stubbornly.

3. He will benefit you with what he has learned of subtle and rare points without feeling indebted.

4. Beware the obstinate one, the one who shows off that "I won," and the one who boasts,

5. As there is evil inside of him, so distinguish [your behavior towards him] by cutting ties and turning away [from him].

بُلِيتُ بِأَرْبَعٍ

I Have Been Tried by Four Things

The soul has a divine origin, and so, it feels tranquility and peace when ascending toward the heavenly. In this worldly life, there are things that pull the soul towards the world and prevent it from striving to reach its natural state. These things are meant to serve as a test for the bearer of the soul and are meant to be overcome.

1. I am tried by four things showering painful arrows from their bows:

2. Iblīs, the worldly life, my lower-self, and desires. Where can an intelligent person flee from desires?

66

القناعة

Contentment

If one has been given the blessing of contentment from Allah ﷻ, then the riches of other people do not faze him. Such a person knows with certainty that his sustenance for the day is in the hands of his Lord. He considers asking others besides his Lord to be the highest form of disgrace.

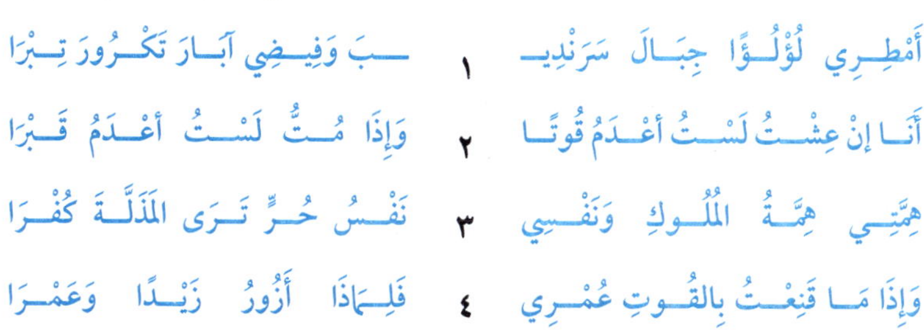

أَمْطِرِي لُؤْلُؤًا جِبَالَ سَرَنْدِيـ ١ ـبَ وَفِيضِي آبَارَ تَكْرُورَ تِبْرَا

أَنَا إِنْ عِشْتُ لَسْتُ أَعْدَمُ قُوتًا ٢ وَإِذَا مُتُّ لَسْتُ أَعْدَمُ قَبْرَا

هِمَّتِي هِمَّةُ الْمُلُوكِ وَنَفْسِي ٣ نَفْسُ حُرٍّ تَرَى الْمَذَلَّةَ كُفْرَا

وَإِذَا مَا قَنِعْتُ بِالْقُوتِ عُمْرِي ٤ فَلِمَاذَا أَزُورُ زَيْدًا وَعَمْرَا

1. Rain down, O the mountains of Serendib,[1] pearls. And pour forth, O the wells of Toucouleur[2], gold nuggets[3].

2. If I live, I will not be deprived of sustenance, and if I die, I will not be deprived of a grave.

3. My resolve is the resolve of kings, and my soul is the soul of nobles—it considers disgrace [to be as despicable as] disbelief.

4. When I am content with whatever sustenance [I have] in my life, then why should I pay visits to Zayd and 'Amr[4] [seeking monetary gain]?

---

[1] The English spelling of Sarandīb, which is the name given for Sri Lanka by the Arabs.
[2] A West African ethnic group native to Senegal, Mali, and Mauritania.
[3] Meaning that it will not affect me in the slightest.
[4] Zayd and 'Amr are generic names used in the Arabic language to refer to "other people."

67

الصَّفْحُ شِيمَةُ كُلِّ حُرٍّ

Pardoning is the Natural Disposition of Every Noble Person

Refusing to pardon one who undertook the great effort needed to humble himself and apologize before you is surely a quality of contemptible people.

إِذَا اعْتَـذَرَ الصَّدِيـقُ إِلَيْـكَ يَوْمًـا ١ مِـنَ التَّقْصِـيرِ عُـذْرَ أَخٍ مُقِـرِّ

فَصُنْـهُ عَـنْ عِتَابِـكَ وَاعْـفُ عَنْـهُ ٢ فَـإِنَّ الصَّفْـحَ شِـيمَةُ كُلِّ حُـرِّ

1. If one day a friend apologizes to you the apology of a brother acknowledging [his] deficiency,

2. Then save him from your rebuke and forgive him, as pardoning is the natural disposition of every noble person.

68

الرِّضَى بِحُكْمِ الدَّهْرِ

Contentment with the Decision of Time

One will experience varying conditions in life, some pleasing and others displeasing. Contentment allows one to bear those conditions without complaint, which then allows one to live a peaceful life in this temporary abode.

وَمَـا كُنْـتُ أَرْضَى مِـنْ زَمَـانِي بِـمَا تَرَى ١ وَلَكِنَّنِـي رَاضٍ بِـمَا حَكَـمَ الدَّهْـرُ

فَـإِنْ كَانَـتِ الأَيَّـامُ خَانَـتْ عُهُودَنَـا ٢ فَـإِنِّي بِهَـا رَاضٍ وَلَكِنَّهَـا قَهْـرُ

1. I was not pleased with the present time due to what you see [of my condition], but I am content with what Time has decreed.

2. Although the days have failed to keep our promises, I am content with them, but [that is with] compulsion.

Once, whilst visiting Iraq, Imam al-Shāfi‘ī reached the town of Samarra. His clothes were tattered and soiled, and his hair was long and disheveled. Thus, he decided to pay a visit to a barber. Seeing the Imam’s shabby condition, the barber refused to attend to him and told him to go to someone else. This displeased Imam al-Shāfi‘ī so he turned to his slave and asked him how much money he had with him. When he replied that ten dinars were at hand, Imam al-Shāfi‘ī told him to give it to the barber. The Imam left while reciting the following couplets:

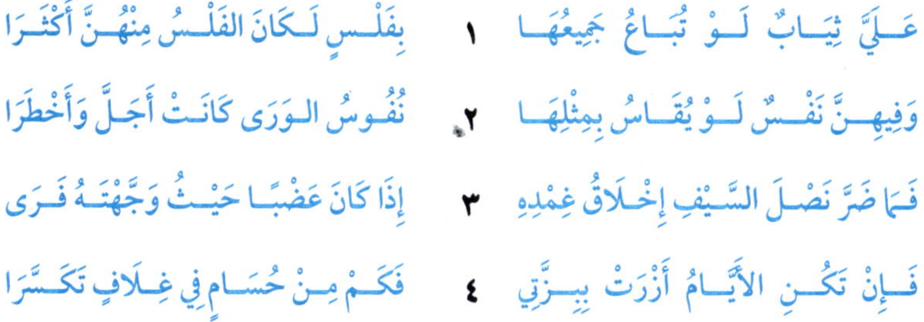

1. On me are clothes; if all of them were to be sold for a penny,

the penny would be [worth] more than them.

2. In them is a soul, if its like was measured with the souls of mankind, it would be nobler and worthier.

3. The corroding of the sword's sheath does not harm its blade. If it is sharp, wherever you direct it, it will slash.

4. Even if the days have belittled my clothing, how many a sharp sword is [found] in a broken scabbard!

70

حَقِيقَةُ الدُّنْيَا وَالدِّرْهَمِ

The Reality of the Worldly Life and the Dirham

Chasing debased and temporary monetary gains and making it one's objective will only lead to grief in the worldly life and Hellfire in the Hereafter. If wealth is acquired with God-consciousness, then the opposite result is hoped for.

١ النَّارُ آخِرُ دِينَارٍ نَطَقْتَ بِهِ ... وَالهَمُّ آخِرُ هَذَا الدِّرْهَمِ الجَارِي

٢ وَالمَرْءُ بَيْنَهُمَا مَا لَمْ يَكُنْ وَرِعًا ... مُعَذَّبُ القَلْبِ بَيْنَ الهَمِّ وَالنَّارِ

1. *Nār*[1] is the end of [the word] "dinar" you utter, and *hamm*[2] is at the end of this circulating "dirham."

2. One who [chases after] them both—if he is not God-fearing—is tormented in the heart with both grief and the Fire.

---

1 In English: the Fire.

2 In English: grief.

تَقَلُّبُ الأَيَّامِ

The Changing of Days

As mentioned in Surah Sharḥ, "So, surely with hardship comes ease." But it should be kept in mind that just like difficulties do not last, so too do happiness and joy not last, as that is the nature of this impermanent worldly life.

عَوَاقِبُ مَكْرُوهِ الأُمُورِ خِيَارُ ١ وَأَيَّامُ شَرٍّ لَا تَدُومُ قِصَارُ

وَلَيْسَ بِبَاقٍ بُؤْسُهَا وَنَعِيمُهَا ٢ إِذَا كَرَّ لَيْلٌ ثُمَّ كَرَّ نَهَارُ

1. The outcome of unfavorable circumstances is [always] good, and the days of evil are short and do not last.
2. Its hardships and bliss are not everlasting; when night returns, then day returns [soon thereafter][1].

غَزَلٌ

Love Poetry

It was said to Imam al-Shāfi'ī ﵀: "You have said much regarding asceticism, but do you have any love poetry?" So, the Imam recited the following couplets:

يَا كَاحِلَ العَيْنِ بَعْدَ النَّوْمِ بِالسَّهَرِ ١ مَا كَانَ كُحْلُكَ بِالْمَنْعُوتِ لِلْبَصَرِ

[1] Meaning that hardships and bliss come and go.

لَوْ أَنَّ عَيْنِي إِلَيْكَ الدَّهْرَ ناظِرَةٌ ٢ حَانَتْ وَفَاتِي وَلَمْ أَشْبَعْ مِنَ النَّظَرِ

سُقْيَا لِدَهْرٍ مَضَى مَا كَان أَطْيَبَهُ ٣ لَوْلَا التَّفَرُّقُ والتَّنْغِيصُ بِالسَّفرِ

إِنَّ الرَّسُولَ الَّذِي يَأْتِي بِلَا عِدَةٍ ٤ مِثْلُ السَّحَابِ الَّذِي يَأْتِي بِلَا مَطَرِ

دَعْنِي أُمَتِّعْ طَرْفِي مِنْكَ بِالنَّظَرِ ٥ فَنُورُ وَجْهِكَ يَجْلُو ظُلْمَةَ البَصَرِ

1. O, the one who applies kohl to [my] eyes by [keeping me] awake after [nights of usual] sleep[1], your kohl is not the one prescribed for strengthening the eyesight.

2. If my eyes were to gaze at you for a [life]time, my death would come and I would not have been satisfied with gazing.

3. The most pleasant of times has passed as watering for Time. If only there was no separation and disturbance through travelling.

4. The messenger that comes without a promise is like a cloud that comes without rain.

5. Let me make my eye enjoy a glance at you, as the light of your face clears the darkness of the sight.

صَبْرُ النَّفْسِ

The Patience of the Lower-Self

It sometimes happens that during times of hardship, the lower-self nags one to fulfill its desires. To yield to it then will only bring

[1] Implying that by spending the nights awake longing for his beloved, black bags have formed around his eyes.

about regret and disgrace in the future. In such a situation, try to scrape out and use any ounce of patience from within.

إِذَا شِـئْتَ أَنْ تَسْـتَقْرِضَ المَـالَ مُنْفِقًـا ١ عَـلَى شَـهَوَاتِ النَّفْـسِ فِي زَمَـنِ العُسْرِ

فَسَلْ نَفْسَكَ الإِقْرَاضَ مِنْ كِيسِ صَبْرِهَا ٢ عَلَيْـكَ وَإِرْفَاقًـا إِلَى زَمَـنِ اليُـسْرِ

وَإِنْ صَـبَرَتْ كُنْـتَ الغَنِـيَّ وَإِنْ أَبَـتْ ٣ فَـكُلُّ مَنُـوعٍ بَعْدَهَـا وَاسِـعُ العُـذْرِ

1. If you want to seek a loan of wealth to spend on the desires of the lower-self in a time of hardship,
2. Then ask your lower-self to loan you from the bag of its patience and to wait until a time of ease.
3. If your lower-self is patient, you will be self-sufficient, and if [your lower-self] refuses, then [it will offer excuses like how] every tight-fisted person has plenty of excuses.

74

دِيَةُ الذَّنْبِ

The Atonement for Sin

When someone apologizes to you, know that this action of theirs must have taken great courage and determination. Thus, appreciate his effort by accepting the apology wholeheartedly and let bygones be bygones.

قِيـلَ لِي: قَـدْ أَسَـا عَلَيْـكَ فُـلَانٌ ١ وَمُقَـامُ الفَتَـى عَـلَى الـذُّلِّ عَـارُ

قُلْـتُ: قَـدْ جَـاءَنِي وَأَحْـدَثَ عُـذْرًا ٢ دِيَـةُ الذَّنْـبِ عِنْدَنَـا الاِعْتِـذَارُ

1. It was said to me, "So-and-so insulted you and a young man

remaining [silent] whilst being disgraced is shameful."

2. I said, "He came to me and gave an apology. The atonement for sin, according to us, is apologizing."

75

صُرُوفُ الدَّهْرِ

The Changing of Time

Those enjoying their lives without any care for others or even their own Hereafter should take lesson from those before them who were seized for their crimes in this life and will most likely face punishment in the Hereafter.

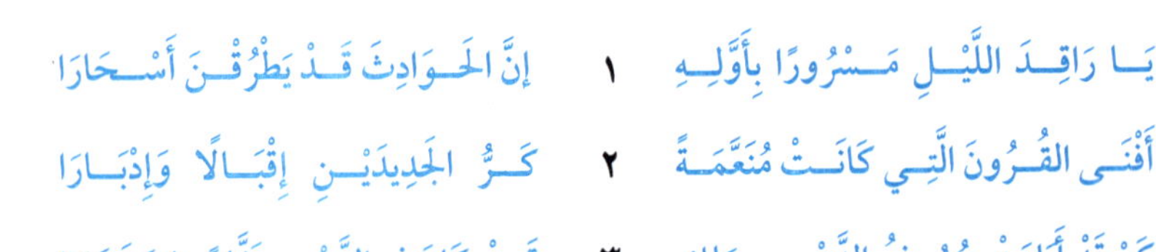

يَا رَاقِدَ اللَّيْلِ مَسْرُورًا بِأَوَّلِهِ ١ إِنَّ الحَوَادِثَ قَدْ يَطْرُقْنَ أَسْحَارَا

أَفْنَى القُرُونَ الَّتِي كَانَتْ مُنَعَّمَةً ٢ كَرُّ الجَدِيدَيْنِ إِقْبَالًا وَإِدْبَارَا

كَمْ قَدْ أَبَادَتْ صُرُوفُ الدَّهْرِ مِن مَلِكٍ ٣ قَدْ كَانَ فِي الدَّهْرِ نَفَّاعًا وَضَرَّارَا

1. O the one who sleeps happily in the early part of the night, [know that] incidents knock [at one's door] at dawn.

2. The coming and going of night and day destroyed generations that were enjoying a pleasant life.

3. How many kings—who in [their] era were abundantly beneficial [to some] and immensely harmful [to others]—did the vicissitudes of fortune destroy!

76

الوَحْدَةُ خَيْرٌ مِنْ جَلِيسِ السُّوءِ

Loneliness is Better Than an Evil Companion

By staying in the company of the wicked, the possibility always remains that one can be enticed towards their sinful deeds. On the other hand, by staying in the worship of the Lord-of-all, one is guaranteed everlasting benefit.

إِذَا لَمْ أَجِدْ خِلًّا تَقِيًّا فَوَحْدَتِي ١ أَلَذُّ وَأَشْهَى مِنْ غَوِيٍّ أُعَاشِرُه

وَأَجْلِسُ وَحْدِي لِلْعِبَادَةِ آمِنًا ٢ أَقَرُّ لِعَيْنِي مِنْ جَلِيسٍ أُحَاذِرُه

1. When I cannot find a righteous friend, then my solitude is more enjoyable and pleasurable to me than associating with an enticer [towards sin].
2. That I sit alone in worship safe is more pleasing to my eyes than a companion I am wary of.

77

العِلْمُ وَالجَهْلُ

Knowledge and Ignorance

Although the fruits of knowledge are great, they do not manifest overnight. Acquiring knowledge in small increments and one day seeing the results is better than faring a lifetime as an ignorant person captive to the knowledge of others.

تَعَلَّمْ مَا اسْتَطَعْتَ تَكُنْ أَمِيرًا ١ وَلَا تَكُ جَاهِلًا تَبْقَى أَسِيرًا

تَعَلَّمْ كُلَّ يَوْمٍ حَرْفَ عِلْمٍ ٢ تَرَ الْجُهَّالَ كُلَّهُمُ حَمِيرًا

1. Learn what you can, you will become a leader; do not be ignorant [otherwise] you will remain captive.

2. Learn [at least] a letter of knowledge every day—you will see all the ignorant ones as donkeys[1].

78

جِنَانُ الْخُلْدِ

Everlasting Gardens

Some people become so involved in pursuing the world that they forget their purpose in this life and the potential rewards awaiting them in the next. What they do not realize is that sacrificing a little now will grant one an immense reward for eternity. To be saved from the Hellfire, one simply needs to keep in mind the potential punishment for sins. In this way, one will be able to abstain from those sins, and thereby gain salvation.

يَا مَنْ يُعَانِقُ دُنْيَا لَا بَقَاءَ لَهَا ١ يُمْسِي وَيُصْبِحُ فِي دُنْيَاهُ سَفَّارًا

هَلَّا تَرَكْتَ لِذِي الدُّنْيَا مُعَانَقَةً ٢ حَتَّى تُعَانِقَ فِي الفِرْدَوْسِ أَبْكَارًا

إِنْ كُنْتَ تَبْغِي جِنَانَ الخُلْدِ تَسْكُنُهَا ٣ فَيَنْبَغِي لَكَ أَنْ لَا تَأْمَنَ النَّارَا

1. O the one who embraces the worldly life [which] has no permanence and spends the mornings and evenings in his worldly life travelling [seeking material gains],

[1] The example of a donkey is often used to show ignorance such as in the verse of the Qur'an, "... like a donkey that carries a load of books." (62:5)

2. Why do you not leave embracing the worldly life so that you may embrace damsels in *Fidaws*[1]?

3. If you desire the gardens of eternity to abide therein, then you should never feel safe from the Fire.

79

السُّكُوتُ تِجَارَةٌ رَابِحَةٌ

Observing Silence is a Profitable Business

One can gain much from observing silence—such as being saved from the many sins of the tongue—but even if one gains nothing, there is nothing to lose.

وَجَدْتُ سُكُوتِي مَتْجرًا فَلَزِمْتُهُ ١ إِذَا لَمْ أَجِدْ رِبْحًا فَلَسْتُ بِخَاسِرِ

وَمَا الصَّمْتُ إِلَّا فِي الرِّجَالِ مَتَاجِرُ ٢ وَتَاجِرُهُ يَعْلُو عَلَى كُلِّ تَاجِرِ

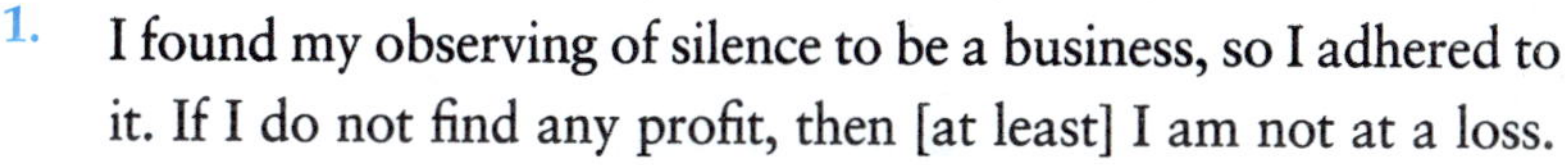

1. I found my observing of silence to be a business, so I adhered to it. If I do not find any profit, then [at least] I am not at a loss.

2. Observing silence is but a business amongst men, and its businessman surpasses every [other] businessman.

80

مَدْحُ طَلَبَةِ العِلْمِ

Praise of Students of Knowledge

One of the noblest occupations is that of a student of sacred knowledge. Words cannot describe the enjoyment one finds in

[1] The name of the highest level of Paradise.

seeking sacred knowledge. It is for this reason that some choose to remain students their whole lives.

أَكْـرِمْ بِمَجْلِـسِ فِتْيَـةٍ ١ رَيْحَانُهُـمْ وَرَقُ السُّـدُورْ

صَبُّـوا أَبَارِيـقَ الهَـوَى ٢ بَـيْنَ القُلُـوبِ عَـلَى الصُّـدُورْ

جَعَلُـوا شَرَابَهُـمُ الحَـدِ ٣ يـثَ وَكَأْسَـهُمْ أَبَـدًا تَـدُورْ

1. How honorable is a gathering of youth! Their fragrance [emanates from] the leaves of the lote tree[1].
2. They have poured the pitchers of affection [for knowledge] upon the hearts in the chests.
3. They make their drink [academic] discussion and their cup forever circulates.

شوقٌ إلى مصر

Longing for Egypt

Imam al-Shāfi'ī ﷺ had travelled across the Islamic world in search of knowledge but he still longed for his homeland as there is no place dearer than the land of one's birth and childhood. The Imam composed the following when he intended to leave Iraq for Egypt. It just so happened that both things he expected occurred; he gained prosperity there and he passed away there as well.

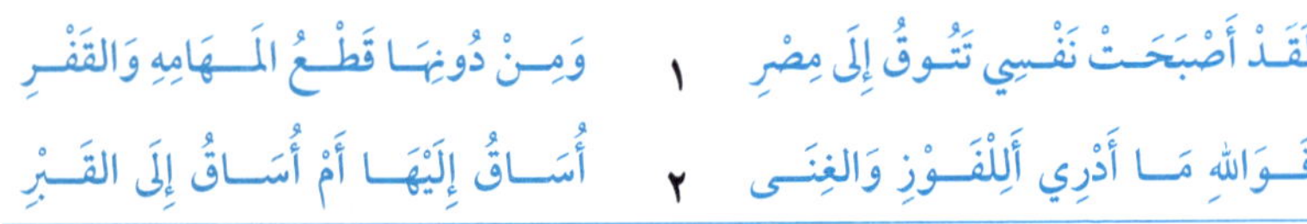

لَقَدْ أَصْبَحَتْ نَفْسِي تَتُوقُ إِلَى مِصْرِ ١ وَمِنْ دُونِهَا قَطْعُ المَهَامِهِ وَالقَفْرِ

فَوَاللهِ مَا أَدْرِي أَلِلْفَوْزِ وَالغِنَى ٢ أُسَاقُ إِلَيْهَا أَمْ أُسَاقُ إِلَى القَبْرِ

1. My soul yearns for Egypt and before it [lies] the crossing of barren lands and deserts.

2. By Allah, I do not know if for success and prosperity I am being taken there or I am being taken to the grave.

82

القَنَاعَةُ دِرْعٌ حَصِينٌ

Contentment is a Strong Armor

Poverty and death are two fears plaguing the minds of those who lack true Īmān. Out of fear of poverty, they waste their lives amassing wealth. Out of fear of death, they pretend as if it is not a reality.

تَدَرَّعْتُ ثَوْبًا لِلقُنُوعِ حَصِينَةً ١ أَصُونُ بِهَا عِرْضِي وَأَجْعَلُهَا ذُخْرَا

وَلَمْ أَحْذَرِ الدَّهْرَ الخَؤُونَ فَإِنَّمَا ٢ قُصَارَاهُ أَنْ يَرْمِي بِيَ المَوْتَ وَالفَقْرَا

فَأَعْدَدْتُ لِلْمَوْتِ الإِلَهَ وَعَفْوَهُ ٣ وَأَعْدَدْتُ لِلْفَقْرِ التَّجَلُّدَ والصَّبْرَا

1. I have worn as armor the protective clothing of one who is content. I protect by it my honor and make it a treasure [to benefit from later].

2. I am not wary of Time ever-treacherous, as the most it can do is pelt me with death and poverty.

3. I have prepared for death: Allah and His forgiveness, and I have prepared for poverty: endurance and patience.

اِلْتِمَاسُ العُذْرِ

Seeking Excuses

There are different types of people you will encounter in life; some work to gain your pleasure sincerely, while others lie to your face. But this does not mean that they do not hold you in esteem.

اِقْبَلْ مَعَاذِيرَ مَنْ يَأْتِيكَ مُعْتَذِرًا ١ إِنْ بَرَّ عِنْدَكَ فِيمَا قَالَ أَوْ فَجَرَا

لَقَدْ أَطَاعَكَ مَنْ يُرْضِيكَ ظَاهِرُهُ ٢ وَقَدْ أَجَلَّكَ مَنْ يَعْصِيكَ مُسْتَتِرَا

1. Accept the excuses of one who comes to you offering them, [regardless] if he seems truthful to you in what he says or untruthful,
2. As [the truthful one] has obeyed you by [making] his apparent please you, and he has honored you by disobeying you in secret.

اليَقَظَةُ والحَذَرُ

Vigilance and Caution

One who thinks that life should be free of any calamities is living a lie. The reality of life is that it presents one with problems and afflictions one does not anticipate. By being vigilant and cautious, one can prepare for the worst and lessen the impact of such situations.

تَـاهَ الأُعَـيْرِجُ وَاسْـتَعْلَى بِـهِ البَطَـرُ ١ فَقُـلْ لَـهُ: خَـيْرُ مَـا اسْـتَعْمَلْتَهُ الحَـذَرُ

أَحْسَـنْتَ ظَنَّـكَ بِالأَيَّـامِ إِذْ حَسُـنَتْ ٢ وَلَمْ تَخَـفْ سُـوءَ مَـا يَـأْتِي بِـهِ القَـدَرُ

وَسَالَمَـتْكَ اللَّيَـالِي فَاغْـتَرَرْتَ بِهَـا ٣ وَعِنْـدَ صَفْـوِ اللَّيَـالِي يَحْـدُثُ الكَـدَرُ

1. [When] the venomous snake[1] has become proud, haughty, and arrogant, then tell it: "The best approach you can take is caution."

2. You thought well of the days when they were well, and you did not fear the evil that fate would bring.

3. The nights made peace with you, but you were deceived by them [even though it is known that] distress occurs during the tranquility of nights.

صُنْ وَجْهَكَ مِنَ الذُّلِّ

Save Your Face From Disgrace

Having a sense of honor is a quality of a Mu'min; he safeguards the honor granted to him through Islam by not disgracing himself before the creation, and he humbles himself solely before the Creator.

كُلْ بِمِلْـحِ الجَرِيـشِ خُبْـزَ الشَّـعِيرِ ١ وَاعْتَقِـبْ لِلنَّجَـاةِ ظَهْـرَ البَعِـيرِ

وَجُـبِ المَهْمَـهَ المَخُـوفَ إلى طَنْـ ٢ ـجَةٍ أَوْ خَلْفَهَـا إِلَى الـدُّرْدُورِ

وَصُـنِ الوَجْـهَ أَن يُـذَلَّ وَأَنْ يَخْـ ٣ ـضَعَ إِلَّا إِلَى اللَّطِيـفِ الخَبِـيرِ

---

[1] Referring to a person.

1. Eat barley bread with crushed salt and for deliverance [from the worries of livelihood] take turns [riding on] camelback.

2. Traverse the terrifying, remote desert to Tangier[1] or further than that to Dardur[2].

3. And save [your] face from disgrace and humbling yourself [before anyone] besides the All-Kind, the All-Aware.

86

سَلامُ فِرَاقٍ

Farewell

Imam al-Shāfi'ī came to know that a man was speaking ill of him behind his back, so he wrote him the following couplets:

سَأَصْبِرُ فَاصْبِرْ وَاقْطَعِ الوَصْلَ بَيْنَنَا ١ وَلَا تَذْكُرَنِّي وَاسْلُ بِاللهِ عَنْ ذِكْرِي

فَقَدْ عِشْتَ دَهْرًا لَسْتَ تَعْرِفُ مَنْ أَنَا ٢ وَعِشْتُ وَلَمْ أَعْرِفْكَ دَهْرًا مِنَ الدَّهْرِ

سَلَامُ فِرَاقٍ لَا مَوَدَّةَ بَيْنَنَا ٣ وَلَا مُلْتَقَى حَتَّى القِيَامَةِ وَالحَشْرِ

1. I will be patient, and you [also] be patient and cut the ties between us. Do not mention me at all, and for the sake of Allah, forget me.

2. You have lived a long time not knowing who I was, and I have lived a long time not knowing who you were.

3. Farewell, there is no affection between us, and there will be no meeting until [the Day of] Judgement and Resurrection.

---

1 A city in Morocco on the northwestern coast of Africa.

2 A place on the coast of the Gulf of Oman.

87

الدَّهْرُ يَوْمَانِ: يَوْمٌ لَكَ وَيَوْمٌ عَلَيْكَ

Time Consists of Two Days: One For You and One Against You

This worldly life is not meant to be continuously enjoyed, and as such, some days are better than others. Although everyone faces difficulties in life, noble and pious people face more difficulties than others.

الدَّهْرُ يَوْمَانِ ذَا أَمْنٌ وَذَا خَطَر	١	وَالعَيْشُ عَيْشَانِ ذَا صَفْوٌ وَذا كَدَرُ
أَمَا تَرَى البَحْرَ تَعْلُو فَوْقَهُ جِيَفٌ	٢	وَتَسْتَقِرُّ بِأَقْصَى قَاعِهِ الدُّرَرُ
وَفِي السَّماءِ نُجُومٌ لَا عِدَادَ لَهَا	٣	وَلَيْسَ يُكْسَفُ إِلَّا الشَّمْسُ وَالقَمَرُ

1. Time [consists of] two days; one of safety and one of danger. And life [consists of] two lives; one pure and one murky.

2. Do you not see the sea? Corpses float upon it while pearls remain at the bottom of its depths.

3. There are innumerable stars in the sky, [but] only the Sun and the Moon are eclipsed.

88

لِلرَّبِّ أَمْرٌ فَوْقَ أَمْرِي

The Lord Has a Decision Over My Decision

Being distant from one's friends requires patience and strong resolve, and in such a situation, one should remember that Allah ﷻ is in control of all things—including that situation. We may strive our utmost to change our condition and still not achieve our goal, but that should not be a cause for despair, as that is the will of Allah.

أُفَكِّرُ فِي نَوَى إِلْفِي وَصَبْرِي ١ وَأَحْمَدُ هِمَّتِي وَأَذُمُّ دَهْرِي

وَمَا قَصَّرْتُ فِي طَلَبٍ وَلَكِنْ ٢ لِرَبِّ النَّاسِ أَمْرٌ فَوْقَ أَمْرِي

1. I contemplate the remoteness of my close friends and my patience. And then I praise my resolve and criticize my era [that I am living in].

2. I was not remiss in seeking [my goal], but the Lord of mankind has a decision over my decision.

89

نُدْرَةُ الأَصْحَابِ الأَوْفِيَاءِ

The Rarity of Reliable Friends

The condition of mankind is bound to worsen as time progresses. And so, finding true friends amongst mankind will get more difficult than ever before. In such times, the best course of action is to remain aloof from people and thus be safe from their harm.

كُنْ سَائِرًا فِي ذَا الزَّمَانِ بِسَيْرِهِ ١ وَعَنِ الوَرَى كُنْ رَاهِبًا فِي دَيْرِهِ

وَاغْسِلْ يَدَيْكَ مِنَ الزَّمَانِ وَأَهْلِهِ ٢ وَاحْذَرْ مَوَدَّتَهُمْ تَنَلْ مِنْ خَيْرِهِ

إِنِّي اطَّلَعْتُ فَلَمْ أَجِدْ لِي صَاحِبًا ٣ أَصْحَبُهُ فِي الدَّهْرِ وَلَا فِي غَيْرِهِ

فَتَرَكْتُ أَسْفَلَهُمْ لِكَثْرَةِ شَرِّهِ ٤ وَتَرَكْتُ أَعْلَاهُمْ لِقِلَّةِ خَيْرِهِ

1. Proceed with the progression of the times, and with mankind be [like] a monk in his monastery.
2. Wash your hands of Time and its people and be wary of loving them, [then only] will you acquire from the goodness of Time.
3. I have looked and have not found in any era a companion I could accompany.
4. I left the lowest of them [in status] because of their extreme evil and I left the highest of them [in status] because of their lack of goodness.

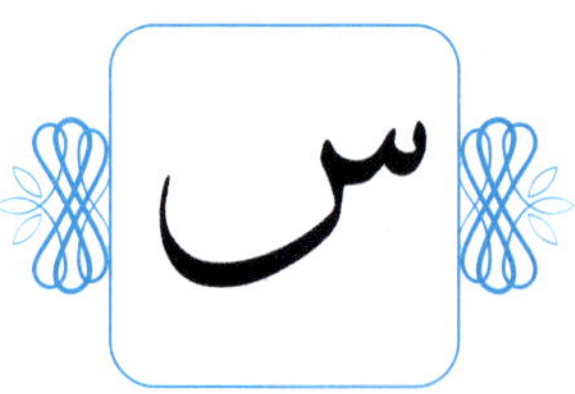

قافية السين
The End-Rhyme of the Letter *Sīn*

القَلَمُ
The Pen

The pen specifically and writing in general is a great bounty of Allah . Allah taught man what he knew not through the pen. Man then uses the pen to accomplish the noble purpose of preserving and imparting knowledge. Another purpose of the pen is to facilitate communication over distances. This great bounty should not be overlooked and, more importantly, should not be misused.

هَـلْ تَذْكُرِيـنَ إِذِ الرَّسَـائِلُ بَيْنَنَـا ١ يَجْرِيـنَ فِي الشَّـجَرِ الَّـذِي لَمْ يُغْـرَسِ

أَيَّـامَ سِرُّكِ فِي يَـدِي وَمِثَالُـهُ ٢ لِي فِي يَدَيْـكِ مِـنَ الضَّمِـيرِ الأَخْـرَسِ

1. Do you remember when letters were flowing between us [written] on [the paper of] a tree which had not been planted?[1]

2. Days when your secret was in my hand and the like for me in your hands from a mute heart.[2]

1 Referring to mail sent by post.
2 Referring to the relationship with a pen when writing with it.

المُنَاجَاة

A Secret Conversation

The etiquettes of supplicating to Allah ﷻ include praising Him, mentioning His favors, showing one's humility, seeking forgiveness, and asking for that which is beneficial in this world and the Hereafter. Through this, one's supplication will be more worthy of being accepted in the sight of Allah ﷻ.

قَلْبِي بِرَحْمَتِكَ اللَّهُمَّ ذُو أُنُسِ ١ فِي السِّرِّ وَالْجَهْرِ وَالإِصْبَاحِ وَالغَلَسِ
وَمَا تَقَلَّبْتُ مِنْ نَوْمِي وَفِي سِنَتِي ٢ إِلَّا وَذِكْرُكَ بَيْنَ النَّفْسِ وَالنَّفَسِ
لَقَدْ مَنَنْتَ عَلَى قَلْبِي بِمَعْرِفَةٍ ٣ بِأَنَّكَ اللهُ ذُو الآلَاءِ وَالقُدُسِ
وَقَدْ أَتَيْتُ ذُنُوبًا أَنْتَ تَعْلَمُهَا ٤ وَلَمْ تَكُنْ فَاضِحِي فِيهَا بِفِعْلِ مُسِي
فَامْنُنْ عَلَيَّ بِذِكْرِ الصَّالِحِينَ وَلَا ٥ تَجْعَلْ عَلَيَّ إِذًا فِي الدِّينِ مِنْ لَبَسِ
وَكُنْ مَعِي طُولَ دُنْيَايَ وَآخِرَتِي ٦ وَيَوْمَ حَشْرِي بِمَا أَنْزَلْتَ فِي عَبَسِ

1. O Allah, my heart is familiar with Your mercy, in public and in private, in [the light of] morning and in darkness.

2. I have not turned in my sleep or in my drowsiness except that Your remembrance was between [my] soul and [my] breath.

3. You have blessed my heart with the recognition that You are Allah, possessor of blessings and glory.

4. I have committed [many] sins which You know [well], but You have never disgraced me due to my evil deeds.

5. Thus, grace me with mention amongst the righteous, and do not put me in any confusion in [any aspect of] *Dīn*.

6. Be with me throughout my worldly life and my Hereafter, as well as on the day of my resurrection due to what You have revealed in [Sūrah] ʿAbasa.[1]

الأَصْدِقَاءُ عِنْدَ الشَّدَائِدِ

Friends at Times of Difficulty

In times of difficulty, having a true friend by your side supporting you makes the ordeal ever the more bearable. But finding such a friend is like sifting for gold by a river; it takes time and careful scrutiny.

صَدِيقٌ لَيْسَ يَنْفَعُ يَوْمَ بَأْسٍ ١ قَرِيبٌ مِنْ عَدُوٍّ فِي القِيَاسِ

وَمَا يُغْنِي الصَّدِيقُ بِكُلِّ عَصْرٍ ٢ وَلَا الإِخْوَانُ إِلَّا لِلتَّآسِي

عَمَرْتُ الدَّهْرَ مُلْتَمِسًا بِجُهْدِي ٣ أَخَا ثِقَةٍ فَأَكْدَاهُ الْتِمَاسِي

تَنَكَّرَتِ البِلَادُ عَلَيَّ حَتَّى ٤ كَأَنَّ أُنَاسَهَا لَيْسُوا بِنَاسِي

1. A friend that does not benefit on a day of harm is logically closer to [being an] enemy.

2. Friends will not avail at all times, and neither will brothers, except for offering condolences.

3. I have lived a [life]time searching with great effort for a

[1] Referring to the condition of solitude one will face on the Day of Judgement as mentioned in verses 33-37 of the 80th Sūrah of the Holy Qur'an.

trustworthy friend, but my search exhausted my efforts.

4. [At times of difficulty] the lands and its inhabitants become strangers for me such that it is as if its people are not people.

93

وَاعِظُ النَّاسِ

One Who Admonishes People

Being free of all faults and sins is impossible for the children of Adam, but self-rectification is a path that can get us as close as possible. This is as opposed to one who does not even acknowledge his own faults and sins, let alone rectify his lower-self. Such a person has no right to admonish others when he himself needs admonition.

يَا وَاعِظَ النَّاسِ عَمَّا أَنْتَ فَاعِلُهُ ١ يَا مَنْ يُعَدُّ عَلَيْهِ العُمْرُ بِالنَّفَسِ

اِحْفَظْ لِشَيْبِكَ مِنْ عَيْبٍ يُدَنِّسُهُ ٢ إِنَّ البَيَاضَ قَلِيلُ الحَمْلِ لِلدَّنَسِ

كَحَامِلٍ لِثِيَابِ النَّاسِ يَغْسِلُهَا ٣ وَثَوْبُهُ غَارِقٌ فِي الرِّجْسِ وَالنَّجَسِ

تَبْغِي النَّجَاةَ وَلَمْ تَسْلُكْ طَرِيقَتَهَا ٤ إِنَّ السَّفِينَةَ لَا تَجْرِي عَلَى اليَبَسِ

رُكُوبُكَ النَّعْشَ يُنْسِيكَ الرُّكُوبَ عَلَى ٥ مَا كُنْتَ تَرْكَبُ مِنْ بَغْلٍ وَمِنْ فَرَسِ

يَوْمَ القِيَامَةِ لَا مَالٌ وَلَا وَلَدٌ ٦ وَضَمَّةُ القَبْرِ تُنْسِي لَيْلَةَ العُرُسِ

1. O the one who admonishes people for [the very thing that] you yourself are doing; O the one whose life is being counted by the breath,

2. Protect [yourself] from a blemish that will stain your old age; the whiteness [of old age] can barely bear stains [of disgrace].

3. [Your example is] like the one who carries people's clothing to wash, whilst his own clothes are drowning in dirt and filth.

4. You seek success, but you have not trodden its path—boats do not sail on dry land.

5. Your riding the funeral bier will make you forget the mules and horses you used to ride.

6. On the Day of Judgement, neither wealth nor children [will avail you]. The embrace of the grave will make you forget [even] the night of [your] wedding.

مَفْخَرَةُ الإِنْسَانِ العِلْمُ

The Source of Pride for Man is Knowledge

The value of knowledge cannot be understated; through it, one can gain material success in the worldly life and, to a higher degree, gain eternal success in the Hereafter. But, like all things in life, it requires sacrifice and effort. Renouncing comforts and luxuries in pursuit of knowledge is guaranteed to produce results.

العِلْمُ مَغْرِسُ كُلِّ فَخْرِ ١ وَاحْذَرْ يَفُوتُكَ فَخْرُ ذَاكَ المَغْرِسِ
وَاعْلَمْ بِأَنَّ العِلْمَ لَيْسَ يَنَالُهُ ٢ مَنْ هَمُّهُ فِي مَطْعَمٍ أَوْ مَلْبَسِ
إِلَّا أَخُو العِلْمِ الَّذِي يُعْنَى بِهِ ٣ فِي حَالَتَيْهِ عَارِيًا أَوْ مُكْتَسِي
فَاجْعَلْ لِنَفْسِكَ مِنْهُ حَظًّا وَافِرًا ٤ وَاهْجُرْ لَهُ طِيبَ الرُّقَادِ وَعَبِّسِ
فَلَعَلَّ يَوْمًا إِنْ حَضَرْتَ بِمَجْلِسٍ ٥ كُنْتَ الرَّئِيسَ وَفَخْرَ ذَاكَ المَجْلِسِ

1. Knowledge is the flowerbed of pride. Be proud of it and

beware of losing the pride of that flowerbed.

2. Know that knowledge cannot be acquired by one whose concern is eating and dressing.

3. [It can only be acquired by] the possessor of knowledge who is preoccupied with it in every condition [whether] naked or clothed.

4. Make a great portion of knowledge for yourself, renounce for it the comfort of sleep, and [exert yourself] with full seriousness [for it].

5. Then hopefully, one day, when you attend a gathering, you shall be the leader and pride of that gathering.

عِزَّةُ النَّفْسِ

Self-Respect

"Preservation of honor" is one of the five objectives of Shariah. This not only entails the preservation of other people's honor, but one's own honor as well. A person ennobled by the Dīn of Islam should avoid any action that would endanger their self-honor in any way.

لَقَلْعُ ضِرْسٍ وَضَرْبُ حَبْسٍ ١ وَنَزْعُ نَفْسٍ وَرَدُّ أَمْسِ

وَقَرُّ بَرْدٍ وَقَوْدُ فَرْدٍ ٢ وَدَبْغُ جِلْدٍ بِغَيْرِ شَمْسِ

وَأَكْلُ ضَبٍّ وَصَيْدُ دُبٍّ ٣ وَصَرْفُ حَبٍّ بِأَرْضِ خَرْسِ

وَنَفْخُ نَارٍ وَحَمْلُ عَارٍ ٤ وَبَيْعُ دَارٍ بِرُبْعِ فَلْسِ

وَبَيْعُ خُفٍّ وَعُدْمُ إِلْفٍ ٥ وَضَرْبُ إِلْفٍ بِحَبْلِ قَلْسِ

أَهْوَنُ مِنْ وَقْفَةِ الحُرِّ ٦ يَرْجُو نَوَالًا بِبَابِ نَحْسِ

1. Surely, uprooting a molar, beating of imprisonment, extracting a soul, bringing back [the bygone] yesterday,

2. [Withstanding] the severity of cold, killing in retaliation, tanning leather without [exposing it to] the Sun,

3. Eating an iguana, hunting a bear, sowing seeds in an infertile land,

4. Blowing out a fire, bearing disgrace, selling a house for a quarter of a penny,

5. Selling leather socks, losing a beloved, striking a beloved with a thick rope,

6. Are [all] easier for a noble person [to bear] than standing at the door of a wretched person hoping for a favor.

قافية الصاد

The End-Rhyme of the Letter *Sād*

العِلْمُ نُورٌ

Knowledge is Divine Light

There is a direct correlation between our actions and our ability to grasp divine knowledge. It is for this reason that some are able to go forward and benefit themselves as well as others with their knowledge, while others fall behind.

شَــكَوْتُ إِلَى وَكِيــعٍ سُــوءَ حِفْظِــي ١ فَأَرْشَــدَنِي إِلَى تَــرْكِ الـــمَعَاصِي

وَأَخْــبَرَنِي بِــأَنَّ العِلْــمَ نُــورٌ ٢ وَنُــورُ اللهِ لَا يُهْــدَى لِعَــاصِي

1. I complained to [my teacher] Wakīʿ[1] of my weak memory, so he instructed me to abstain from sins,

2. And he told me that knowledge is divine light, and the divine light of Allah is not granted to a sinner.

[1] Wakīʿ bin al-Jarrāḥ (d. 176 A.H.) was a prominent *muḥaddith* and one of Imam al-Shāfiʿī's teachers.

الخُلَفَاءُ الرَّاشِدُون

The Rightly Guided *Khalīfahs*

The Abbasid Caliphate is famously known as the Golden Age of Islam based on the worldly advancements achieved in that era. It would be more prudent to say that the Golden Age of Islam was the era of the Prophet ﷺ and his Companions: the Rightly Guided Khalīfahs. That era was when Islam was at its utmost perfection and is the era from which we are to take guidance and lesson.

١ شَهِدتُّ بِأَنَّ اللهَ لَا رَبَّ غَيْرُهُ ... وَأَشْهَدُ أَنَّ البَعْثَ حَقٌّ وَأُخْلِصُ

٢ وأَنَّ عُرَى الإِيمَانِ قَوْلٌ مُبَيَّنٌ ... وَفِعْلٌ زَكِيٌّ قَدْ يَزِيدُ وَيَنْقُصُ

٣ وَأَنَّ أَبَا بَكْرٍ خَلِيفَةُ رَبِّهِ ... وَكَانَ أَبُو حَفْصٍ عَلَى الخَيْرِ يَحْرِصُ

٤ وَأُشْهِدُ رَبِّي أَنَّ عُثْمَانَ فَاضِلٌ ... وَأَنَّ عَلِيًّا فَضْلُهُ مُتَخَصِّصُ

٥ أَئِمَّةُ قَوْمٍ يُقْتَدَى بِهُدَاهُمُ ... لَحَى اللهُ مَنْ إِيَّاهُمُ يَتَنَقَّصُ

٦ فَمَا لِغُوَاةٍ يَشْتُمُونَ سَفَاهَةً ... وَمَا لِسَفِيهٍ لَا يَحِيصُ وَيَخْرُصُ

1. I have testified that there is no deity besides Allah, and I have testified that the Resurrection is a true reality, and I am sincere [in this].

2. And [I have testified] that the [foundational] handles of *Īmān* are a clear statement[1] and pure deeds, [and that *Īmān*] increases and decreases.

3. And [I have testified] that Abū Bakr was the true *khalīfah* of

1 Stating the *shahādah* (the testimony of faith).

his Lord, and Abū Hafṣ[1] was always eager to do good.

4. I make my Lord witness that 'Uthmān was an eminent person and that 'Alī had unique merit.

5. [These are] the leaders of the people whose guidance is followed. May the curse of Allah be upon those who degrade them.

6. What is wrong with the astray who curse [them] out of foolishness, and what is wrong with the foolish one who does not leave [these actions] and [continues to] fabricate [lies about them]?

[1] The agnomen of 'Umar bin al-Khaṭṭāb.

قافية الضاد
The End-Rhyme of the Letter *Ḍād*

الجُودُ
Generosity

Shayṭān deludes us into thinking that we will donate more when we have more, but that is just one of the many false hopes he pollutes our hearts with. The time to donate generously is now, not just in the future.

إِذَا لَمْ تَجُـودُوا وَالأُمُـورُ بِكُـمْ تَمْـضِي ١ وَقَـدْ مَلَكَـتْ أَيْدِيكُمُ البَسْـطَ والقَبْضَا
فَـمَاذَا يُرَجَّـى مِنْكُـمُ إِنْ عَزَلْتُـمُ ٢ وَعَضَّتْكُـمُ الدُّنْيَـا بِأَنْيابِهَـا عَضَّـا
وَتَسْـتَرْجِعُ الأَيَّـامُ مَـا وَهَبَتْكُـمُ ٣ وَمِـنْ عَـادَةِ الأَيَّـامِ تَسْـتَرْجِعُ القَرْضَـا

1. If you did not act generously while matters were run by you and while your hands controlled giving and withholding,

2. What can be expected of you if you are dismissed [from a position], and the world bites you with its teeth severely?

3. Time will take back what it had gifted you, as its habit is to take back loans.

99

هَكَذَا الصَّدَاقَةُ

Friendship is Like This

When you have gained a true friend, and he wrongs you in some way, it is better to overlook that misdeed and attempt to repair the weakened bonds of friendship, lest those bonds break entirely. Most friendships come and go, but a true friendship deserves to be preserved and cherished.

Imam al-Shāfiʿī said the following to a friend who broke ties with him:

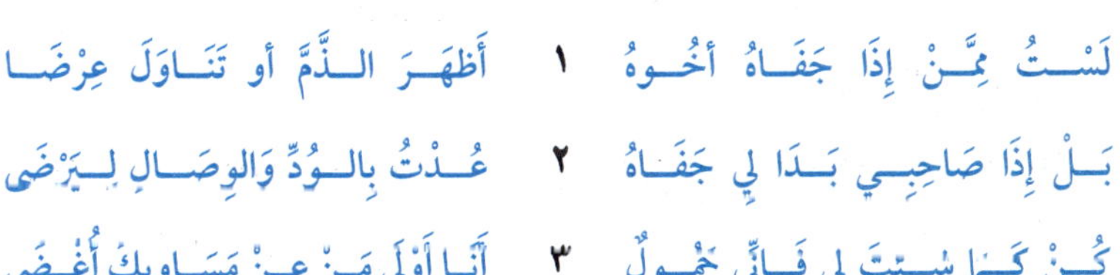

لَسْتُ مِمَّنْ إِذَا جَفَاهُ أَخُوهُ ١ أَظْهَرَ الذَّمَّ أَو تَنَاوَلَ عِرْضَا

بَلْ إِذَا صَاحِبِي بَدَا لِي جَفَاهُ ٢ عُدْتُ بِالوُدِّ وَالوِصَالِ لِيَرْضَى

كُنْ كَمَا شِئْتَ لِي فَإِنِّي حَمُولٌ ٣ أَنَا أَوْلَى مَنْ عَنْ مَسَاوِيكَ أَغْضَى

1. I am not from amongst those who, when his friend breaks ties with him, he finds fault [in him] and attacks [his] honor.

2. Rather, when my friend's breakage of ties becomes apparent to me, I return [the favor] with affection and reunion so that he may be happy.

3. Be as you wish to be with me, as I am tolerant [and] it is most befitting that I be the one to overlook your misdeeds.

100

حُبُّ آلِ مُحَمَّدٍ ﷺ

Love for the Noble Family of Muhammad ﷺ

Out of jealousy and wretchedness, the Khawārij claimed Imam al-Shāfi'ī to be a Shiite. Thus, he denounced them and composed the following couplets refuting their allegations. Throughout Hajj, the Imam constantly recited these couplets.

يَا رَاكِبًا قِفْ بِالْمُحَصَّبِ مِنْ مِنًى ١ وَاهْتِفْ بِقَاعِدِ خَيْفِهَا وَالنَّاهِضِ

سَحَرًا إِذَا فَاضَ الْحَجِيجُ إِلَى مِنًى ٢ فَيْضًا كَمُلْتَطِمِ الْفُرَاتِ الْفَائِضِ

إِنِّي أُحِبُّ بَنِي النَّبِيِّ الْمُصْطَفَى ٣ وَأَعُدُّهُ مِنْ وَاجِبَاتِ فَرَائِضِي

إِنْ كَانَ رَفْضًا حُبُّ آلِ مُحَمَّدٍ ٤ فَلْيَشْهَدِ الثَّقَلَانِ أَنِّي رَافِضِي

1. O rider! Stop at [the valley of] al-Muḥaṣṣab in Mina and announce to the ones sitting and standing in the masjid of Khayf therein—

2. In the early morning, when the pilgrims pour forth into Mina like the clashing [waves] of the abounding Euphrates—

3. "I love the children of the prophet Muṣṭafā, and I consider it to be one of my necessary obligations,

4. If loving the noble family of Muhammad is Shiism, then mankind and jinn-kind should bear witness that I am a Shia."

قافية العين
The End-Rhyme of the Letter *'Ayn*

101

وُجُوبُ صَدَقَةٍ
The Obligation of Charity

There are other forms of charity besides monetary charity. Donating one's time and actions should be done, especially by those unable to donate monetarily.

١ وَجَبَتْ عَلَيَّ زَكَاةُ مَا مَلَكَتْ يَدِي   وَزَكَاةُ جَاهِي أَنْ أُعِينَ وَأَشْفَعَا

٢ فَإِذَا سُئِلْتَ فَجُدْ وَإِنْ لَمْ تَسْتَطِعْ   فَاجْهَدْ بِجُهْدِكَ كُلِّهِ أَنْ تَنْفَعَا

1. It is necessary for me to give alms for what my hands own, [as well as for] my honor, which is that I assist and intercede.

2. If you are asked, then be generous. And if you cannot, then strive your utmost to benefit.

النَّصائِحُ القَيِّمَةُ

Valuable Advice

If one ponders and acts upon these four pieces of advice, one will live a life of the wise.

1.	Sufficient for me is my knowledge if it is beneficial.	١. حَسْبِي بِعِلْمِي إِنْ نَفَعْ
2.	There is only disgrace in greed.	٢. مَا الذُّلُّ إِلَّا فِي الطَّمَعْ
3.	Whoever is conscious of Allah repents,	٣. مَنْ رَاقَبَ اللهَ رَجَعْ
4.	From the evil that he commits.	٤. عَنْ سُوءِ مَا كَانَ صَنَعْ
5.	No bird flew and soared high,	٥. مَا طَارَ طَيْرٌ وَ ارْتَفَعْ
6.	Except that it fell just like it flew.	٦. إِلَّا كَمَا طَارَ وَقَعْ

ع

لَا تَطْمَعْ

Do Not Be Greedy

Greed is considered to be one of the "Seven Deadly Sins" by Christians. This belief of theirs can be understood as having a divine origin, as the Qur'an and Hadith both condemn this disease of the heart. It is such that it enslaves the minds of those who are free.

العَبْدُ حُرٌّ إِنْ قَنِعْ ١ وَالحُرُّ عَبْدٌ إِنْ طَمِعْ

فَاقْنَعْ وَلَا تَطْمَعْ فَلَا ٢ شَيْءٌ يَشِينُ سِوَى الطَّمَعْ

1. A slave is free if he is content, and a free man is a slave if he is greedy,
2. So be content and do not be greedy, as nothing disgraces [one] besides greed.

104

سَكْرَةُ المَوتِ

The Agony of Death

The reality of the throes of death is that the lower-self feels pain when being separated from what it loves and craves, i.e., the worldly life. It is possible to decrease this pain by working to tame our inner-selves and prepare it for this awaited separation.

مِنَ المَوْتِ لَا ذُو الصَّبْرِ يُنْجِيهِ صَبْرُهُ	١	وَلَا لِجَزُوعٍ كَارِهِ المَوْتِ مَجْزَعُ
أَرَى كُلَّ ذِي عُمْرٍ وَإِنْ طَالَ عُمْرُهُ	٢	وَعَاشَ لَهُ سُمٌّ مِنَ المَوْتِ مُنْقَعُ
وَكُلُّ امْرِئٍ لَاقٍ مِنَ المَوْتِ سَكْرَةً	٣	لَهَا سَاعَةٌ فِيهَا يَذِلُّ وَيَخْضَعُ
فَلِلَّهِ فَانْصَحْ يَا ابْنَ آدَمَ إِنَّهُ	٤	مَتَى مَا تُخَادِعْهُ فَنَفْسَكَ تَخْدَعُ

1. From death, a patient one's patience will not save him, nor will the impatient one who despises death have a place of refuge.
2. I see every aged person—even though he lived a long life—for him will be the venomous poison of death.
3. Every person will face the agony of death; it has a time wherein he will be lowly and humble.
4. So be sincere with Allah, O son of Adam, as when you [try to] deceive Him, then you are [in reality] deceiving yourself.

الصَّدِيقُ أَدْرَى بِنَفْعِ صَدِيقِهِ

A Friend Knows Best What Benefits His Friend

When Imam Imam al-Shāfiʿī ﷺ was detained in Iraq on false charges, he sent the following verses to request Imam Muhammad bin al-Ḥasan al-Shaybānī ﷺ—the great student of Imam Abū Ḥanīfah ﷺ who was very well respected and had a high status in the court of the Abbasid *khalīfah* Harūn al-Rashīd—to intercede on his behalf.

لَسْتُ أَدري مَا حِيْلَتِي غَيْرَ أَنِّي ١ أَرْتَجِي مِنْ جَمِيلِ جَاهِكَ صُنْعَا

وَالفَتَى إِنْ أَرَادَ نَفْعَ صَدِيقٍ ٢ فَهْوَ يَدْرِي فِي أَمْرِهِ كَيْفَ يَسْعَى

1. I do not know what my strategy is, except that I hope for what is best [for me] from your high position.
2. If a young man wants to benefit a friend, then he knows [best] how to proceed in his matter.

حُبُّ الصَّالِحِين

Love for the Righteous

Even if one does not feel that he is righteous (as one should never feel), loving righteous people is a step towards righteousness itself. Likewise is the case with wretched people; one should detest them even though one knows that he may be one of them.

أُحِبُّ الصَّالِحِينَ وَلَسْتُ مِنْهُمْ ١ لَعَلِّي أَنْ أَنَالَ بِهِمْ شَفَاعَهْ

وَأَكْرَهُ مَنْ تِجَارَتُهُ المَعَاصِي ٢ وَلَوْ كُنَّا سَوَاءً فِي البِضَاعَهْ

1. I love the righteous while I am not one of them. Hopefully, through [loving] them, I will acquire [their] intercession [on the Day of Judgement].

2. I detest the one whose trade is sinning even though we are equal in merchandise.[1]

107

اتَّقِ دَعْوَةَ المَظْلُومِ

Fear the Supplication of the Oppressed

Just like it is next to impossible to dodge the arrow of an expert archer, it is equally impossible to escape the supplication of the oppressed. Whether one is the oppressor or the one oppressed, do not underestimate such a supplication.

وَرُبَّ ظَلُومٍ قَدْ كُفِيتُ بِحَرْبِهِ ١ فَأَوْقَعَهُ المَقْدُورُ أَيَّ وُقُوعِ
فَمَا كَانَ لِي الإِسْلَامُ إِلَّا تَعَبُّدًا ٢ وَأَدْعِيَةً لَا تُتَّقَى بِدُرُوعِ
وَحَسْبُكَ أَنْ يَنْجُو الظَّلُومُ وَخَلْفَهُ ٣ سِهَامُ دُعَاءٍ مِنْ قِسِيِّ رُكُوعِ
مُرَيَّشَةً بِالهُدْبِ مِنْ كُلِّ سَاهِرٍ ٤ مُنَهَّلَةً أَطْرَافُهَا بِدُمُوعِ

1. Many an oppressor I was sufficed from fighting him, as destiny had landed him in many calamities.

2. Islam, for me, is worship and such supplication which cannot be protected [from] with armor.

3. It is far-fetched that the oppressor escapes while behind him

[1] Referring to his sins.

is the arrow of supplication from the quiver of one who bows [and prostrates in salah],

4. Feathered with the eyelashes of every wakeful one and its sides watered with tears.

108

الحَسُودُ ذُو وَجْهَيْنِ

The Jealous One is Two-Faced

One sign that someone is jealous of you is that they speak ill of you behind your back. But this action of their's should not prompt you to do the same, as that is a reprehensible sin.

وَذِي حَسَدٍ يَغْتَابُنِي حَيْثُ لَا يَرَى ١ مَكَانِي وَيُثْنِي صَالِحًا حَيْثُ أَسْمَعُ

تَوَرَّعْتُ أَنْ أَغْتَابَهُ مِنْ وَرَائِهِ ٢ وَمَا هُوَ إِذْ يَغْتَابُنِي مُتَوَرِّعُ

1. Many a jealous person speaks ill of me where he does not see me and praises me lavishly where I listen.

2. I have refrained from speaking ill of him behind his back, but he does not refrain from speaking ill of me.

109

مِنَ الوَرَعِ اشْتِغَالُكَ بِعُيُوبِكَ

Concerning Oneself With One's Shortcomings is a Part of Piety

Being concerned with the shortcomings of others is a futile usage of time, and if done in the company of others, then it is a harmful usage of time as one may be backbiting the other or even slandering him. To stop yourself from doing so, remember that you yourself are spiritually sick and that you need to tend to your own health first.

المَـــرْءُ إِنْ كَانَ عَاقِــلًا وَرِعًــا ١ يَشْــغَلُهُ عَــنْ عُيُوبِهِــمْ وَرَعُــهْ

كَـمَا العَلِيــلُ السَّــقِيمُ يَشْــغَلُهُ ٢ عَــنْ وَجَـعِ النَّـاسِ كُلِّهِـمْ وَجَعُــهْ

1. If a man is intelligent and pious, his piety will distract him from [indulging in] the shortcomings of others,
2. Like how a sick, ailing person's own pain distracts him from everyone else's pain.

تَرْكُ الشَّرِّ

Disregarding Evil

Imam al-Shāfi'ī ﷺ wrote a letter to someone saying: "Hearts are the fields of the tongues, so plant a noble word, because if it does not sprout completely, some of it surely will. Some speech is harder than rocks, more piercing than needles, more bitter than aloe, rounder than a millstone, and sharper than spears. Many times I forgive a hot-headed person due to his heat, fearing that he would be hotter, more bitter, and viler. That is why I say:

لَقَـدْ أَسْـمَعُ القَـوْلَ الَّـذِي كَانَ كُلَّـمَا ١ تُذَكِّرُنِيــهِ النَّفْــسُ قَلْبِــيَ يُصَــدَّعُ

فَأُبْــدِي لِــمَنْ أَبْـدَاهُ مِنِّـي بَشَاشَــةً ٢ كَأَنِّيَ مَــسْرُورٌ بِــمَا مِنْــهُ أَسْــمَعُ

وَمَا ذَاكَ مِنْ عُجْبٍ بِهِ غَيْرَ أَنَّنِي ٣ أَرَى أَنَّ تَرْكَ بَعْضِ الشَّرِّ لِلشَّرِّ أَقْطَعُ

1. Indeed I [even] listen to such a statement that whenever the lower-self reminds me of it, my heart pains.
2. I display, from my [inner] self, a happy demeanor to the one who expresses [that statement], as if I am happy with what I hear from him.
3. That is not out of conceit; rather, I believe that disregarding some evil is [more effective] in eradicating evil.

111

دَعْوَةٌ إلى السَّعْيِ وتَرْكِ الخَوفِ

An Invitation to Strive and Disregard Fear

Remaining in one place complacent will not bring about any positive change in one's life. To bring about change, one will need to face potential dangers and calamities.

الْمَرْءُ فِي كُوْرَتِهِ ضَائِعٌ ١ وَاللَّيْثُ فِي غَيْضَتِهِ جَائِعُ

فَاخْرُجْ تَرَ النَّاسَ وَتَلْقَ الغِنَى ٢ فَالْمَوْتُ لَا يَدْفَعُهُ دَافِعُ

1. A man [remaining] in his village is wasted and a lion [remaining] in his jungle is hungry,
2. So leave [your comfort zone] and you will see people and will find prosperity, [and do not fear death] as death cannot be repelled by anyone.

112

آدابُ النُّصْحِ

Etiquettes of Giving Advice

There are some etiquettes associated with giving advice to others with the intent of reforming them. One important etiquette is to not correct the mistakes of others in public, as instead of bringing about reform, it will create feelings of being belittled. Instead, by giving advice in private, the advice will touch the person's heart and will hopefully bring about true reform.

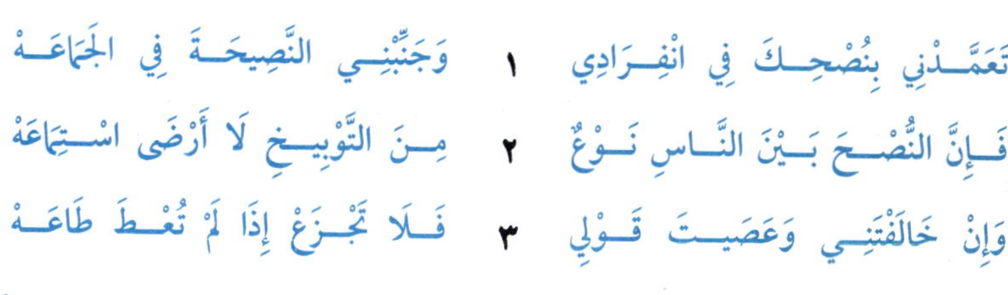

تَعَمَّدْنِي بِنُصْحِكَ فِي انْفِرَادِي ١ وَجَنِّبْنِي النَّصِيحَةَ فِي الْجَمَاعَهْ

فَإِنَّ النُّصْحَ بَيْنَ النَّاسِ نَوْعٌ ٢ مِنَ التَّوْبِيخِ لَا أَرْضَى اسْتِمَاعَهْ

وَإِنْ خَالَفْتَنِي وَعَصَيْتَ قَوْلِي ٣ فَلَا تَجْزَعْ إِذَا لَمْ تُعْطَ طَاعَهْ

1. Approach me with your advice in private and spare me the advice in a gathering,
2. As advising amongst people is a type of rebuke that I am not happy to listen to.
3. And if you oppose me and disobey my statement, then do not be unhappy if you are not given obedience.

113

مَتَى يَكُونُ رَأْيُكَ نَافِعًا

When Your Opinion Will Be Beneficial

Not everyone is receptive to the opinions of others, and so, before giving one's opinion, one must ascertain whether such an opinion is even being sought or not.

وَلَا تُعْطِيَنَّ الرَّأْيَ مَنْ لَا يُرِيدُهُ ١ فَلَا أَنْتَ مَحْمُودٌ وَلَا الرَّأْيُ نَافِعُهْ

1. Never give an opinion to one who does not want it, as you will not be appreciated, nor will the opinion benefit him.

مُدَاوَاةُ الهَوَى

Treating Affection

A man came to Imam al-Shāfiʿī with a piece of paper which said:

سَلِ الْمُفْتِيَ الْمَكِّيَّ مِنْ آلِ هَاشِمٍ ١ إِذَا اشْتَدَّ وَجْدٌ بِامْرِئٍ كَيْفَ يَصْنَعُ

1. Ask the Meccan muftī from the noble family of Hāshim, "When one's love [for someone] intensifies, what is he to do?"

Imam al-Shāfiʿī wrote underneath:

يُدَاوِي هَوَاهُ ثُمَّ يَكْتُمُ وَجْدَهُ ١ وَيَصْبِرُ فِي كُلِّ الأُمُورِ وَيَخْضَعُ

1. He [should] treat his affection, then conceal his love, have patience in all matters, and surrender [himself to fate]

The man took the paper and went away. Thereafter, he returned and had written in response to Imam al-Shāfiʿī:

فَكَيْفَ يُدَاوِي وَالهَوَى قَاتِلُ الفَتَى ١ وَفِي كُلِّ يَوْمٍ غُصَّةً يَتَجَرَّعُ

1. How can he treat the affection while it is killing the young man and he is swallowing agony every day?

Finally, Imam al-Shāfi'ī ﷺ wrote:

1. If he cannot be patient with what afflicts him, then nothing is more beneficial for him than death.

قافية الفاء

The End-Rhyme of the Letter *Fā'*

صُعُوبَةُ الوُصُولِ إلى الهَدَفِ

The Difficulty of Reaching One's Goal

Although the obstacles in the way to one's goal may seem tremendous and the means inadequate, there is nothing impossible when one has firm determination coupled with the help of Allah.

كَيْفَ الوُصُولُ إِلَى سُعَادَ ودونَهَا ١ قُلَلُ الجبالِ ودونهنَّ حُتُوفُ

الرِّجْلُ حَافِيَةٌ وَمَا لِي مَرْكَبٌ ٢ وَالكَفُّ صِفْرٌ وَالطَّرِيقُ مَخُوفُ

1. How can I reach Suʿād[1] when before her are the summits of mountains and before them are [potential] deaths?

2. The feet are bare, I have no conveyance, the palm is empty, and the path is feared.

[1] A generic name of a woman. What is meant is any desirable goal.

أبُو حَنِيفَة

Imam Abū Ḥanīfah

Although one might disagree with someone, one must still maintain due respect. Imam al-Shāfi‘ī did not belittle Imam Abū Ḥanīfah despite disagreeing with him on nearly everything, but rather, he praised him and made duā’ for him.[1]

لَقَدْ زَانَ الْبِلَادَ وَمَنْ عَلَيْهَا ١ إِمَامُ الْمُسْلِمِينَ أَبُو حَنِيفَهْ

بِأَحْكَامٍ وَآثَارٍ وَفِقْهٍ ٢ كَآيَاتِ الزَّبُورِ عَلَى الصَّحِيفَهْ

فَمَا بِالْمَشْرِقَيْنِ لَهُ نَظِيرٌ ٣ وَلَا بِالْمَغْرِبَيْنِ وَلَا بِكُوفَهْ

فَرَحْمَةُ رَبِّنَا أَبَدًا عَلَيْهِ ٤ مَدَى الْأَيَّامِ مَا قُرِئَتْ صَحِيفَهْ

1. The Imam of the Muslims, Abū Ḥanīfah, has beautified the land and its inhabitants,

2. Through rulings, narrations, and jurisprudence like [how] the verses of the Psalms [beautify] the paper.

3. Neither in the East, nor the West, nor in Kūfah is the like of him.

4. May our Lord’s mercy forever be upon him for as long as the days remain in which his papers[2] are read.

1 This poem has also been attributed to Imam Abū Ḥanīfah’s great student ‘Abdullāh b. Mubārak.
2 Referring to the books containing his teachings.

لَيْسَ الأمْرُ بِالقُوَّةِ

It is Not Strength that Matters

One should not consider their strength to be a source of pride for them if they are not using it in a manner that will benefit themselves or others in this life or the next. Likewise, one should not consider their weakness as a hindrance to striving to achieve success in this life and the next.

أُكَلَ العُقَـابُ بِقُـوَّةٍ جِيَـفَ الفَـلَا ١ وَجَنَى الذُّبَابُ الشَّهْدَ وَهْوَ ضَعِيفُ

1. The eagle, though strong, feeds on the corpses of the jungle [whereas] the bee, though weak, produces [such a great bounty as] honey.

المُتَنَسِّكُون

Those Who Impersonate the Ascetics

Some people don the garb of piety for the paltry material gain of this world. They will wish on Judgement Day that they had not only donned that garb, but also had rectified their inner selves, and thus, would have gained success and salvation.

وَدَعِ الَّذِيـنَ إِذَا أَتَـوْكَ تَنَسَّـكُوا ١ وَإِذَا خَلَـوْا فَهُـمُ ذِئَـابُ خِـرَافِ

1. Abandon those who, when they come to you, display piety and, when they are alone, are wolves [that devour] sheep.

119

إذا لَمْ يَكُنْ صَفْوُ الوِدَادِ طَبِيْعَةً

When Pure Love is Not Natural

Friendship is not a relationship in which one is bound to the other like a familial relationship. If one sees that their friendship is not conducive to their well-being, one should leave that friendsh and seek sincere friendship elsewhere.

إِذَا الْمَرْءُ لَا يَرْعَاكَ إِلَّا تَكَلُّفًا ١ فَدَعْهُ وَلَا تُكْثِرْ عَلَيْهِ التَّأَسُّفَا

فَفِي النَّاسِ أَبْدَالٌ وَفِي التَّرْكِ رَاحَةٌ ٢ وَفِي الْقَلْبِ صَبْرٌ لِلْحَبِيبِ وَلَوْ جَفَا

فَمَا كُلُّ مَنْ تَهْوَاهُ يَهْوَاكَ قَلْبُهُ ٣ وَلَا كُلُّ مَنْ صَافَيْتَهُ لَكَ قَدْ صَفَا

إِذَا لَمْ يَكُنْ صَفْوُ الْوِدَادِ طَبِيعَةً ٤ فَلَا خَيْرَ فِي خِلٍّ يَجِيءُ تَكَلُّفَا

وَلَا خَيْرَ فِي خِلٍّ يَخُونُ خَلِيلَهُ ٥ وَيَلْقَاهُ مِنْ بَعْدِ الْمَوَدَّةِ بِالْجَفَا

وَيُنْكِرُ عَيْشًا قَدْ تَقَادَمَ عَهْدُهُ ٦ وَيُظْهِرُ سِرًّا كَانَ بِالْأَمْسِ قَدْ خَفَا

سَلَامٌ عَلَى الدُّنْيَا إِذَا لَمْ يَكُنْ بِهَا ٧ صَدِيقٌ صَدُوقٌ صَادِقُ الْوَعْدِ مُنْصِفَا

1. When a person only takes care of you reluctantly, leave him and do not express much regret over him,
2. Because amongst people there are [better] replacements and in leaving [him] there is comfort. There is patience in the heart for the beloved, even if he has treated [you] harshly.
3. It is not [necessary] that every person you love, his heart [also] loves you. Nor [is it necessary] that every person you are sincere to is [also] sincere to you.
4. When pure love is not natural, then there is no goodness in a

close friend that comes reluctantly.

5. And there is no goodness in a close friend who betrays his close friend and meets him after love with harshness,

6. And [who] denies life [spent together] the time of which has long passed, and [who] reveals secrets he had concealed yesterday.

7. Farewell to this worldly life if there is no truthful, trustworthy, and righteous friend in it.

قافية القاف
The End-Rhyme of the Letter *Qāf*

الشَّبَابُ الضَّائِعُ

Wasted Youth

It's a great source of pain and remorse when one sees youth wasting away their lives in useless worldly pursuits. But nevertheless, one should not look down upon them, but rather one should advise them, supplicate for them, and learn from their mistakes.

إِذَا رَأَيْتَ شَبَابَ الحَيِّ قَدْ نَشَأُوا ١ لَا يَحْمِلُونَ قِلَالَ الحِبْرِ وَالوَرَقَا

وَلَا تَرَاهُمْ لَدَى الأَشْيَاخِ فِي حِلَقٍ ٢ يَعُونَ مِنْ صَالِحِ الأَخْبَارِ مَا اتَّسَقَا

فَعُدَّ عَنْهُمْ وَدَعْهُمْ إِنَّهُمْ هَمَجُ ٣ قَدْ بَدَّلُوا بِعُلُوِّ الهِمَّةِ الحُمَقَا

1. When you see the youth of the tribe having grown up and not carrying inkwells and paper,
2. And you do not see them before the elders in circles learning by heart the sound reports that are in good order,

3. Then abandon them and leave them, as they are riffraff who have exchanged high aspirations for stupidity.

121

إفْشَاءُ السِّرِّ

Disclosing Secrets

Secrets are one of the most difficult things to safeguard, not only for the one entrusted with them, but also for the one to whom they belong. If one cannot trust himself with his secrets, then he should not be surprised to see others disclose them.

لَمْ يَبْقَ فِي النَّاسِ إِلَّا المَكْرُ والمَلَقُ ١ شَوْكٌ إِذَا لَمَسُوا زَهْرٌ إِذَا رَمَقُوا

فَإِنْ دَعَتْكَ ضَرُورَاتٌ لِعِشْرَتِهِمْ ٢ فَكُنْ جَحِيمًا لَعَلَّ الشَّوْكَ يَحْتَرِقُ

1. If a man discloses his secrets with his tongue and then reprimands others for doing so, then he is foolish.

2. If a man's chest is constricted from [keeping] his own secret, then the chest of the one he entrusted the secret with will be even more constricted.

122

فَسَادُ طَبَائِعِ النَّاسِ

Corruption of People's Natures

Many people have false pretenses when engaging with others. When encountering such people, the best course of action is to remain unfazed by their statements and politely but firmly stand one's ground.

لَمْ يَبْقَ فِي النَّاسِ إِلَّا المَكْرُ والمَلَقُ ١ شَوْكٌ إِذَا لَمَسُوا زَهْرٌ إِذَا رَمَقُوا

فَإِنْ دَعَتْكَ ضَرُورَاتٌ لِعِشْرَتِهِمْ ٢ فَكُنْ جَحِيمًا لَعَلَّ الشَّوْكَ يَحْتَرِقُ

1. Only plotting and flattery remain amongst people; thorns when they touch, flowers when they glance.

2. If necessities compel you to live with them, then be a blazing fire; hopefully, the thorn will burn.

الاغْتِرَابُ عِلَاجٌ في بَعْضِ الأحْيَانِ

Emigration is Sometimes a Cure

People are sometimes faced with conditions in which the only solution for them is to leave their home. Although it might be difficult, leaving one's home refines one's character and expands one's horizons.

اِرْحَلْ بِنَفْسِكَ مِنْ أَرْضٍ تُضَامُ بِهَا ١ وَلَا تَكُنْ مِنْ فِرَاقِ الأَهْلِ فِي حُرَقِ

مَنْ ذَلَّ بَيْنَ أَهَالِيهِ بِبَلْدَتِهِ ٢ فَالِاغْتِرَابُ لَهُ مِنْ أَحْسَنِ الخُلُقِ

فَالعَنْبَرُ الخَامُ رَوْثٌ فِي مَوَاطِنِهِ ٣ وَفِي التَّغَرُّبِ مَحْمُولٌ عَلَى العُنُقِ

وَالكُحْلُ نَوْعٌ مِنَ الأَحْجَارِ تَنْظُرُهُ ٤ فِي أَرْضِهِ وَهْوَ مَرْمِيٌّ عَلَى الطُّرُقِ

لَمَّا تَغَرَّبَ حَازَ الفَضْلَ أَجْمَعَهُ ٥ فَصَارَ يُحْمَلُ بَيْنَ الجَفْنِ وَالحَدَقِ

1. Depart a land in which you are treated unjustly and do not be in pain from parting with the people.

2. Whoever has been disgraced amongst his people and his town, then emigration [is a result of] his good character.

3. As unrefined ambergris is dung in its origins, and when separated, it is carried on people's necks.

4. Kohl is a type of rock that you see in its land, thrown on the paths,

5. [But] when it separates [from its origin], it gains great virtue and becomes [such that] it is carried between the eyelid and the pupil.

المُدَارَاةُ والتَّقِيَّةُ

Flattery and Prudence

It's not always possible to overcome an enemy through arguing and fighting. Each situation calls for using a technique unique to it. Flattery is one such technique.

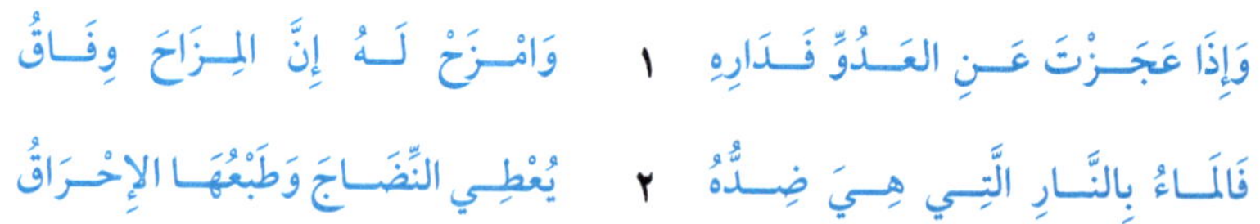

وَإِذَا عَجَزْتَ عَنِ العَدُوِّ فَدَارِهِ ١ وَامْزَحْ لَهُ إِنَّ المِزَاحَ وِفَاقُ

فَالْمَاءُ بِالنَّارِ الَّتِي هِيَ ضِدُّهُ ٢ يُعْطِي النِّضَاجَ وَطَبْعُهَا الإِحْرَاقُ

1. When you are incapable of [overcoming] an enemy, then flatter him and joke with him, as joking [brings about] harmony.

2. As water with fire—which is its opposite—gives [the benefit of] cooking while [fire's] nature is burning.

125

حَالُ الغَرِيبِ

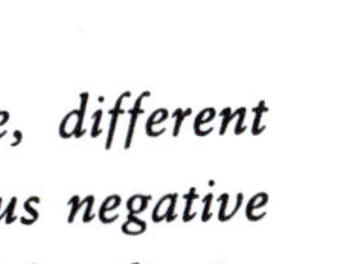

The Condition of the Outsider

Being in a strange new land, amongst strange, different people, makes a person uncomfortable. The various negative feelings one has makes one long for the comfort and familiarity of one's home country and family. But given time, a person can come to love that new land and those different people, as humans are an adaptable species.

إِنَّ الغَرِيبَ لَهُ مَخَافَةُ سَارِقٍ ١ وَخُضُوعُ مَدْيُونٍ وَذِلَّةُ مُوثَقِ

فَإِذَا تَذَكَّرَ أَهْلَهُ وبِلَادَهُ ٢ فَفُؤَادُهُ كَجَنَاحِ طَيْرٍ خَافِقِ

1. An outsider has the fearfulness of a thief, the submissiveness of one in debt, and the lowliness of one who is imprisoned.
2. When he remembers his family and his country, then his heart is like the fluttering wings of a bird.

126

الإغْضَاءُ عَنْ هَفَوَاتِ النَّاسِ فِي سَفَرٍ

Overlooking People's Mistakes on a Journey

Although one should overlook the mistakes of others in general, this principle especially applies when one is on a journey with other people. The greater benefit of social harmony amongst travel companions should be given preference over attempting to rectify the faults of others.

إِذَا رَافَقْتَ فِي الأَسْفَارِ قَوْمًا ١ فَكُنْ لَهُمْ كَذِي الرَّحِمِ الشَّفِيقِ
بِعَيْبِ النَّفْسِ ذَا بَصَرٍ وَعِلْمٍ ٢ وَأَعْمَى العَيْنِ مِنْ عَيْبِ الرَّفِيقِ
وَلَا تَأْخُذْ بِعَثْرَةِ كُلِّ قَوْمٍ ٣ وَلَكِنْ قُلْ: هَلُمَّ إِلَى الطَّرِيقِ
فَإِنْ تَأْخُذْ بِعَثْرَتِهِمْ يَقِلُّوا ٤ وَتَبْقَى فِي الزَّمَانِ بِلَا صَدِيقِ

1. When you accompany people on journeys, then be like a compassionate relative to them;

2. Of [your] own faults, perceptive and aware, and blind to the faults of the companions.

3. Do not take hold of the mistakes of every people, but rather say, "Onward on the path."

4. If you [continuously] take hold of their mistakes, they will decrease, and you will remain in life without any friends.

ضَرُورَةُ كِتَابَةِ العِلْمِ

The Necessity of Writing Knowledge

As our memories weakened over the generations, writing allowed us to preserve externally what we could not preserve internally i.e., vast amounts of knowledge. Even if we intend to memorize something, writing it down should be the first step toward that goal.

العِلْمُ صَيْدٌ وَالكِتَابَةُ قَيْدُهُ ١ قَيِّدْ صُيُودَكَ بِالحِبَالِ الوَاثِقَهْ
فَمِنَ الحَمَاقَةِ أَنْ تَصِيدَ غَزَالَةً ٢ وَتَتْرُكَهَا بَيْنَ الخَلَائِقِ طَالِقَهْ

1. Knowledge is game, and writing is its cage; capture your game with strong ropes,

2. As it is stupidity that you catch a gazelle and then let it loose amongst people.

الوَفَاءُ بِالحَقِّ

Fulling a Right

Justice is a central facet of Islam and is one of the objectives behind establishing Islamic rule on Earth. Giving people their rights falls under this supreme virtue.

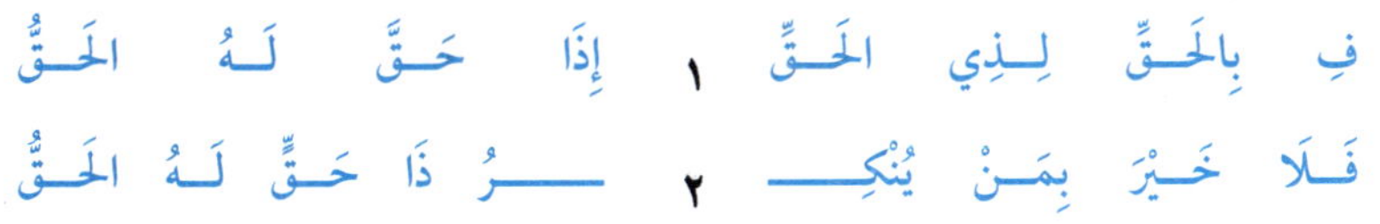
فِ بِالحَقِّ لِـذِي الحَـقِّ ١ إِذَا حَـقَّ لَـهُ الحَـقُّ
فَـلَا خَـيْرَ بِمَـنْ يُنْكِـــرُ ٢ ذَا حَـقٍّ لَـهُ الحَـقُّ

1. Fulfill the right of the one who has a right when the right becomes due for him,

2. As there is no good for one who denies a rightfully entitled person his right.

التَّوَكُّلُ فِي طَلَبِ الرِّزْقِ

Reliance on Allah ﷻ in Seeking Provision

When we have a belief that Allah ﷻ has power over everything, then providing sustenance for one of His slaves is an automatic given, and so, we have no need to worry about our sustenance. Whatever provision is destined for us by Allah, will surely reach us without us even asking for it. This does not mean that we forgo working to acquire sustenance, but rather it means that we put in our effort and leave the results to Allah.

تَوَكَّلْتُ فِي رِزْقِي عَلَى اللهِ خَالِقِي	١	وَأَيْقَنْتُ أَنَّ اللهَ لَا شَكَّ رَازِقِي
وَمَا يَكُ مِنْ رِزْقِي فَلَيْسَ يَفُوتُنِي	٢	وَلَوْ كَانَ فِي قَاعِ البِحَارِ العَوَامِقِ
سَيَأْتِي بِهِ اللهُ العَظِيمُ بِفَضْلِهِ	٣	وَلَوْ لَمْ يَكُنْ مِنِّي اللِّسَانُ بِنَاطِقِ
فَفِي أَيِّ شَيْءٍ تَذْهَبُ النَّفْسُ حَسْرَةً	٤	وَقَدْ قَسَّمَ الرَّحْمَنُ رِزْقَ الخَلَائِقِ

1. I placed my trust in Allah, my Creator, regarding my sustenance, and I am certain that Allah is no doubt my Sustainer.
2. Whatever is to be my sustenance will not escape me, even if it is at the bottom of deep oceans.
3. Allah the Great, out of His grace, will bring it forth, even if my tongue does not utter [a single word].
4. For what does the lower-self grieve while the Beneficent has allotted the provision of creation?

130

العَقْلُ وَحْدَه لا يُغْنِي

Intelligence Alone Does Not Enrich

One should humble oneself and realize that their intelligence does not determine how much sustenance they will receive. The sustenance of mankind and the rest of creation is a preordained decree of al-Razzāq, Who bestows upon whomsoever He wills, however much He wills, and whenever He wills.

لَوْ كُنْتَ بِالعَقْلِ تُعْطَى مَا تُرِيدُ إِذَنْ ١ لَمَا ظَفِرْتَ مِنَ الدُّنْيَا بِمَرْزُوقِ

رُزِقْتَ مَالًا عَلَى جَهْلٍ فَعِشْتَ بِهِ ٢ فَلَسْتَ أَوَّلَ مَجْنُونٍ وَمَرْزُوقِ

1. If, through your intelligence, you could be given all that you wanted, then you would not find anyone in the world receiving sustenance [due to the lack of sufficient intelligence].

2. You have been provided with wealth despite ignorance and have subsisted on it; you are not the first foolish person who is receiving sustenance.

العِلْمُ ما حَفِظْتَ

True Knowledge is What You Have Memorized

True knowledge is not what one has written. Books and notebooks can be taken, lost, or destroyed, but one's memory cannot be touched by anyone. Recall the famous story of Imam al-Ghazālī ﷺ *and the highway robber.*[1]

عِلْمِي مَعِي حَيْثُمَا يَمَّمْتُ يَنْفَعُنِي ١ قَلْبِي وِعَاءٌ لَهُ لَا بَطْنُ صُنْدُوقِ

إِنْ كُنْتُ فِي البَيْتِ كَانَ العِلْمُ فِيهِ مَعِي ٢ أَوْ كُنْتُ فِي السُّوقِ كَانَ العِلْمُ فِي السُّوقِ

1. My knowledge is with me; wherever I intend [to go], it benefits me. My heart is its vessel, not [books] inside a wooden box.

---

1 Refer to *Itḥāf al-Sa'ādah al-Muttaqīn bi Sharḥ Iḥyā' 'Ulūm al-Dīn* by Murtaḍā al-Zabīdī ﷺ for the full story.

2. If I am at home, the knowledge is there with me, or if I am in the market, the knowledge is [with me] in the market [as well].

132

الضَّرَرُ مِنْ غَيْرِ قَصْدٍ

Unintentional Harm

Sometimes it may be that you intend to benefit someone, but because of the way you attempt to do so, your action is considered a form of disobedience and disrespect. Thus, it is necessary to properly conduct one's actions, lest they be misinterpreted.

1. He intended to benefit but then unintentionally caused harm; [at times] obedience [turns out] to be disobedience.

133

بَيْنَ الحِجَا والغِنَى

Between Intelligence and Wealth

Once, the poet Abū al-Qāsim ʿAyyāsh b. al-Azraq came to Imam al-Shāfiʿī ﵀ and said, "O Abū ʿAbdillāh, will you not be fair with us? You have this jurisprudence in whose essence you excel, and we have this poetry, but you have interfered with us in it. So either you leave us alone, or you allow us to participate in jurisprudence. I have brought a few verses, which, if you can compose the equivalent of, I will surely repent from composing poetry. And if you are unable to do so, then you repent from poetry." The Imam told him to present what he had. He presented:

مَـا هِمَّتِـي إِلَّا مُقَارَعَـةُ العِـدا ١ خَلُـقَ الزَّمَـانُ وَهِمَّتِـي لَمْ تَخْلُـقِ

وَالنَّـاسُ أَعْيُنُهُـمْ إِلَى سَـلْبِ الفَتَـى ٢ لَا يَنْظُـرُونَ إِلَى الحِجَـا وَالأَوْلَـقِ

لَـوْ كانَ بِالحِيَـلِ الغِنَـى لَوَجَدْتَنِـي ٣ بِنُجُـومِ أَقْطَـارِ السَّـمَاءِ تَعَلُّقِـي

1. My ambition is only [for] fighting enemies; Time becomes old while my ambition does not.

2. People's eyes [look towards] dispossessing the young man. They do not look at intelligence and foolishness.

3. If wealth was through schemes, then you would find me hanging onto the stars belonging to the regions of the sky.[1]

Imam al-Shāfiʿī then responded extemporaneously[2] :

إِنَّ الَّـذِي رُزِقَ اليَسَـارَ وَلَمْ يُصِـبْ ١ حَمْـدًا وَلَا أَجْـرًا لَغَـيْرُ مُـوَفَّـقِ

مَـا هِمَّتِـي إِلَّا مُطَالَبَـةُ العُـلَى ٢ خَلُـقَ الزَّمَـانُ وَهِمَّتِـي لَمْ تَخْلُـقِ

وَالجَـدُّ يُـدْنِي كُلَّ أَمْـرٍ شَاسِـعٍ ٣ والجَـدُّ يَفْتَـحُ كُلَّ بَـابٍ مُغْلَـقِ

فَـإِذَا سَـمِعْتَ بِـأَنَّ مَجْـدُودًا حَـوَى ٤ عُـودًا فَـأَوْرَقَ فِي يَدَيْـهِ فَصَـدِّقِ

وَإِذَا سَـمِعْتَ بِـأَنَّ مَحْرُومًـا أَتَـى ٥ مَـاءً لِيَشْرَبَـهُ فَغَـاضَ فَحَقِّـقِ

وَمِـنَ الدَّلِيـلِ عَـلَى القَضَـاءِ وَكَوْنِـهِ ٦ بُـؤْسُ اللَّبِيـبِ، وَطِيـبُ عَيْـشِ الأَحْمَقِ

وَأَحَـقُّ خَلْـقِ اللهِ بِالهَـمِّ امْـرُؤٌ ٧ ذُو هِمَّـةٍ يُبْـلَى بِـرِزْقٍ ضَيِّـقِ

وَلَرُبَّـمَا عَرَضَـتْ لِنَفْسِـي فِكْـرَةٌ ٨ فَـأَوَدُّ مِنْهَـا أَنَّنِـي لَمْ أُخْلَـقِ

---

[1] Meaning that he would acquire all that could be acquired in the world.

[2] The Imam fit in the verses of Abū al-Qāsim ʿAyyāsh b. al-Azraq in between his own verses as verses 2, 9, and 13.

لَوْ كانَ بِالحِيَلِ الغِنَى لَوَجَدْتُنِي ٩ بِنُجُومِ أَقْطَارِ السَّمَاءِ تَعَلُّقِي

لَكِنَّ مَنْ رُزِقَ الحِجَا حُرِمَ الغِنَى ١٠ ضِدَّان مُفْتَرِقَانِ، أَيَّ تَفَرُّقِ

إِنَّ اللَّدِيغَ لَخَائِفٌ مُتَوَجِّسٌ ١١ يَخْشَى وَيَرْهَبُ كُلَّ حَبْلٍ أَبْرَقِ

وَالمَرْءُ كَالمَخْبُوِّ تَحْتَ لِسَانِهِ ١٢ وَلِسَانُهُ مِفْتَاحُ بَابٍ مُغْلَقِ

وَالنَّاسُ أَعْيُنُهُمْ إِلَى سَلْبِ الفَتَى ١٣ لَا يَنْظُرُونَ إِلَى الحِجَا وَالأَوْلَقِ

1. One who has been provided with ease and then does not acquire rewards nor praise is surely unsuccessful.

2. My ambition is only seeking loftiness; Time becomes old while my ambition does not.

3. Good fortune brings every distant matter close and opens every closed door.

4. If you hear that a fortunate person held wood in his hands, then it bore fruit, then believe [it]!

5. And if you hear that an unfortunate person came to a source of water to drink and then it receded, then believe [that as well]!

6. A proof of predestination and its existence is the suffering of the intelligent and the pleasant life of the foolish.

7. The one with the most right to grieve, from the creation of Allah, is a man with ambition tested with constrained provision.

8. Sometimes [such negative] thoughts occur to me due to which I wish I were never created.

9. If wealth was through schemes, then you would find me

hanging onto the stars belonging to the regions of the sky[1].

10. But whoever has been provided with intelligence [has also been] deprived of wealth; two opposites that forever remain separated.

11. Someone bitten is surely fearful and perceptive; he fears and runs from every shining rope[2].

12. Man is like [a flame] extinguished under his tongue; his tongue is the key to a locked door.

13. People's eyes [look towards] dispossessing a young man [of what he has]. They do not look at intelligence and foolishness.

1 Meaning that he would acquire all that could be acquired in the world.
2 Referring to something that appears to be a snake.

قافية الكاف

The End-Rhyme of the Letter *Kāf*

الاتِّكَالُ على النَّفْسِ

Self-Reliance

No one knows your needs better than you do, and people are not always going to be there for you, so be self-sufficient amongst people and needy before the One who is always with you and knows you better than yourself.

مَـا حَـكَّ جِلْـدَكَ مِثْـلُ ظُفْـرِكَ ١ فَتَـوَلَّ أَنْـتَ جَمِيـعَ أَمْـرِكْ

وَإِذَا قَصَـدْتَّ لِحَاجَـةٍ ٢ فَاقْصِـدْ لِـمُعْتَرِفٍ بِقَـدْرِكْ

1. Nothing scratches your skin like your own nail, so manage all your affairs yourself.

2. When you approach [someone] for a need, then approach one who recognizes your worth.

135

رَدُّ الجَمِيلِ بِالسَّيِّئ

Repaying Good with Evil

Good conduct entails repaying evil with good, by which "the one you had mutual enmity with him will turn as if he were a close friend."[1] *Doing the opposite will result in the opposite.*

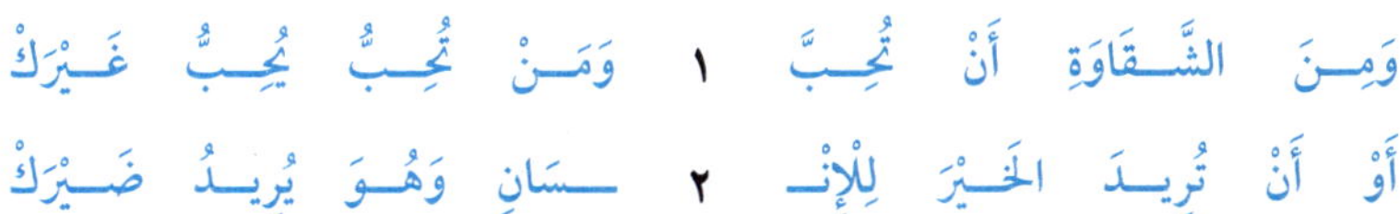

وَمِنَ الشَّقَاوَةِ أَنْ تُحِبَّ ١ وَمَنْ تُحِبُّ يُحِبُّ غَيْرَكْ

أَوْ أَنْ تُرِيدَ الخَيْرَ لِلْإِنْسَانِ ٢ وَهُوَ يُرِيدُ ضَيْرَكْ

1. Misfortune is that you love while the one you love loves another,
2. Or that you want good for someone whilst he wants harm for you.

136

رَأْسُ الغِنَى

The Essence of Wealth

Contentment frees one from engaging in actions that degrade one's character, such as asking at people's doors or following them for some worldly benefit.

رَأَيْتُ القَنَاعَةَ رَأْسَ الغِنَى ١ فَصِرْتُ بِأَذْيَالِهَا مُمْتَسِكْ

فَلَا ذَا يَرَانِي عَلَى بَابِهِ ٢ وَلَا ذَا يَرَانِي بِهِ مُنْهَمِكْ

فَصِرْتُ غَنِيًّا بِلَا دِرْهَمٍ ٣ أَمُرُّ عَلَى النَّاسِ شِبْهَ المَلِكْ

1. I realized that contentment is the highest [form] of wealth, so I held firmly to its hem.

[1] Qur'an: 41:34

2. This one will not see me upon his door, and that one will not see me preoccupied with him.

3. I have become wealthy without even a dirham, and I pass by the people like a king.

الفَسَادُ الكَبِيرُ

A Great Depravity

People should assess the person they refer to in matters of religion. It is important that he be learned as well as of good character, as it is common for the ignorant and the shameless to gain a large following.

فَسَادٌ كَبِيرٌ عَالِمٌ مُتَهَتِّكٌ ١ وَأَكْبَرُ مِنْهُ جَاهِلٌ مُتَنَسِّكُ

هُمَا فِتْنَةٌ فِي العَالَمِينَ عَظِيمَةٌ ٢ لِمَنْ بِهِمَا فِي دِينِهِ يَتَمَسَّكُ

1. A shameless scholar is a great [source of] corruption, and a greater [source of] corruption is an ignorant worshipper.

2. Both are a great trial in the world for one who holds fast to them in his religious matters.

الزَّيتُ المُبَارَكُ

Blessed Oil

The Imam once said, “When I was young, my mother would often feed me oil. Once, I told her, 'Mother, this oil has burnt my liver.' She then said, 'Son, eat it because it is blessed.' Upon this, I said:

تُأَدِّمُنِـــي بِالزَّيْـــتِ قَالَــتْ: مُبَــارَكُ ١ وَقَــدْ أَحْــرَقَ الأَكْبَـادَ هَـذَا المُبَـارَكُ

1. She feeds me oil and says, '[It is] blessed,' whereas it is this blessed oil that has burnt my liver."

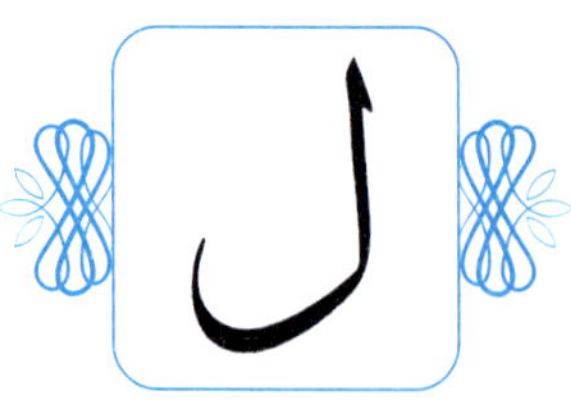

قافية اللام
The End-Rhyme of the Letter *Lām*

الوَقْتُ المُنَاسِبُ لِلْعِلْمِ
The Appropriate Time for Knowledge

When one is young, one can mold and develop one's mind for any purpose. This molding should be done consciously and with the supervision of an expert in a particular field, by which one can begin to gain expertise as well. If one is unaware of the tenderness of their mind, then it's entirely possible that one's mind is subconsciously molded by the wrong ideas and beliefs prevalent in society.

تَعَلَّمْ يَا فَتَى وَالعُودُ رَطْبٌ ١ وَطِيْفُكَ لَيِّنٌ وَالطَّبْعُ قَابِلْ

فَإِنَّ الجَهْلَ وَاضِعُ كُلِّ عَالٍ ٢ وَإِنَّ العِلْمَ رَافِعُ كُلِّ خَامِلْ

فَحَسْبُكَ يَا فَتَى شَرَفًا وَعِزًّا ٣ سُكُوتُ الحَاضِرِينَ وَأَنْتَ قَائِلْ

1. Learn, O young man, while the stem [of your youth] is moist, your thoughts are soft, and the natural disposition is accepting,

2. As ignorance puts down every exalted [person] and knowledge

elevates every undistinguished [person].

3. Sufficient for you, O young man, as honor and glory is the silence of those present while you are speaking.

140

المَوتُ أَفْضَلُ مِنْ ذُلِّ السُّؤَالِ

Death is Better than the Disgrace of Begging

Begging before people is disgracing, whereas begging before Allah ﷻ is humbling.

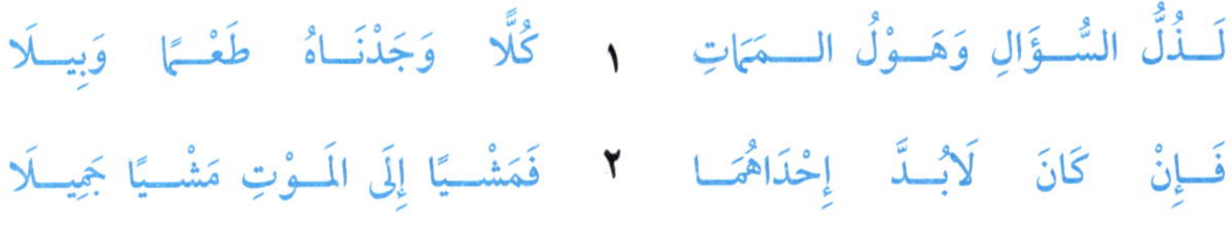

لَذُلُّ السُّؤَالِ وَهَوْلُ الْمَمَاتِ ١ كُلًّا وَجَدْنَاهُ طَعْمًا وَبِيلَا

فَإِنْ كَانَ لَابُدَّ إِحْدَاهُمَا ٢ فَمَشْيًا إِلَى الْمَوْتِ مَشْيًا جَمِيلَا

1. The disgrace of begging and the terror of death; we found both to have a horrible taste.

2. If [choosing] one of the two was necessary, then [I would choose] walking happily towards death.

141

حُبُّ آلِ البَيتِ فَرْضٌ مِنْ اللّٰهَ

Loving the Noble Family is Compulsory

Our love for the Prophet ﷺ is so intense that it spreads to all those who were associated with him, especially his noble family. Not loving them would, in fact, be going against the command of Allah ﷻ.

يَـا آلَ بَيْـتِ رَسُـولِ اللهِ حُبُّكُـمُ ١ فَـرْضٌ مِـنَ اللهِ فِي القُـرآنِ أَنْزَلَـهُ

يَكْفِيكُـمُ مِـنْ عَظِيـمِ الفَخْـرِ أَنَّكُـمُ ٢ مَـنْ لَمْ يُصَـلِّ عَلَيْكُـمْ لَا صَـلَاةَ لَـهُ

1. O the noble family of the Messenger of Allah, loving you is an obligation from Allah revealed in the Qur'an.

2. It will suffice for you as a great [source of] pride that one who does not send salutations upon you, his prayer is not valid.

المَرْءُ بِمَا يَعْلَمُه

Man is Revered Due to His Knowledge

Knowledge is such that it can elevate one's rank in society, but that should not be the purpose behind seeking knowledge. One seeks knowledge for the pleasure of Allah ﷻ and to follow the way of His Prophet ﷺ ; any other worldly benefit is an additional blessing from Allah ﷻ .

تَعَلَّـمْ فَلَيْـسَ المَـرْءُ يُولَـدُ عَالِمًـا ١ وَلَيْـسَ أَخُـو عِلْـمٍ كَمَـنْ هُـوَ جَاهِـلُ

وَإِنَّ كَبِـيرَ القَـوْمِ لَا عِلْـمَ عِنْـدَهُ ٢ صَغِـيرٌ إِذَا الْتَفَّـتْ عَلَيْـهِ الجَحَافِـلُ

وَإِنَّ صَغِـيرَ القَـوْمِ إِنْ كَانَ عَالِمًـا ٣ كَبِـيرٌ إِذَا رُدَّتْ إِلَيْـهِ الـمَحَافِلُ

وَلَا تَـرْضَ مِـنْ عَيْـشٍ بِـدُونٍ وَلَا يَكُنْ ٤ نَصِيبُـكَ إِرْثٌ قَدَّمَتْـهُ الأَوَائِـلُ

1. Seek knowledge, for no man is born knowledgeable; one who possesses knowledge is unlike one who is ignorant.

2. The elder of a nation who lacks knowledge is insignificant

when armies face him.

3. The youth of a nation, if he is knowledgeable, is significant when gatherings turn to him [to learn from him].

4. Do not be content with a lowly life and do not let your [only] share [of knowledge] be inheritance left over by the predecessors.

الطَّبِيبُ السَّقِيْمُ

The Sickly Doctor

Once, when Imam al-Shāfi'ī ﷺ was sick, a doctor was called to check up on him. While the doctor was examining him, the Imam noticed a malady on the body of the doctor, who was completely unaware of it. And so, the Imam looked down and recited the following:

جَاءَ الطَّبِيبُ يَجُسُّنِي فَجَسَسْتُهُ ١ فَإِذَا الطَّبِيبُ لِمَا بِهِ مِنْ حَالْ

وَغَدَا يُعالِجُنِي بِطُولِ سَقَامِهِ ٢ وَمِنَ العَجَائِبِ أَعْمَشٌ كَحَّالْ

1. The doctor came to examine me, and I [also] examined him. And so, the condition he was afflicted with [became apparent to me].

2. He began to treat me [in spite of] his longstanding sickness. How strange is it that one afflicted with eye disease is an eye doctor!

144

الإمَامُ أَحْمَدُ بْنُ حَنْبَلَ

Imam Aḥmad bin Hanbal

Sometimes a student may possess qualities that earn the respect of his teacher, and sometimes—greater than that—a teacher may praise such a student with words that become a means of preserving his character as a lesson for generations to come.

قَالُوا: يَزُورُكَ أَحْمَدٌ وَتَزُورُهُ ١ قُلْتُ الفَضَائِلُ لَا تُفَارِقُ مَنْزِلَهُ

إِنْ زَارَنِي فَبِفَضْلِهِ أَوْ زُرْتُهُ ٢ فَلِفَضْلِهِ فَالفَضْلُ فِي الحَالَيْنِ لَهُ

1. People said, "Aḥmad visits you and you visit him." I replied, "Virtues do not part his residence."
2. If he visits me, then it is out of his virtue, or if I visit him, then it is because of his virtue. Thus, virtue in both situations is his.

145

الفَضْلُ لِلَّذِي يَتَفَضَّلُ

Graciousness is Due for the One Who is Gracious

Graciousness is defined as "excellence of manners or social conduct," and as such, it is a praiseworthy characteristic befitting every Muslim.

The Imam related the following verse from his father:

عَلَى كُلِّ حَالٍ أَنْتَ بِالفَضْلِ آخِذٌ ١ وَمَا الفَضْلُ إِلَّا لِلَّذِي يَتَفَضَّلُ

1. In every condition, hold fast to graciousness; graciousness is only due for one who is gracious.

146

حَمْلُ النَّفْسِ على مَا يَزِينُهَا

Beautifying the Lower-Self

Rectifying your lower-self, dealing with others in a pleasing manner, being patient about your sustenance, and finding true friends will all lead to a tranquil life in this world.

صُنِ النَّفْسَ وَاحْمِلْهَا عَلَى مَا يَزِينُهَا ١ تَعِشْ سَالِمًا وَالقَوْلُ فِيكَ جَمِيلُ

وَلَا تُولِيَنَّ النَّاسَ إِلَّا تَجَمُّلًا ٢ نَبَا بِكَ دَهْرٌ أَوْ جَفَاكَ خَلِيلُ

وَإِنْ ضَاقَ رِزْقُ اليَوْمِ فَاصْبِرْ إِلَى غَدٍ ٣ عَسَى نَكَبَاتُ الدَّهْرِ عَنْكَ تَزُولُ

فَيَغْنَى غَنِيُّ النَّفْسِ إِنْ قَلَّ مَالُهُ ٤ وَيَغْنَى فَقِيرُ النَّفْسِ وَهْوَ ذَلِيلُ

وَلَا خَيْرَ فِي وُدِّ امْرِئٍ مُتَلَوِّنٍ ٥ إِذَا الرِّيحُ مَالَتْ، مَالَ حَيْثُ تَمِيلُ

وَمَا أَكْثَرَ الإِخْوَانَ حِينَ تَعُدُّهُمْ ٦ وَلَكِنَّهُمْ فِي النَّائِبَاتِ قَلِيلُ

1. Protect the lower-self and make it take upon that which will beautify it; you will live safely, and [people will] speak well of you.

2. Simply be patient with people, [even if] Time displeases you or your bosom friend treats you harshly.

3. If today's sustenance is constrained, then be patient till tomorrow. Hopefully, the misfortunes of time will leave you.

4. The one who is rich at heart will be rich even if his wealth decreases, and the one who is poor at heart will be rich while being contemptible.

5. There is no goodness in the love of a whimsical person; when the wind changes its direction, he changes direction with it.

6. How plentiful are friends when you count them, but in [times of] misfortunes, they are few.

147

مُدَارَاةُ الحُسَّادِ

Courteousness to the Envious

When one has been blessed with bestowals from the Beneficent One, then one is bound to become the target of envious eyes. Only one thing will cool the burning fire of envy in their hearts and that is death.

وَدَارَيْتُ كُلَّ النَّاسِ لَكِنَّ حَاسِدِي ١ مُدَارَاتُهُ عَزَّتْ وَعَزَّ مَنَالُهَا

وَكَيْفَ يُدَارِي المَرْءُ حَاسِدَ نِعْمَةٍ ٢ إِذَا كَانَ لَا يُرْضِيهِ إِلَّا زَوَالُهَا

1. I treated all people courteously except the one envious of me; treating him courteously was difficult [previously], and difficult is its obtainment [in the future].

2. How can a person treat courteously one who is envious of [his] blessings when only their vanishing will please him?

148

عُلُوُّ الذِّكْرِ

Fame

Fame is a neutral concept; one can become famous for good or become infamous for bad. In both cases, fame has the potential to destroy a person, either inwardly by inflating his ego in the first case or outwardly by degrading his status in the second case.

المَرْءُ يَحْظَى ثُمَّ يَعْلُو ذِكْرُهُ ١ حَتَّى يُزَيَّنَ بِالَّذِي لَمْ يَفْعَلِ

وَتَرَى الشَّقِيَّ إِذَا تَكَامَلَ غَيُّهُ ٢ يَشْقَى وَيُنْحَلُ بِالَّذِي لَمْ يَفْعَلِ

1. A man acquires good fortune and then his fame spreads until he is adorned with [such good deeds] that he did not even perform.

2. And you will see the unfortunate one, when his transgression reaches its peak, he becomes wretched and is [wrongly] attributed with [such sins] that he did not even commit.

149

اِسْتِعَارَةُ الكُتُبِ

Borrowing Books

Imam al-Shāfi'ī requested to borrow some of Imam Muḥammad bin al-Ḥasan al-Shaybānī's books, but he was unable to give them for some reason or another. Imam al-Shāfi'ī then wrote to him the following couplets. Thereafter, Imam

Muḥammad ﷺ came himself with the books and gave them over to him.

ـنُ مَنْ رَآهُ مِثْلَهُ	١	يَا، قُلْ لِمَنْ لَمْ تَرَ عَيْـ
مَا قَدْ رَأَى مَنْ قَبْلَهُ	٢	وَمَنْ كَأَنَّ مَنْ قَدْ رَآهُ
حَيْثُ عَقَلْنَا عَقْلَهُ	٣	وَمَنْ كَلَامُنَا لَهُ
فَاقَ الكَمَالَ كُلَّهُ	٤	لِأَنَّ مَا يُجِنُّهُ
أَنْ يَمْنَعُوهُ أَهْلَهُ	٥	العِلْمُ يَنْهَى أَهْلَهُ
لِأَهْلِهِ لَعَلَّهُ	٦	لَعَلَّهُ يَبْذُلُهُ

1. O, say to he who, the eye of the one who sees him, has not seen the like of him,
2. He who, one who sees him is as if he has seen those before him,
3. He who, our speech is for him because we comprehend [the level of] his intellect,
4. Because what he conceals has surpassed perfection completely:
5. "Knowledge prohibits its people from depriving its [other] people of it.
6. Hopefully, he will give it generously to its people, hopefully."

150

تَوَاضُعُ العُلَمَاءِ

The Humility of the Scholars

For every knowledgeable person, there is always someone with greater knowledge until the All-Knowing. Knowing this, along with the various experiences one has in life, should keep one humble and grounded in reality.

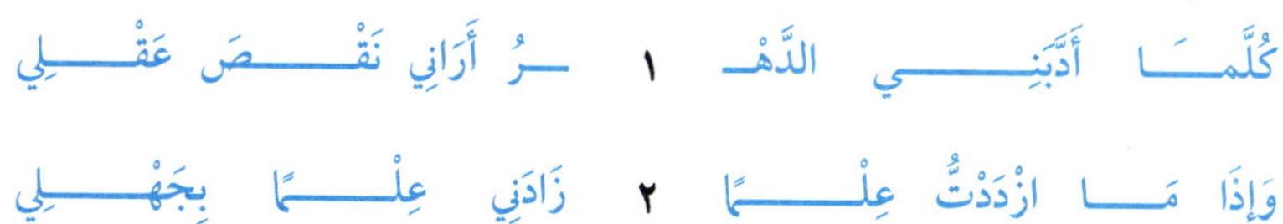

كُلَّمَا أَدَّبَنِي الدَّهْـ ١ ـرُ أَرَانِي نَقْصَ عَقْلِي

وَإِذَا مَا ازْدَدْتُّ عِلْمًا ٢ زَادَنِي عِلْمًا بِجَهْلِي

1. Whenever Time disciplined me, it showed me the deficiency of my intellect.
2. Whenever my knowledge increased, it increased my knowledge of my ignorance.

عُلُوُّ الهِمَّةِ

High-Aiming Ambition

Sometimes one has high aspirations, but those aspirations are unreachable due to some other constraints, such as a lack of financial means. In such a situation, one should not give up but should rather strive to remove that constraint with the help of Allah ﷻ.

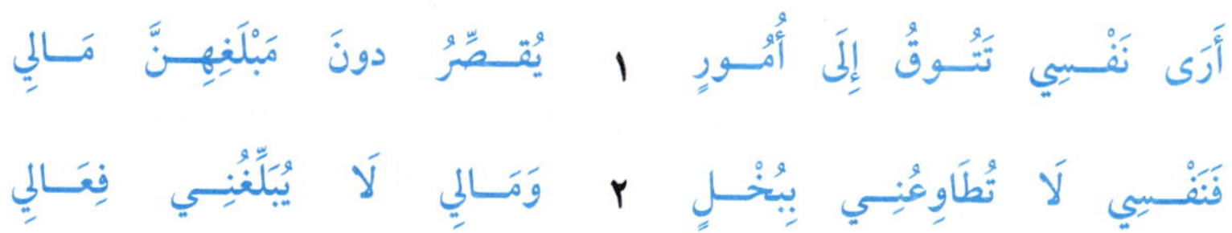

أَرَى نَفْسِي تَتُوقُ إِلَى أُمُورٍ ١ يُقَصِّرُ دونَ مَبْلَغِهِنَّ مَالِي

فَنَفْسِي لَا تُطَاوِعُنِي بِبُخْلٍ ٢ وَمَالِي لَا يُبَلِّغُنِي فِعَالِي

1. I see that I long for such matters for which my wealth falls short in acquiring.

2. My lower-self does not obey me [in being] stingy and my wealth is not [enough] to convey me to my deeds.

يَأْتِي العِلْمُ بِالتَّفَرُّغِ

Knowledge Comes with Dedication

It has been observed that those who look after their families are unable to devote as much time to their studies as they should. It is for this reason that getting married while studying has been discouraged.

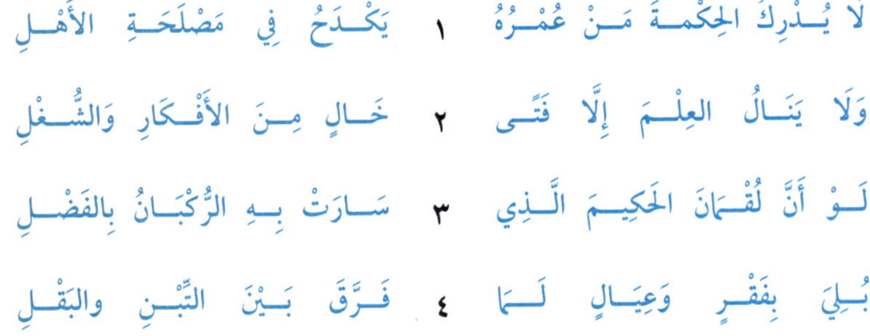

لَا يُدْرِكُ الحِكْمَةَ مَنْ عُمْرُهُ ١ يَكْدَحُ فِي مَصْلَحَةِ الأَهْلِ

وَلَا يَنَالُ العِلْمَ إِلَّا فَتًى ٢ خَالٍ مِنَ الأَفْكَارِ وَالشُّغْلِ

لَوْ أَنَّ لُقْمَانَ الحَكِيمَ الَّذِي ٣ سَارَتْ بِهِ الرُّكْبَانُ بِالفَضْلِ

بُلِيَ بِفَقْرٍ وَعِيَالٍ لَمَا ٤ فَرَّقَ بَيْنَ التِّبْنِ والبَقْلِ

1. That person cannot acquire wisdom whose life [is spent] toiling for the welfare of his family.
2. Only a young man, free of thoughts and preoccupations, can acquire knowledge.
3. If Luqmān the wise, whose virtue has spread far and wide,
4. Had been tested with poverty and a [earning for] a family, he would not even be able to differentiate between grass and vegetables.

153

المُبْتَدِعُون

The Innovators

Innovation (bid'ah) is defined as considering an act to be a part of Dīn when it is not so. This has been deemed reprehensible by the Prophet ﷺ. An act done for the sake of Dīn does not fall under this. Thus, merely doing something new would not immediately be considered an innovation in the technical sense of the word. One would have to determine the intent and purpose behind the action before passing a verdict.

لَمْ يَبْرَحِ النَّاسُ حَتَّى أَحْدَثُوا بِدَعًا ١ فِي الدِّينِ بِالرَّأْيِ لَمْ يُبْعَثْ بِهَا الرُّسُلُ

حَتَّى اسْتَخَفَّ بِدِينِ اللهِ أَكْثَرُهُمْ ٢ وَفِي الَّذِي حُمِّلُوا مِنْ حَقِّهِ شُغُلُ

1. People continued [in their wrong ways] until they created innovations in the *Dīn* with [their own] opinions with which the messengers were not sent[1].
2. So much so that most of them valued the *Dīn* of Allah lightly and were distracted from [fulfilling] His right with which they were tasked with.

154

ذَكَاءٌ ودُعَاءٌ

Intelligence and Supplication

When the *khalīfah* Hārūn al-Rashīd appointed al-Amīn and al-

1 All the messengers of Allah ﷺ called towards the message of *tawḥīd* although their Shariahs were different.

Ma’mūn as his successors in Makkah, a young boy stood up and said: “O Commander of the Faithful,

لَا قَصَّرَا عَنْهَا وَلَا بَلَغَتْهُمَا ١ حَتَّى يَطُولَ بِهَا لَدَيْكَ طِوَالُهَا

1. [May Allah] not let them be incapable [of the *khilāfah*] and may it not reach them until its duration lasts long by you [O Hārūn al-Rashīd].”

The people then asked who this youth is, who combined both congratulation and consolation in one verse. It was answered: “This is a Qurayshī young man named Muḥammad bin Idrīs al-Shāfi‘ī.”

155

مُشَاكَلَةُ النَّاسِ

Resembling People

Once, while Imam al-Shāfi‘ī was on a journey, nightfall forced him to alight at a masjid, and so he spent the night there. In the masjid, there were some ignorant people conversing using obscene language, so he quoted the following couplets:

وَأَنْزَلَنِي طُولُ النَّوَى دارَ غُرْبَةٍ ١ إِذَا شِئْتُ لَاقَيْتُ امْرَأً لَا أُشَاكِلُهُ

أُحَامِقُهُ حَتَّى تُقَالَ سَجِيَّةٌ ٢ وَلَوْ كَانَ ذَا عَقْلٍ لَكُنْتُ أُعَاقِلُهُ

1. The long distance made me alight at an unknown abode where, if I [ever] wanted, I could [easily] find [many] a man who I was dissimilar to [in temperament].

2. I would agree with him in his stupidity until it will be said [that it is my] natural disposition, and if he was intelligent, I would agree with him in his intelligence.

156

البُعْدُ عَنْ أَبْوَابِ المُلُوكِ

Avoiding the Doors of Kings

Across the centuries, the scholars of Dīn throughout the Muslim lands were always wary of going to kings and seeking benefit from them. They feared that doing so would compromise their role as custodians of the Dīn and the Dīn would then be at the whims of the kings.

إِنَّ الْمُلُوكَ بَلَاءٌ حَيْثُمَا حَلُّوا ١ فَلَا يَكُنْ لَكَ فِي أَبْوَابِهِمْ ظِلُّ

مَاذَا تُؤَمِّلُ مِنْ قَوْمٍ إِذَا غَضِبُوا ٢ جَارُوا عَلَيْكَ وَإِنْ أَرْضَيْتَهُمْ مَلُّوا؟

فَاسْتَغْنِ بِاللهِ عَنْ أَبْوَابِهِمْ كَرَمًا ٣ إِنَّ الْوُقُوفَ عَلَى أَبْوَابِهِمْ ذُلُّ

1. Kings are trials wherever they settle, so do not [even] let your shadow be at their doors.

2. What do you hope from people who, when they get angry [at you] they oppress you and when you please them, they become bored?

3. So become independent, through Allah, of their doors out of dignity, for standing at their doors is a disgrace.

مَنْ طَلَبَ العُلَى سَهِرَ اللَّيَالِي

Whoever Seeks High Status Spends the Nights Awake

In any transaction, the more you put in, the more you will get as a result. If you wish to have a high status before Allah, then you must put in the due effort, whether that be in studying the Dīn or in worshipping Him.

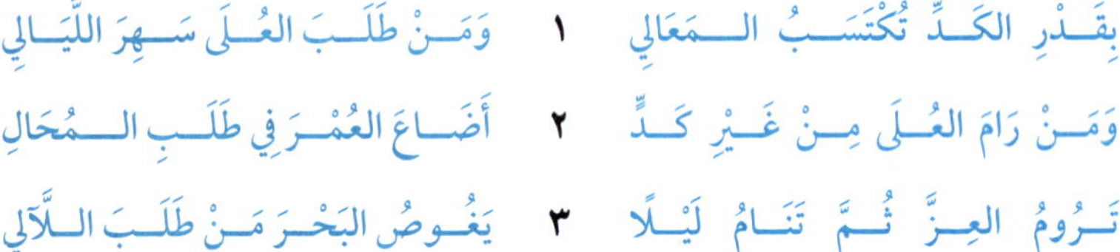

1. According to [one's] effort are noble things acquired and whoever seeks high status spends the nights awake.
2. Whoever desires high status without any effort has wasted [his] life in seeking the impossible.
3. You desire honor [but] then you sleep [throughout] the night; the one seeking pearls dives into the ocean!

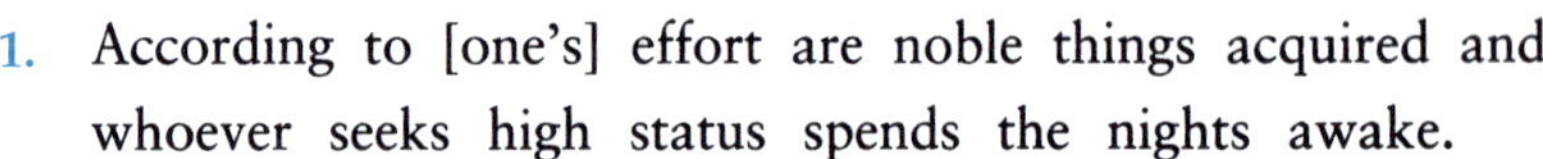

الفَقِيهُ والرَّئِيسُ والغَنِيُّ

The Jurist, the Leader, and the Wealthy

There is no "one-size-fits-all" standard for judging the merit of people. People's merits are gauged differently based on their statuses or roles in society. For every person one encounters in life, one must apply the appropriate standard.

إِنَّ الفَقِيهَ هُوَ الفَقِيهُ بِفِعْلِهِ ١ لَيْسَ الفَقِيهُ بِنُطْقِهِ وَمَقَالِهِ

وَكَذَا الرَّئِيسُ هُوَ الرَّئِيسُ بِخُلْقِهِ ٢ لَيْسَ الرَّئِيسُ بِقَوْمِهِ وَرِجَالِهِ

وَكَذَا الغَنِيُّ هُوَ الغَنِيُّ بِحَالِهِ ٣ لَيْسَ الغَنِيُّ بِمُلْكِهِ وَبِمَالِهِ

1. A jurist is defined by his actions, not by his speech and his sayings.
2. Similarly, a leader is defined by his character, not by his people and his men.
3. Likewise, a wealthy person is defined by his condition, not by his power and his wealth.

159

حُبُّه لِأَبِي بَكْرٍ ﵁ وعَلِيٍّ ﵁

His Love For Abū Bakr ﵁ and 'Alī ﵁

Following the position of our pious predecessors, we assign a higher rank to Abū Bakr ﵁ than 'Alī ﵁ but we love them both as Companions of the Holy Prophet ﷺ. We avoid deviating from the middle way by speaking against or hating one of the two.

إِذَا نَحْنُ فَضَّلْنَا عَلِيًّا فَإِنَّنَا ١ رَوَافِضُ بِالتَّفْضِيلِ عِنْدَ ذَوِي الجَهْلِ

وَفَضْلُ أَبِي بَكْرٍ إِذَا مَا ذَكَرْتُهُ ٢ رُمِيتُ بِنَصْبٍ عِنْدَ ذِكْرِيَ لِلْفَضْلِ

فَلَا زِلْتُ ذَا رَفْضٍ وَنَصْبٍ كِلَاهُمَا ٣ بِحُبَّيْهِمَا حَتَّى أُوَسَّدَ فِي الرَّمْلِ

1. When we honor 'Alī, then by doing so, we are *Rawāfiḍ*[1] according to the ignorant ones.
2. And when I mention the merit of Abū Bakr, I am accused of being a *Nāṣibiyy*.[2]
3. Thus, I remain both a *Rāfiḍiyy* and a *Nāṣibiyy* by loving them both until I am laid to rest in the sand.

1 The plural of "*Rāfiḍiyy*" which is someone who has extreme love for 'Alī.
2 Someone who harbors hatred for 'Alī.

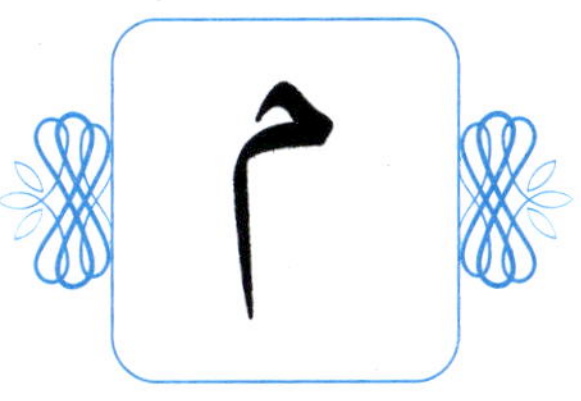

قافية الميم
The End-Rhyme of the Letter *Mīm*

ابْكِ على عَيبِكَ
Cry for Your Own Faults

Even if one has a noble intention behind pointing out and rectifying the faults of others, it would be more prudent to work on oneself first. This requires the ability to introspect, which is the first step toward rectifying one's lower self.

عَجِبْتُ لِمَنْ يَبْكِي عَلَى عَيْبِ غَيْرِهِ ١ دُمُوعًا وَلَا يَبْكِي عَلَى عَيْبِهِ دَمَا

وَأَعْجَبُ مِنْ هَذَا يَرَى عَيْبَ غَيْرِه ٢ عَظِيمًا وَفِي عَيْنَيْهِ مِنْ عَيْبِهِ عَمَى

1. I am amazed at the one who cries tears at the faults of others and does not cry [tears of] blood at his own faults.
2. And more astonishing than that is [one who] sees the faults of others as being big while his eyes are blind to his own faults.

161

عِفُّوا تَعِفَّ نِسَاؤُكُمْ

Be Chaste and Your Women Will Remain Chaste

One of the objectives of the Shariah is "safeguarding lineage," which entails that the foundation of society i.e., the family, be preserved. To that end, fornication and adultery have been declared forbidden by Allah as they destroy families and therefore society as a whole.

عِفُّوا تَعِفَّ نِسَاؤُكُمْ فِي المَحْرَمِ ١ وَتَجَنَّبُوا مَا لَا يَلِيقُ بِمُسْلِمِ

إِنَّ الزِّنَا دَيْنٌ فَإِنْ أَقْرَضْتَهُ ٢ كَانَ الوَفَا مِنْ أَهْلِ بَيْتِكَ فَاعْلَمِ

1. Be chaste from forbidden acts and your women will remain chaste [as well], and avoid that which is unbefitting a Muslim.

2. Fornication is a debt, so if you lend it, know that the fulfillment will be from your own house.

162

بِالْعِلْمِ تُبْنَى الأَمْجَادُ

Grandeur is Built on Knowledge

When a person acquires knowledge of Dīn, people look up to him and turn to him for guidance. Thus, he bears the responsibility of steering them in the right direction through his actions and words. If he fails to fulfill this responsibility, then he will have to answer for it on a Day unlike any other.

رَأَيْتُ العِلْمَ صَاحِبُهُ كَرِيمٌ ١ وَلَوْ وَلَدَتْهُ آبَاءٌ لِئَامُ

وَلَيْسَ يَزَالُ يَرْفَعُهُ إِلَى أَنْ ٢ يُعَظِّمَ أَمْرَهُ القَوْمُ الكِرَامُ

وَ يَتَّبِعُونَهُ فِي كُلِّ حَالٍ ٣ كَرَاعِي الضَّأْنِ تَتْبَعُهُ السَّوَامُ

فَلَوْلَا العِلْمُ مَا سَعِدَتْ رِجَالٌ ٤ وَلَا عُرِفَ الحَلَالُ وَلَا الحَرَامُ

1. I saw that the possessor of knowledge is honorable even if he is born into a lowly family.
2. [His knowledge] keeps elevating him until the noble people respect him.
3. They follow him in every condition, like how livestock follows the shepherd.
4. If it were not for knowledge, men would not be happy and the lawful and the unlawful would not be known.

163

لا عيش إلّا عَيش الآخرَة

There is Only the Life of the Hereafter

If one's soul is properly rectified, it yearns for the true life ahead and for meeting the Lord. Even the wait of a second more is unbearable for that exalted soul. Sadly, our souls cling to the Earthly domain and forget the reality of the Hereafter.

يَا نَفْسُ مَا هُوَ إِلَّا صَبْرُ أَيَّامِ ١ كَأَنَّ مُدَّتَهَا أَضْغَاثُ أَحْلَامِ

يَا نَفْسُ [جُوزِي] عَنِ الدُّنْيَا مُبَادَرَةً ٢ وَخَلِّ عَنْهَا فَإِنَّ العَيْشَ قُدَّامِي

1. O [my] soul, it is but the patience of [a few] days, as if its

duration is [just] that of confused dreams.

2. O [my] soul, pass by and leave the worldly life on an impulse, as the [true] life is ahead of me.

164

الأمْرَاضُ مِنْ ثَلاثٍ

Three Things Are the Cause of Sickness

One's body is a trust from Allah and keeping a trust entails safeguarding it from that which may harm it. Although some things may be permissible in Shariah, that does not mean that one should indulge in them as much as one pleases.

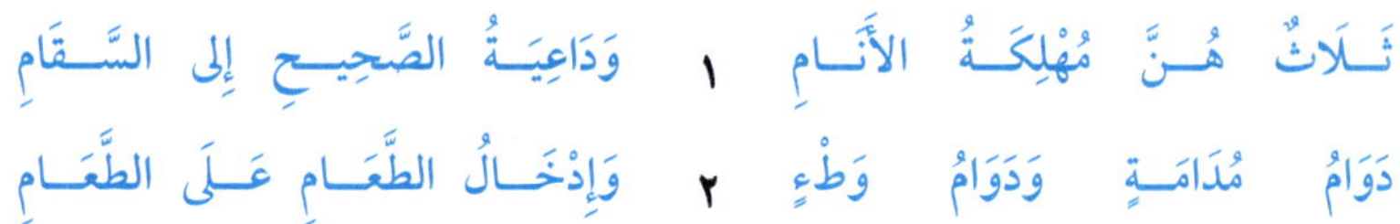

ثَـلَاثٌ هُـنَّ مُهْلِكَـةُ الأَنَـامِ ١ وَدَاعِيَـةُ الصَّحِيـحِ إلى السَّـقَامِ

دَوَامُ مُدَامَـةٍ وَدَوَامُ وَطْءٍ ٢ وَإِدْخَـالُ الطَّعَـامِ عَـلَى الطَّعَـامِ

1. Three are destructive to man and invite the healthy to sicknesses:

2. Continuous drinking of liquor, constant sexual intercourse, and forcing food upon food.

165

مَنْحُ العِلْمِ ومَنْعِه

The Bestowing and Depriving of Knowledge

Although one must be careful when deciding who to impart knowledge to, one must also not go to the extreme of concealing and withholding knowledge from a true seeker. For this, we have been given a stern warning from the Prophet ﷺ: "Whoever conceals knowledge which Allah has made beneficial for mankind's affairs of religion, Allah will bridle him with reins of fire on the Day of Resurrection."(Ibn Mājah)

أَأَنْثُرُ دُرًّا وَسْطَ سَارِحَةِ البَهَم	١	وَأَنْظِمُ مَنْثُورًا لِرَاعِيَةِ الغَنَمْ؟
لَعَمْرِي لَئِنْ ضُيِّعْتُ فِي شَرِّ بَلْدَةٍ	٢	فَلَسْتُ مُضِيعًا فِيهِمُ غُرَرَ الكَلِمْ
سَأَكْتُمُ عِلْمِي عَنْ ذَوِي الجَهْلِ طَاقَتِي	٣	وَلَا أَنْثُرُ الدُّرَّ النَّفِيسَ عَلَى الغَنَمْ
فَإِنْ فَرَّجَ اللهُ اللَّطِيْفُ بِلُطْفِهِ	٤	وَصَادَفْتُ أَهْلًا لِلْعُلُومِ وَلِلْحِكَمْ
بَثَثْتُ مُفِيدًا وَاسْتَفَدْتُّ وِدَادَهُمْ	٥	وَإِلَّا فَمَكْنُونٌ لَدَيَّ وَمُكْتَتَمْ
وَمَنْ مَنَحَ الجُهَّالَ عِلْمًا أَضَاعَهُ	٦	وَمَنْ مَنَعَ المُسْتَوْجِبِينَ فَقَدْ ظَلَمْ
وَكَاتِمُ عِلْمِ الدِّينِ عَمَّنْ يُرِيدُهُ	٧	يَبُوءُ بِأَوْزَارٍ وَإِثْمٍ إِذَا كَتَمْ

1. Should I scatter pearls in the midst of herders of lambs and string them together for shepherds?

2. May my life be blessed, that even if I am to be wasted in the worst land, I will not waste the finest words [of knowledge] amongst them.

3. I will conceal my knowledge from the ignorant ones [to the best of] my ability, and I will not scatter precious pearls before sheep.

4. If Allah the All-Subtly Kind makes ease out of His benevolence and I find those worthy of knowledge and wisdom,

5. I will disseminate beneficial [knowledge] and I will gain their love. If not, [the knowledge] will be stored and concealed with me.

6. Whoever has bestowed the ignorant with knowledge has wasted

م

it, and whoever has deprived the deserving has wronged.

7. The one who conceals the knowledge of *Dīn* from the one seeking it will bear burdens and sin if he conceals.

166

لِلشَّامِتِين يَومٌ

A Day for Those Who Rejoice Over Other's Misfortunes

It is a sad reality that many of those favored by Allah ﷻ gain enemies who want nothing less than death for them. They forget that they, too, will face death and will thereby be questioned by the One whose friends they have harmed.

قَضَيْتُ نَحْبِي فَسُرَّ قَوْمٌ ١ حَمْقَى بِهِمْ غَفْلَةٌ وَنَوْمُ

كَأَنَّ يَوْمِي عَلَيَّ حَتْمٌ ٢ وَلَيْسَ لِلشَّامِتِينَ يَوْمُ

1. I have completed my time [in this worldly life], so a foolish group of people afflicted with heedlessness and slumber rejoiced.

2. As if my day [of death] is something forced upon me only and those who rejoice over others' misfortunes do not have a day.

167

قَدْ بَلَوتُك

I Tested You

Imam al-Shāfi‘ī ﵀ was asked for something but he refused. He then recited the following:

وَلَقَدْ بَلَوْتُكَ وَابْتَلَيْتَ خَلِيقَتِي ١ وَلَقَدْ كَفَاكَ مُعَلِّمِي تَعْلِيمِي

1. Indeed, I have tested you and you [also] have tested my temperament. Thus, sufficient for [me against] you is what my teacher has taught me.

168

وَدَاعُ الدُّنْيَا وَالتَّأَهُّبُ لِلآخِرَةِ

Bidding Farewell to the World and Preparing for the Hereafter

Imam al-Shāfi'ī ﵀ was asked about his health during his sickness from which he passed away, so the Imam replied, "I am departing from the worldly life, separating from my close friends, drinking from the cup of death, arriving before Allah. By Allah, I do not know whether my soul will proceed to Paradise or to Hell. Thus, I console my soul." Thereafter, he started crying and recited:

إِلَيْكَ إِلَهَ الخَلْقِ أَرْفَعُ رَغْبَتِي ١ وَإِنْ كُنْتُ يَا ذَا المَنِّ وَالجُودِ مُجْرِمَا

وَلَمَّا قَسَا قَلْبِي وَضَاقَتْ مَذَاهِبِي ٢ جَعَلْتُ الرَّجَا مِنِّي لِعَفْوِكَ سُلَّمَا

تَعَاظَمَنِي ذَنْبِي فَلَمَّا قَرَنْتُهُ ٣ بِعَفْوِكَ رَبِّي كَانَ عَفْوُكَ أَعْظَمَا

وَمَا زِلْتَ ذَا عَفْوٍ عَنِ الذَّنْبِ لَمْ تَزَلْ ٤ تَجُودُ وَ تَعْفُو مِنَّةً وَ تَكَرُّمَا

وَلَوْلَاكَ مَا يَقْوَى لِإِبْلِيسَ عَابِدٌ ٥ فَكَيْفَ وَقَدْ أَغْوَى صَفِيَّكَ آدَمَا

فَيَا لَيْتَ شِعْرِي هَلْ أَصِيرُ لِجَنَّةٍ ٦ فَأَهْنَا وَإِمَّا لِلسَّعِيرِ فَأَنْدَمَا

٧ وَإِنِّي لَآتِي الذَّنْبَ أَعْرِفُ قَدْرَهُ وَ أَعْلَمُ أَنَّ اللهَ يَعْفُو وَيَرْحَمَا
٨ فَإِنْ تَعْفُ عَنِّي تَعْفُ عَنْ مُتَمَرِّدٍ ظَلُومٍ غَشُومٍ لَا يُزَايِلُ مَأْثَمَا
٩ فَإِنْ تَنْتَقِمْ مِنِّي فَلَسْتُ بِآيِسٍ وَلَوْ أُدْخِلَتْ نَفْسِي بِجُرْمِي جَهَنَّمَا
١٠ فَجُرْمِي عَظِيمٌ مِنْ قَدِيمٍ وَحَادِثٌ وَعَفْوُكَ يَا ذَا العَفْوِ أَعْلَى وَأَجْسَمَا
١١ خَفِ اللهَ وارْجُهُ لِكُلِّ عَظِيمَةٍ وَلَاتُطِعِ النَّفْسَ اللَّجُوجَ فَتَنْدَمَا
١٢ وَكُنْ بَيْنَ هَاتَيْنِ مِنَ الخَوْفِ والرَّجَا وَأَبْشِرْ بِعَفْوِ اللهِ إِنْ كُنْتَ مُسْلِمَا
١٣ فَلِلَّهِ دَرُّ العَارِفِ الفَرْدِ إِنَّهُ تَسُحُّ لِفَرْطِ الوَجْدِ أَجْفَانُهُ دَمَا
١٤ يُقِيمُ إِذَا مَا اللَّيْلُ جَنَّ ظَلَامُهُ عَلَى نَفْسِهِ مِنْ شِدَّةِ الخَوْفِ مَأْتَمَا
١٥ فَصِيحًا إِذَا مَا كَانَ فِي ذِكْرِ رَبِّهِ وَفِي مَا سِوَاهُ فِي الوَرَى كَانَ أَعْجَمَا
١٦ وَيَذْكُرُ أَيَّامًا مَضَتْ مِنْ شَبَابِهِ وَمَا كَانَ فِيهَا بِالجَهَالَةِ أَجْرَمَا
١٧ فَصَارَ قَرِينَ الهَمِّ طُولَ نَهَارِهِ وَيَخْدُمُ مَوْلَاهُ إِذَا اللَّيْلُ أَظْلَمَا
١٨ يَقُولُ حَبِيبِي أَنْتَ سُؤْلِي وَبُغْيَتِي كَفَى بِكَ لِلرَّاجِينَ سُؤْلًا وَمَغْنَمَا
١٩ أَلَسْتَ الَّذِي غَذَّيْتَنِي وَكَفَلْتَنِي وَمَا زِلْتَ مَنَّانًا عَلَيَّ وَ مُنْعِمَا
٢٠ عَسَى مَنْ لَهُ الإِحْسَانُ يَغْفِرُ زَلَّتِي وَ يَسْتُرُ أَوْزَارِي وَمَا قَدْ تَقَدَّمَا

1. To You, Lord of the creation, I extend my wish [of forgiveness] even though I am, O the Gracious and Generous One, guilty.
2. When my heart hardened and my paths narrowed, I made my hope in Your forgiveness a ladder.
3. My sins appeared great to me, but when I compared them to Your forgiveness, my Lord, Your forgiveness was greater.
4. You have always been Most-Forgiving of sins. You will always

be bountiful and forgiving out of favor and generosity.

5. If it were not for You, no worshipper would have power over Iblīs. How [when] he misled your sincere [slave] Ādam?

6. How I wish I knew whether I will proceed to Paradise and then be delighted or to Hell and then regret!

7. I commit a sin aware of its worth, and [also] knowing that Allah forgives and is merciful.

8. If You forgive me, You will be forgiving a disobedient, oppressing, wrongdoing [slave who] continues to sin.

9. If You punish me, then I will not be despondent [of Your mercy], even if I am made to enter Hell due to my sins.

10. My past and present sins are great, but your forgiveness, O the Most Forgiving One, is much greater.

11. Fear Allah and have hope in Him in every calamity. Do not follow the stubborn lower-self and then [later] regret.

12. Remain between these two: fear and hope, and rejoice at the forgiveness of Allah if you are a Muslim.

13. How excellent is the one alone, acquainted [with Allah], that his eyelids flow blood due to extreme ardor!

14. When the night spreads its darkness, he mourns for his lower-self out of extreme fear.

15. Eloquent when he is in the remembrance of his Lord and inarticulate amongst creation regarding anything besides Him.

16. He remembers the days of his youth that have passed and

what [sins] he committed in them out of ignorance.

17. Throughout his day, he is sorrowful,[1] and he serves his Master when the night falls.

18. He says, "O my beloved, You are my wish and desire. You are sufficient as a wish and desire for the hopeful ones.

19. Are you not the One who sustained me and supported me? You remain beneficent and gracious towards me.

20. Hopefully, the benevolent One will forgive my mistakes and will hide my sins and whatever that has passed."

169

وُجُوبُ صَوْنِ العِلْمِ

The Obligation of Preserving Knowledge

Knowledge is a great bestowal from Allah ﷻ, and so it should be valued and safeguarded just like any other bestowal of His. Just like how you would not give your most prized possession to anyone on the street, likewise, do not impart knowledge to those not deserving of it.

العِلْمُ مِنْ فَضْلِهِ، لِمَنْ خَدَمَهْ ١ أَنْ يَجْعَلَ النَّاسَ كُلَّهُمْ خَدَمَهْ

فَوَاجِبٌ صَوْنُهُ عَلَيْهِ كَمَا ٢ يَصُونُ فِي النَّاسِ عِرْضَهُ وَدَمَهْ

فَمَنْ حَوَى العِلْمَ ثُمَّ أَوْدَعَهُ ٣ بِجَهْلِهِ غَيْرَ أَهْلِهِ ظَلَمَهْ

1. One of the merits of knowledge is that it makes everyone

[1] This is due to his being unable to engross himself in the worship of his Lord as he does at night.

servants of the one who serves it.

2. Necessary is its preservation upon him, just as it protects his dignity and blood amongst people.

3. The one who amasses knowledge and then entrusts it to those unworthy of it out of ignorance has [truly] wronged it.

Safeguard Your Brother's Honor

A Muslim's honor, family, property, etc., fall under his sanctity, and it is the responsibility of every Muslim not to violate the sanctity of his brother, regardless of whether that is through words or through actions.

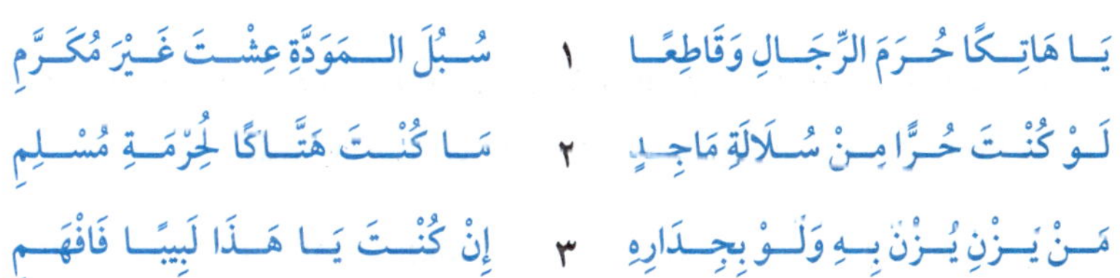

1. O the one violating the sanctity of men and cutting the means of affection, may you not live honorably.

2. Had you been noble and of honorable descent, you would not have been violating the sanctity of a Muslim.

3. Whoever fornicates will be fornicated with[1], even within his own walls. If you are intelligent, then understand this!

1 Meaning that sometimes the recompense for one who fornicates is that those associated with him will be fornicated with.

التَذَلُّل والاستِغَاثَة

Humility and Seeking Help

When turning to Allah, seeking His forgiveness, mercy, and grace, one should acknowledge and mention one's utter need for Allah along with mentioning things sacred to Allah. This is, in fact, the secret to having one's supplications accepted by Allah.

بِمَوْقِفِ ذُلِّي دُونَ عِزَّتِكَ العُظْمَى	١	بِمَخْفِيِّ سِرٍّ لَا أُحِيطُ بِهِ عِلْمَا
بِإِطْرَاقِ رَأْسِي، بِاعْتِرَافِي بِذِلَّتِي	٢	بِمَدِّ يَدِي، أَسْتَمْطِرُ الجُودَ وَالرُّحْمَى
بِأَسْمَائِكَ الحُسْنَى الَّتِي بَعْضُ وَصْفِهَا	٣	لِعِزَّتِهَا يَسْتَغْرِقُ النَّثْرَ وَالنَّظْمَا
بِعَهْدٍ قَدِيمٍ مِنْ أَلَسْتُ بِرَبِّكُمْ؟	٤	بِمَنْ كَانَ مَجْهُولًا فَعَلَّمْتَهُ بِالأَسْمَا
أَذِقْنَا شَرَابَ الأُنْسِ يَا مَنْ إِذَا سَقَى	٥	مُحِبًّا شَرَابًا لَا يُضَامُ وَلَا يَظْمَا

1. By standing with humility before Your great might, by the hidden secrets which I cannot comprehend,

2. By bowing my head, acknowledging my disgrace, and spreading my hands, I beg for the rain of generosity and mercy.

3. By Your beautiful names, that—due to their greatness—even describing some of them would fill up prose and poetry,

4. By the ancient covenant of '*ahd alast* taken from one who was unknown, and You taught him the names [of things][1],

---

1 Referring to Adam and his offspring.

5. Let us taste the drink of [Your] love, O the one who, when He gives to drink those who love [Him], they are not disgraced nor do they feel thirsty[1] .

172

الجُودُ والفَاقَةُ

Generosity and Poverty

Whatever we consume now will not avail us in the Hereafter, but what we give to others could potentially serve as the means of our salvation. Feeding another even half a date and remaining hungry ourselves could tip the scale in our favor and save us from the Hellfire.

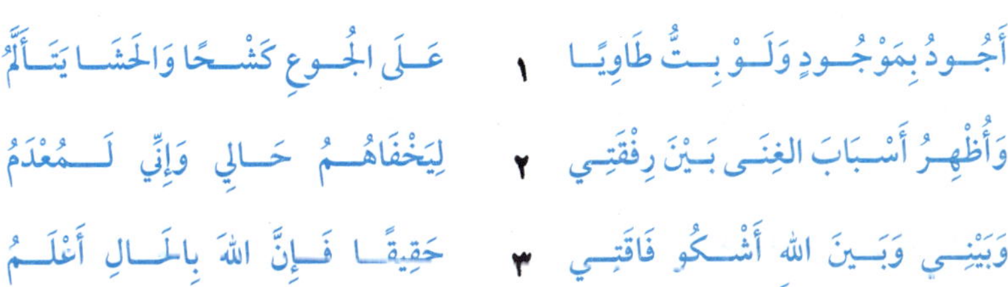

أَجُودُ بِمَوْجُودٍ وَلَوْ بِتُّ طَاوِيًا ١ عَلَى الجُوعِ كَشْحًا وَالحَشَا يَتَأَلَّمُ

وَأُظْهِرُ أَسْبَابَ الغِنَى بَيْنَ رِفْقَتِي ٢ لِيَخْفَاهُمُ حَالِي وَإِنِّي لَمُعْدَمُ

وَبَيْنِي وَبَيْنَ اللهِ أَشْكُو فَاقَتِي ٣ حَقِيقًا فَإِنَّ اللهَ بِالحَالِ أَعْلَمُ

1. I give away whatever I have [to those in need] even if I have to spend the night locking hunger in my bosom while [my] intestines pain.

2. I display means of wealth before my friends to hide my condition from them—that I am destitute.

3. [Only] between myself and Allah do I truly complain of my poverty, for verily He knows best [my] condition.

---

1 Meaning that they are made self-sufficient by Allah and are no longer dependent on others.

الغِيرَةُ على العِلْمِ

Vigilant Care for Knowledge

Just as one ought to be protective of one's family, one should be protective of one's knowledge as well. Both are a trust from Allah ﷻ and cannot be entrusted to anyone or everyone.

وَمَا أَنَا بِالغَيْرَانِ مِنْ دُونِ أَهْلِهِ ١ إِذَا أَنَا لَمْ أُصْبِحْ غَيُورًا عَلَى عِلْمِي

طَبِيبُ فُؤَادِي مُذْ ثَلَاثِينَ حِجَّةً ٢ وَصَيْقَلُ ذِهْنِي وَالْمُفَرِّجُ عَنْ هَمِّي

1. I am not deserving of [being described as] one who has vigilant care for his family if I do not have vigilant care for my knowledge.

2. [My knowledge] has been the doctor of my heart for thirty years, the polisher of my intellect, and the reliever of my worries.

اِعْرِفْ عَدُوَّكَ مِنْ صَدِيقِكَ

Know Your Enemy From Your Friend

An oft-forgotten aspect of friendship is taking into consideration the social circle of one's friends. If they keep your enemies as their friends, then be wary of your friendship with them. This will help in distinguishing a true friend from a potential enemy.

صَدِيقُكَ مَنْ يُعَادِي مَنْ تُعَادِي ١ بِطُولِ الدَّهْرِ مَا سَجَعَ الحَمَامُ

وَيُوفِي الدَّيْنَ عَنْكَ بِغَيْرِ مَطْلٍ ٢ وَلَا يَمْنُنْ بِهِ أَبَدًا دَوَامُ

فَإِنْ صَافَى صَدِيقُكَ مَنْ تُعَادِي ٣ وَيَفْرَحُ حِينَ تَرْشُقُكَ السِّهَامُ

فَذَاكَ هُوَ العَدُوُّ بِغَيْرِ شَكٍّ ٤ تَجَنَّبْهُ فَصُحْبَتُهُ حَرَامُ

فَإِنَّا قَدْ سَمِعْنَا بَيْتَ شِعْرٍ ٥ شَبِيهِ الدُّرِّ زَيْنُهُ النِّظَامُ:

إِذَا وَافَى صَدِيقُكَ مَنْ تُعَادِي ٦ فَقَدْ عَادَاكَ وَانْفَصَلَ الكَلَامُ

1. Your friend is one who has enmity for the one who you have enmity for, forever and for eternity[1].
2. He fulfills a debt on your behalf without delay and does not ever remind you of that [favor].
3. If your friend has a sincere affection for one who you have enmity for and rejoices when arrows strike you,
4. Then that is your enemy, without a doubt. Avoid him as his companionship is forbidden,
5. As we have heard the verse of poetry resembling pearls whose beauty is proper arrangement:
6. “If your friend fulfills [the wishes of] one who you have enmity for, then he has taken you as an enemy and there’s nothing left to say.”

1 Literally: “So long as the pigeon coos.”

175

الحُبُّ الصَادِقُ

Sincere Affection

Sincere affection is one in which not only are feelings mutual but conditions are shared as well. Showing concern for a beloved's affliction gives them the strength to move on and showing happiness at a beloved's happiness increases their happiness.

عُدْتُ حَبِيبِي وَبِهِ عِلَّةٌ ١ فَعُدْتُ وَالعِلَّةُ لِي لَازِمَهْ

وَعَادَنِي مِنْ عِلَّتِي سَالِمًا ٢ فَعَادَتِ النَّفْسُ بِهِ سَالِمَهْ

وَالنَّفْسُ إِنْ صَحَّتْ وَمَحْبُوبُهَا ٣ غَيْرُ صَحِيحٍ وُجِدَتْ ظَالِمَهْ

وَكَيْفَ لَا تَجْرِي عَلَى حُكْمِهِ ٤ وَهِيَ بِأَحْكَامِ الهَوَى عَالِمَهْ

1. I visited my beloved while he had an affliction and so I returned and all the while, that affliction had become bound with me.

2. He visited me due to my affliction [while being] healthy and so due to him [my] soul went back to being healthy.

3. A soul, if it is well while its beloved is not so, will be found oppressing.

4. And how can it not proceed according to [love's] ruling when it is aware of the rulings of love?

قافية النون

The End-Rhyme of the Letter *Nun*

اِغْتِنَامُ الفُرَصِ

Taking Advantage of Opportunities

The Prophet ﷺ advised us to take advantage of five before five. (Muṣannaf Ibn Abī Shaybah) Of those are: youth before old age, free time before preoccupation, and life before death. All three of these are included in these two verses:

إِذَا هَبَّتْ رِيَاحُكَ فَاغْتَنِمْهَا ١ فَعُقْبَى كُلِّ خَافِقَةٍ سُكُونُ

وَلَا تَغْفُلْ عَنِ الإِحْسَانِ فِيهَا ٢ فَمَا تَدْرِي السُّكُونُ مَتَى يَكُونُ

1. When your wind blows,[1] then take advantage of it, as the outcome of every shaking thing is a state of rest[2],

2. And do not neglect to do good in [those opportune moments], as you do not know when the state of rest will be[3].

1 Meaning that you are full of zeal and vigor and/or that the conditions are favorable.
2 Meaning lassitude or weakness.
3 Referring to death.

177

اِحْفَظْ لِسَانَكَ

Safeguard Your Tongue

Of our body parts, the tongue has the potential to commit the most sins. It is for this reason that the Noble Prophet ﷺ stated, "A slave utters a statement displeasing to Allah, without considering it of any importance, and because of it he sinks in the Hellfire." (Bukhārī)

اِحْفَظْ لِسَانَكَ أَيُّهَا الإِنْسَانُ ١ لَا يَلْدَغَنَّكَ إِنَّهُ ثُعْبَانُ

كَمْ فِي المَقَابِرِ مِنْ قَتِيلِ لِسَانِهِ ٢ كَانَتْ تَهَابُ لِقَاءَهُ الأَقْرَانُ

1. Safeguard your tongue, O mankind—let it not bite you as it is a serpent.

2. How many in the graves are those killed by their [own] tongues! [They were such that even] their peers were afraid to meet them.

178

البَلَاءُ مِنْ أَنْفُسِنَا

Trials are From Our Own Selves

People usually find someone or something else to blame for their faults, to the extent that they even blame time itself. But we have been prohibited from doing so, as Allah ﷻ says, "Do not curse time."(Bukhari) Instead, we should take account of ourselves and realize the extent and effect of our actions.

نَعِيبُ زَمَانَنَا وَالعَيْبُ فِينَا ١ وَمَا لِزَمَانِنَا عَيْبٌ سِوَانَا

وَنَهْجُو ذَا الزَّمَانَ بِغَيْرِ ذَنْبٍ ٢ وَلَوْ نَطَقَ الزَّمَانُ لَنَا هَجَانَا

فَدُنْيَانَا التَّصَنُّعُ وَالتَّرَائِي ٣ وَنَحْنُ بِهِ نُخَادِعُ مَنْ يَرَانَا

وَلَيْسَ الذِّئْبُ يَأْكُلُ لَحْمَ ذِئْبٍ ٤ وَيَأْكُلُ بَعْضُنَا بَعْضًا عِيَانَا

لَبِسْنَا لِلْخِدَاعِ مُسُوكَ ضَأْنٍ ٥ فَوَيْلٌ لِلْمُغِيرِ إِذَا أَتَانَا

1. We fault our era, whereas the faults are ours. [In reality,] our era has no fault besides us.

2. We disparage Time without any misdeed [from it]. If Time could speak to us, it would disparage us [instead].

3. Our worldly life is affectation and ostentation, and with it, we deceive those who see us.

4. The wolf does not devour the meat of [another] wolf, while we openly devour one another.

5. We have donned the hides of sheep to deceive [others], so destruction be upon the assailant when he comes [to attack] us.

179

المَالُ المُنْقِذُ

The Wealth Which Saves

Wealth spent for the sake of Allah ﷻ is not truly "spent," but rather, it is sent over to benefit in the next life. Such spending should be done throughout one's life, not just before passing on and thereby depriving those who would need it most, i.e., one's own family.

يَـا جَامِـعَ المَـالِ تَرْجُـو أَنْ تَفُـوزَ بِـهِ ١ كُلْ مَـا أَكَلْـتَ وَقَـدِّمْ لِلْمَوَازِيـنِ

وَلَا تَكُـنْ كَالَّـذِي قَدْ قَـالَ إِذْ حَضَرَتْ ٢ وَفَاتُـهُ: ثُلْـثُ مَـالِي لِلْمَسَـاكِينِ

1. O the one who gathers wealth hoping to gain success by it, eat what you have eaten and send forth [whatever is left over] for the scales [of deeds on the Day of Resurrection].

2. Do not be like the one who, when his death draws near, says: "A third of my wealth shall be for the needy."

العِلْمُ عَمِيقٌ بَحْرُه

The Ocean of Knowledge is Deep

As one wades further into the ocean of knowledge, one looks back and realizes how less he knew, and looks ahead and realizes how much there is to know. He must continuously decide whether to swim further, remain in place, or—Allah-forbid—swim back. By swimming further, one will surely acquire the pearls of knowledge in the depths of the ocean.

لَـنْ يَبْلُـغَ العِلْـمَ جَمِيعًـا أَحَـدٌ ١ لَا وَلَـوْ حَاوَلَـهُ أَلْـفَ سَـنَهْ

إِنَّـمَا العِلْـمُ عَمِيـقٌ بَحْـرُهُ ٢ فَخُـذُوا مِـنْ كُلِّ شَيءٍ أَحْسَـنَهْ

1. Never will one acquire all of knowledge, even if he attempts to do so for a thousand years.

2. The ocean of knowledge is deep, so take the best [you can] from every [field].

المَشيئَةُ الإلهيَّة

Divine Will

The wisdom behind the will of Allah ﷻ is one of His greatest secrets. If one ponders over it, he may lose his way. Instead, one should be grateful to Allah ﷻ for willing us into existence, willing us to have faith in Him, and willing us to be blessed with many favors.

مَا تَمَّ حِلْمٌ وَلَا عِلْمٌ بِلَا أَدَبٍ ١ وَلَا تَجَاهَلَ فِي قَوْمٍ حَلِيمَانِ

وَمَا التَّجَاهُلُ إِلَّا ثَوْبُ ذِي دَنَسٍ ٢ وَلَيْسَ يَلْبَسُهُ إِلَّا سَفِيهَانِ

1. What You willed occurred even if I did not wish it. And what I wished, if You did not will it to be, did not occur.

2. You have created [Your] slaves for [a purpose] You know well. [Your] knowledge encompasses the young and the old.

3. Of [Your slaves] are the fortunate, the unfortunate, the unattractive, and the beautiful.

4. Of them are the rich and the poor, and each one will be retained for his deeds.[1]

5. You have favored this one, and this one You have disgraced. You have helped that one, and that one You have left helpless.

---

[1]Referring to the verse: "Every soul, for what it has earned, will be retained." (74:38)

182

ذَمُّ التَّجَاهُلِ

Disparagement of Acting Ignorant

Imam al-Shāfiʿī ﷺ once said: "Knowledge is freedom and a seeker of knowledge is a slave. If he serves knowledge, he will own it. And if he has arrogance before it, then knowledge will not yield to one who does not humble himself before it." He then recited:

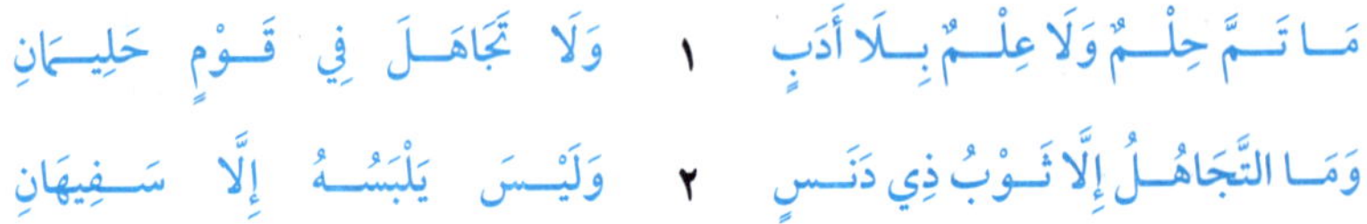

مَا تَمَّ حِلْمٌ وَلَا عِلْمٌ بِلَا أَدَبٍ ١ وَلَا تَجَاهَلَ فِي قَوْمٍ حَلِيمَانِ

وَمَا التَّجَاهُلُ إِلَّا ثَوْبُ ذِي دَنَسٍ ٢ وَلَيْسَ يَلْبَسُهُ إِلَّا سَفِيهَانِ

1. Understanding and knowledge are incomplete without good manners, and one forbearing person of a nation does not do an act of ignorance upon another forbearing person.

2. Acting ignorant is but the cloth of a dirty person and only two foolish persons would wear it.

183

تَعْزِيَةٌ

Consolation

Consoling is a well-attested sunnah of the Prophet ﷺ. Consoling others at their loss reminds us of the temporariness of this life as well as prepares us to face a similar affliction in our lives.

إِنِّي أَعَزِّيكَ لَا أَنِّي عَلَى طَمَعٍ ١ مِنَ الخُلُودِ، وَلَكِنْ سُنَّةُ الدِّينِ
فَمَا المُعَزَّى بِبَاقٍ بَعْدَ صَاحِبِهِ ٢ وَلَا المُعَزِّي وَإِنْ عَاشَا إِلَى حِينِ

1. I am consoling you, not out of a desire for immortality [for myself], but [rather because] it is a practice of *Dīn*.

2. The one being consoled will not remain after [the death of] his companion nor the one consoling, even if both live until a [later] time.

184

خُلُقِي الكَرَمُ

My Disposition is Generosity

Once, Imam al-Shāfi'ī ﵀ was taken to the court of the *khalīfah* Harūn al-Rashīd, who said to him: "O brother Shāfi'ī, have you renounced your allegiance and revolted with the 'Alawiyyah against us? The Imam replied, "O Commander of the Faithful, would I leave a cousin who says that I am his cousin and go to people who say that I am their slave?" So the *khalīfah* let him go and sent him 80,000 dirhams. The Imam then saw a barber and had his hair cut, and gave the barber the 80,000 dirhams. When Harūn al-Rashīd came to know of this, he scolded Imam al-Shāfi'ī ﵀, upon which the Imam recited the following:

وَلَوْ تُنَازِعُنِي كَفِّي إِلَى خُلُقٍ ١ يُزْرِي لَقُلْتُ لَهَا: أَلْقِيهِ أَوْ بِينِي
خِيَمِي كَرِيمٌ وَنَفْسِي لَا تُحَدِّثُنِي ٢ أَنَّ الإِلَهَ بِلَا رِزْقٍ ... يُخَلِّينِي
هَذَا وَمَا زَالَ إِلَيَّ مِنْ أَذَى طَمَعٍ ٣ وَمِنْ مَلَامَةِ أَهْلِ اللَّوْمِ يُغْرِينِي
بَلْ مَا اشْتَرَيْتُ بِمَالِي قَطُّ مَحْمَدَةً ٤ إِلَّا تَيَقَّنْتُ أَنِّي غَيْرُ مَغْبُونِ

وَلَا دُعِيتُ إِلَى مَجْدٍ وَمَكْرُمَةٍ ٥ إِلَّا أَجَبْتُ: أَلَا مَنْ ذَا يُنَادِينِي
لَبَّيْكَ يَا كَرَمِي، لَبَّيْكَ ثَانِيَةً ٦ لَبَّيْكَ ثَالِثَةً، مِنْ حَيْثُ تَدْعُونِي

1. If my palm were to urge me to a disposition that brings disgrace, I would say to it: "Discard it or distance yourself [from me]."

2. My natural disposition is generosity, and my lower-self does not say to me that Allah would leave me without wealth.

3. This notwithstanding, the pain of greed remains with me, and the reproach of those who reproach continues to provoke me.

4. Rather, I have never bought anything praiseworthy with my wealth except that I became certain that I was not cheated[1] .

5. And I am not invited to glory and honor[2] except that I respond: "Lo, who is the one summoning me?"

6. At your service my generosity, "At your service" a second time, "At your service" a third time, from wherever you call me.

سؤالٌ وجوابٌ

Question and Answer

Scholars encounter different types of people throughout their lives. Some pose genuine and intelligent questions, while others pose questions with no purpose other than to make themselves heard. The duty of a scholar is to not take such questions seriously,

[1] Meaning that I knew that Allah will give me a better recompense.

[2] Referring to noble deeds.

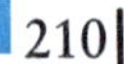

but rather to respond to the questioner in the manner he deserves.

A man asked Imam al-Shāfiʿī ﷺ a question by writing the following:

مَـــاذَا تَقُــولُ هَــدَاكَ اللهُ فِي رَجُــلٍ ١ أَمْسَـى يُحِـبُّ عَجُـوزًا بِنْـتَ تِسْـعِينِ

1. May Allah guide you. What do you say about a man who fell in love with a ninety-year-old woman?

Imam al-Shāfiʿī ﷺ answered:

نَبْكِـي عَلَيْـهِ فَقَـدْ حُـقَّ البُـكَاءُ لَـهُ ١ حُـبُّ العَجُـوزِ بِـتَرْكِ الخُـرَّدِ العَـيْنِ

1. We weep for him, as weeping is due for him; loving an old woman by leaving the virgin maidens [with beautiful] eyes.

186

شُرُوطُ تَحْصِيلِ العِلْمِ سِتَّةٌ

The Conditions of Acquiring Knowledge Are Six

Knowledge does not come about without any preconditions. One must possess the necessary qualities and conditions to be able to acquire knowledge, especially knowledge of the Dīn.

أَخِـي لَـنْ تَنَـالَ العِلْـمَ إِلَّا بِسِـتَّةٍ ١ سَـأُنْبِيكَ عَـنْ تَفْصِيلِهَـا بِبَيَـانِ

ذَكَاءٌ وَحِـرْصٌ وَاجْتِهَـادٌ وَبُلْغَـةٌ ٢ وَصُحْبَـةُ أُسْـتَاذٍ وَطُـولُ زَمَـانِ

1. My brother, you cannot acquire knowledge unless [you have] six [things], the details of which I will clearly inform you:

2. Intelligence, enthusiasm, hard work, financial capability, the company of a teacher, and a long period of time.

القَنَاعَةُ وصِيَانَةُ النَّفْسِ

Contentment and Safeguarding Oneself

Self-sufficiency is a means by which one's respect in society is safeguarded. It entails being content with what one has been bestowed and not turning to others for more. Those who unnecessarily depend on others face disgrace at every turn and those discontented may be depriving themselves of further bestowals from Allah.

قَنِعْتُ بِالقُوتِ مِنْ زَمَانِي ١ وَصُنْتُ نَفْسِي عَنِ الهَوَانِ
خَوْفًا مِنَ النَّاسِ أَنْ يَقُولُوا ٢ فَضْلُ فُلَانٍ عَلَى فُلَانِ
مَنْ كُنْتُ عَنْ مَالِهِ غَنِيًّا ٣ فَلَا أُبَالِي إِذَا جَفَانِي
وَمَنْ رَآنِي بِعَيْنِ نَقْصٍ ٤ رَأَيْتُهُ بِالَّتِي رَآنِي
وَمَنْ رَآنِي بِعَيْنِ تَمٍّ ٥ رَأَيْتُهُ كَامِلَ المَعَانِي

1. I was content with the sustenance of my time, and I safeguarded myself from disgrace,

2. Fearing that people might say, "The favor of so-and-so on so-and-so."

3. Whoever I am independent of his wealth, I will not mind when he shuns me.

4. Whoever looks at me with eyes of contempt, I look at him with the same [eyes].

5. Whoever looks at me with eyes of respect, I look at him as being perfect in all ways.

188

الشَّوقُ إلى مَسْقِطِ الرَّأسِ

Yearning for One's Birthplace

There is nothing that one yearns for more than one's homeland, as that is where one's family, friends, and memories reside. But believers also yearn for something greater than that, which is the homeland of their grandfather Adam ﷺ.

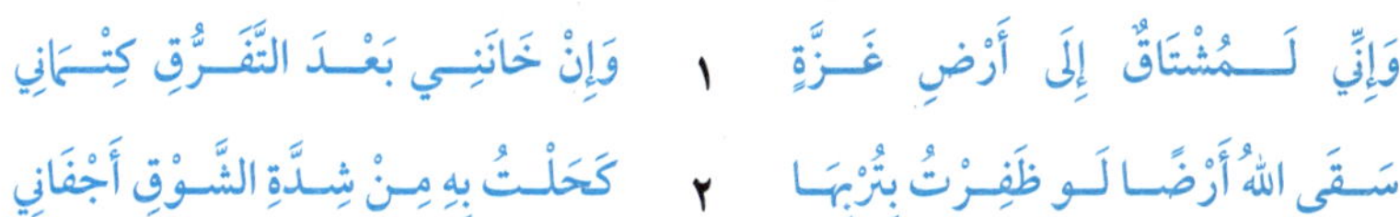

وَإِنِّي لَـمُشْتَاقٌ إِلَى أَرْضِ غَـزَّةٍ ١ وَإِنْ خَانَنِـي بَعْـدَ التَّفَـرُّقِ كِتْـمَانِي

سَـقَى اللهُ أَرْضًـا لَـو ظَفِـرْتُ بِتُرْبِـهَا ٢ كَحَلْـتُ بِهِ مِـنْ شِـدَّةِ الشَّـوْقِ أَجْفَانِي

1. I am yearning for the land of Gaza, [and although I tried to conceal my feelings] after separation [from the land,] my concealment has betrayed me.
2. May Allah water [that] land; if I could obtain its soil, I would apply it as kohl to my eyelids out of extreme yearning.

189

إيَّاكَ والمَنَّ

Beware of Reminding of Favors

Favors for others should be done solely with the intention of earning the pleasure of Allah ﷻ. One who reminds others of the favors he did for them is in danger of losing his reward, as the purpose behind those favors becomes wounding a person's honor or gaining something in return.

رَأَيْتُـكَ تَكْوِينِـي بِمِيسَـمِ مِنَّـةٍ ١ كَأَنَّـكَ كُنْـتَ الأَصْـلَ فِي يَـوم تَكْوِينِي

فَدَعْنِي مِنَ الْمَنِّ الوَخِيمِ فَلُقْمَةٌ ٢ مِنَ العَيْشِ تَكْفِينِي إِلَى يَوْمِ تَكْفِينِي

1. I have seen that you are [always] burning me with the brand of favors.[1] [You act] as if you were the root [cause of my existence] on the day of my creation.[2]

2. So spare me [your] hurtful reminders of favors upon me; a morsel of provision will suffice me in life until the day of my enshrouding.[3]

كُلُّكَ سَوءَاتٌ ولِلنَّاسِ أعْيُنٌ

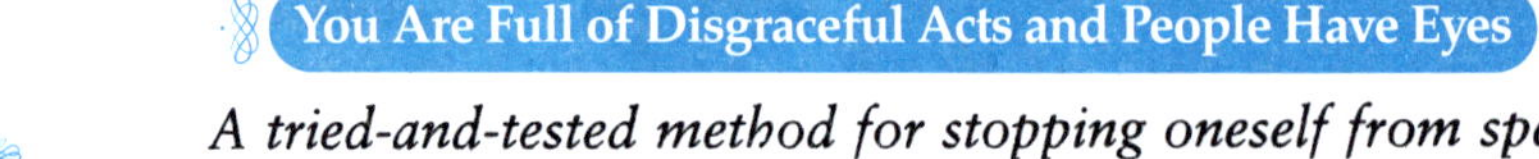

A tried-and-tested method for stopping oneself from speaking about the faults of others is to remind yourself that you, too, have faults and that people are always watching. The small and short pleasure gained in gossiping is not worth seeing one's deeds being given to another on the Day of Recompense.

إِذَا رُمْتَ أَنْ تَحْيَا سَلِيمًا مِنَ الرَّدَى ١ وَدِينُكَ مَوْفُورٌ وَعِرْضُكَ صَيِّنُ

فَلَا يَنْطِقَنْ مِنْكَ اللِّسَانُ بِسَوْأَةٍ ٢ فَكُلُّكَ سَوْءَاتٌ وَلِلنَّاسِ أَلْسُنُ

وَعَيْنُكَ إِنْ أَبْدَتْ إِلَيْكَ مَعَايِبًا ٣ فَدَعْهَا، وَقُلْ يَا عَيْنُ لِلنَّاسِ أَعْيُنُ

وَعَاشِرْ بِمَعْرُوفٍ، وَسَامِحْ مَنِ اعْتَدَى ٤ وَدَافِعْ وَلَكِنْ بِالَّتِي هِيَ أَحْسَنُ

1. If you aim to live a life free of ruination, your *Dīn* perfectly intact, and your dignity preserved,

2. Then your tongue should not speak about the disgraceful

---

1 Meaning that he keeps reminding of the favors that he has done.

2 Meaning that you mention your favors upon me excessively as if you did such a big favor as bringing me into existence.

3 Referring to the burial shroud.

act [of anyone], as you are [also] full[1] of disgraceful acts and people have tongues.

3. If your eye reveals the shortcomings [of others] to you, then disregard them and say, "O eye, people [also] have eyes," [by which they can observe your own shortcomings].

4. Live amicably [with people], tolerate whoever oversteps, and repel [evil] but do so with that which is best.

أفْضَلُ العُلُومِ
The Greatest Knowledge

Imam al-Shāfiʿī once said: "When I see someone of the people of Hadith, it is as if I am seeing a Companion of the Messenger of Allah. May Allah reward them; they have safeguarded for us the source and thus they have merit over us."

1. All knowledge besides the Qur'an, Hadith, and Fiqh[2] are [mere] occupations.

2. True knowledge is wherein there is "*Qāla Ḥaddathanā*."[3] Anything besides that is the whisperings of the devils.

---

1 Literally: "All of you"

2 Literally: "Understanding of *Dīn*"

3 This a phrase commonly used by scholars of Hadith to express the source of a statement being made. Using this, Imam al-Shāfiʿī refers to that knowledge which is passed on to us from the Prophet through a chain of narrators.

192

سُوءُ الظَّنِّ

Negative Expectations

In a society brimming with misdeeds and evil people, having negative expectations about people and their intentions is a means by which one stays safe from their harm. But this is based on one's environment; if one lives amongst the righteous, then the opposite approach is more commendable.

لَا يَكُنْ ظَنُّكَ إِلَّا سَيِّئًا ١ إِنَّ سُوءَ الظَّنِّ مِنْ أَقْوَى الفِطَنْ

مَا رَمَى الإِنسَانَ فِي مَخْمَصَةٍ ٢ غَيْرُ حُسْنِ الظَّنِّ وَالقَوْلُ الحَسَنْ

1. Let your expectations only be negative, for [having] negative expectations is [a sign] of great intelligence.
2. Only positive expectations and good words have landed man in starvation.

193

الصَّمْتُ خَيرٌ مِنْ حَشْوِ الكَلامِ

Silence is Better Than Futile Speech

Observing silence beautifies one's character, decreases the chances of falling into sin, and hopefully will make one's reckoning on the Last Day far easier.

لَا خَيْرَ فِي حَشْوِ الكَلا ١ مِ إِذَا اهْتَدَيْتَ إِلَى عُيونِهْ

وَالصَّمْتُ أَجْمَلُ بِالفَتَى ٢ مِنْ مَنْطِقٍ فِي غَيْرِ حِينِهْ

وَعَلَى الفَتَى بِطِبَاعِهِ ٣ سِمَةٌ تَلُوحُ عَلَى جَبِينِهْ

مَنْ ذَا الَّذِي يَخْفَى عَلَيْ ٤ كَ إِذَا نَظَرْتَ إِلَى قَرِينِهْ

1. There is no good in futile talk when you have become aware of its essence.
2. Silence is more beautiful for a young man than speech on an improper occasion.
3. A sign of a young man's character is apparent on his forehead.
4. Who [remains] hidden from you once you have seen his companion?

ن

194

جُنُونُ الجُنُونِ

Extreme Insanity

Some conditions are beyond one's control and it would be best to leave them in the hands of Allah ﷻ.

A man came to Imam al-Shāfiʿī ﵀ and spoke to him. Afterwards, the Imam said:

جُنُونُكَ مَجْنُونٌ وَلَسْتُ بِوَاجِدٍ ١ طَبِيبًا يُدَاوِي مِنْ جُنُونِ جُنُونِ

1. Your insanity[1] is insane, and I cannot find a doctor to cure extreme insanity.

[1] Possibly referring to ardent love for someone.

اِتَّقِ غَضَبَ الحَلِيمِ

Fear the Anger of the Forbearing One

Imam al-Shāfiʿī ﷺ relates: "I used to have a friend named Ḥuṣayn who was kind to me and would keep in touch with me. Later, he was made governor of al-Sībīn, so he shunned me and forgot about me. So, I wrote the following verses to him:"

خُذْهَا إِلَيْكَ فَإِنَّ وُدَّكَ طَالِقٌ	١	مِنِّي وَلَيْسَ طَلَاقُ ذَاتِ البَيْنِ
فَإِنِ ارْعَوَيْتَ فَإِنَّهَا تَطْلِيقَةٌ	٢	وَيَدُومُ وُدُّكَ لِي عَلَى ثِنْتَيْنِ
وَإِنِ الْتَوَيْتَ شَفَعْتُهَا بِمِثَالِهَا	٣	وَتَكُونُ تَطْلِيقَيْنِ فِي حَيْضَيْنِ
فَإِذَا الثَّلَاثُ أَتَتْكَ مِنِّي طَائِعًا	٤	لَمْ تُغْنِ عَنْكَ وِلَايَةُ السِّيبِينِ
لَمْ أَرْضَ أَنْ أَهْجُو حُصَيْنًا وَحْدَهُ	٥	حَتَّى أُسَوِّدَ وَجْهَ كُلِّ حُصَيْنِ

1. Take it and leave, as your love is divorced from me but not an irrevocable divorce.

2. If you repent, then it will be a single divorce, and your love for me will remain with two divorces [left].

3. And if you remain crooked, I will add [to the one divorce] another the like thereof, and there will have been two divorces in two monthly periods.

4. When the third [divorce] comes to you from me willingly, the governorship of al-Sībīn will not avail you in the slightest.

5. I will not be content with disparaging only one Ḥuṣayn until I blacken the face of every Ḥuṣayn.

أُهِينُ لَهُمْ نَفْسِي

I Humble My Lower-Self for Them

Once, Imam al-Shāfi'ī ﵀ was teaching in the masjid, whereupon the Sun began to shine directly on him. Some of his friends passed by and asked, "Are you sitting in the Sun, Abū Abdullāh?" So al-Shāfi'ī ﵀ recited:

أُهِـينُ لَهُـم نَفْـسِي وَأُكْرِمُهـا بِهِـمْ ١ وَلَا تُكْـرَمُ النَّفْـسُ الَّتِـي لَا تُهِينُهَـا

1. I humble my lower-self for them, and [as a result] honor it through them; the lower-self which you do not humble cannot be honored.

سَفِينَةُ المُؤْمِن

The Ship of a Believer

The true slaves of Allah ﷻ ponder over the worldly life and realize its true worth. They realize that the only thing that will avail them in the life to come is their righteous deeds.

إِنَّ لِلهِ عِبَـادًا فُطَنَـا ١ تَرَكُـوا الدُّنْيَـا وَخَافُـوا الفِتَنَـا

نَظَـرُوا فِيهَـا فَلَمَّا عَلِمُـوا ٢ أَنَّهَـا لَيْسَـتْ لِحَـيٍّ وَطَنَـا

جَعَلُوهَـا لُجَّـةً وَاتَّخَـذُوا ٣ صَالِـحَ الأَعْمَالِ فِيهَـا سُفُنَا

1. Allah has [certain] intelligent slaves; they have discarded the

worldly life and fear [its] temptations.

2. They contemplated it, and when they realized that it is not the [permanent] abode of the living,

3. They took it to be a sea and regarded righteous deeds as ships therein.

نَدَامَةُ الأعْرَابِي

Regret of a Bedouin

Once, a Bedouin sold his slave girl but then regretted doing so and asked to rescind the transaction before he left the place of the sale, but the other person refused. They both then went to Imam al-Shāfi‘ī to resolve their dispute. The bedouin explained the situation with the following verses:

بَـاعَ مِـنَ العُـسْرَةِ وَالدَّيـنِ ١ بِـاللهِ مَـا قَولُـكَ فِي بَايِـعٍ
عَـلَى جَمَـالِ الخُـرَّدِ العَـينِ ٢ غَزَالَـةً تَـاهَ بِهَـا حُسْـنُهَا
طَفَـا لَهَـا مِـنْ حـرَقِ البَـينِ ٣ وَكَانَ يَهْوَاهَـا فَلَـمَّا نَـأَتْ
يَـا أَعْلَـمَ الأُمَّـةِ بِالدِّيـنِ ٤ فَهَـلْ لَـه الرَّجْعَـةُ فِي بَيعِهَـا

1. By Allah, what do you say about a seller who sold due to poverty and debt,

2. A gazelle whose beauty made her arrogant towards large-eyed virgins?

3. He was [extremely] fond of her and when she became distant, the fire of separation manifested [in him] for her.

4. So, does he have the right to rescind her sale, O the most knowledgeable of the Ummah in the *Dīn*?

Imam al-Shāfiʿī ﵀ responded:

نَعَمْ لَهُ الرَّجْعَةُ فِي بَيْعِهَا ١ وَلَوْ بِقِنْطَارٍ مِنَ العَيْنِ

وَلَا تَعُدْ أُخْرَى إِلَى بَيْعِهَا ٢ وَلَوْ أَلَحَّ الفَقْرُ فِي الدَّيْنِ

1. Yes, he does have the right to rescind her sale even if it were for a kantar[1] of assets.

2. And do not return to selling her a second time, even if poverty forces [you to fall] into a debt.

199

العِلْمُ يَسْتَتْبِعُ الهُدَى

Knowledge Follows Guidance

Knowledge is not sought for knowledge's sake; it is learned for acting upon. Before attempting to change the hearts of others through knowledge, one must first change one's own self by acting upon that knowledge.

إِذَا لَمْ يَزِدْ عِلْمُ الفَتَى قَلْبَهُ هُدًى ١ وَسِيرَتَهُ عَدْلًا وَأَخْلَاقَهُ حُسْنَا

فَبَشِّرْهُ أَنَّ اللهَ أَوْلَاهُ نِقْمَةً ٢ يُسَاءُ بِهَا مِثْلُ الَّذِي عَبَدَ الوَثْنَا

1 An amount equivalent to about 100 pounds or 45 kilograms.

1. When the knowledge of a young man does not increase his heart in guidance nor his way of life in uprightness, nor his character in excellence,

2. Then give him the glad tidings that Allah will bring upon him punishment by which he will be tormented like those who worshipped idols.

200

مَرَارَةُ مِنَنِ الرِّجَالِ

The Bitterness of the Favors of Men

Resorting to ask another for a favor hurts one's pride, but to then be reminded of that favor, again and again, is like having the knife twisted in that wound.

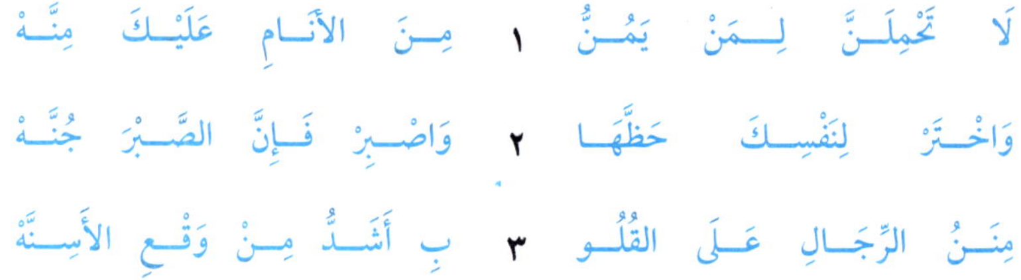

لَا تَحْمِلَنَّ لِمَنْ يَمُنُّ ١ مِنَ الأَنَامِ عَلَيْكَ مِنَّهْ

وَاخْتَرْ لِنَفْسِكَ حَظَّهَا ٢ وَاصْبِرْ فَإِنَّ الصَّبْرَ جُنَّهْ

مِنَنُ الرِّجَالِ عَلَى القُلُو ٣ بِ أَشَدُّ مِنْ وَقْعِ الأَسِنَّهْ

1. Those of the human race who [continuously] remind you of their favor upon you, never carry the burden of their favor.

2. Choose for your lower-self its [destined] share and bear patience, as patience is a shield.

3. [Being reminded of] the favors of men is more severe on the hearts than the blow of spears.

سَأَصْبِرُ لِلحِمَامِ

I Will Be Patient at the Time of Death

Whilst residing in Egypt, Imam al-Shāfiʿī ﷺ suffered from a severe fever. Some of his friends came to visit him. They touched his forehead and said to him that he was all well. Upon this, the Imam recited the following:

أَقُولُ لِعَائِدِيَّ وَشَجَّعُونِي ١ وَغَرَّهُمُ فُتُورُ حِمَى جَبِينِي

تَعَزَّوْا بِالتَّصَبُّرِ عَنْ أَخِيكُمْ ٢ فَضَجُّوا بِالْبُكَاءِ وَوَدَّعُونِي

فَلَمْ أَدَعِ الأَنِينَ لِقِلِّ سُقْمِي ٣ وَلَكِنِّي ضَعُفْتُ عَنِ الأَنِينِ

سَأَصْبِرُ لِلْحِمَامِ وَقَدْ أَتَانِي ٤ وَإِلَّا فَهْوَ آتٍ بَعْدَ حِينِ

وَإِنْ أَسْلَمْ يَمُتْ قَبْلِي حَبِيبٌ ٥ وَمَوْتُ أَحِبَّتِي قَبْلِي يَسُونِي

1. I say to my visitors [who were] encouraging me and [whom] the decreasing heat of my forehead had deceived,
2. "Console yourselves with patience for your brother." So, they [began an] uproar by crying and bid me farewell.
3. [The truth is that] I did not stop groaning because my illness decreased but rather because I am [too] weak to groan.
4. I will have patience upon death and [I feel that] it has drawn close to me, and if not, then it will come to me after some time.
5. If I am saved, then [it's possible that] my beloved will die before me and the death of my loved ones before me [would] pain me.

202

تَرْكُ الهُمُومِ

Discarding Worries

Having sleepless nights over things that are out of one's control goes against the status of a Mu'min, for a Mu'min sleeps sound knowing that all his affairs are in the hands of One who controls all.

سَهِرَتْ أَعْيُنٌ، وَنَامَتْ عُيُونُ ١ فِي أُمُورٍ تَكُونُ أَوْ لَا تَكُونُ

فَادْرَأِ الهَمَّ مَا اسْتَطَعْتَ عَنِ النَّفْـ ٢ ـسِ فَحُمْلَانُكَ الهُمُومَ جُنُونُ

إِنَّ رَبًّا كَفَاكَ بِالأَمْسِ مَا كَا ٣ نَ سَيَكْفِيكَ فِي غَدٍ مَا يَكُونُ

1. Eyes have stayed awake while [other] eyes have slept [whilst contemplating] over matters that may or may not occur.

2. Repel worry from yourself as much as you can, as your bearing of worries [is tantamount to] insanity.

3. The Lord was sufficient for you yesterday for what was, and He will be sufficient for you tomorrow for what is to be.

203

الرِّضَى بِمَا أَنْتَ فِيهِ

Contentment in Whatever Condition You May Be

A simple way by which one can remain content is to

imagine oneself in a condition worse than the present one. It is said that contentment is not a feeling but rather a decision one must make.

إِذَا شِـئْتَ أَنْ تَحْيَـا غَنِيًّـا فَلَاتَكُـنْ ١ عَـلَى حَالَـةٍ إِلَّا رَضِيـتَ بِدُونِهَـا

1. If you wish to live wealthy, then do not be in a conditi[on] except that you would be content with what is lower than it.

204

زِنْ بِمَا وُزِنْتَ بِه

Examine as You Were Examined

To live peacefully amongst people, one must treat different people differently. There are those worthy of honor and companionship and those not so. But even if you cannot find anyone, know that Allah ﷻ is always there to turn to.

زِنْ مَـنْ يَزِنْـكَ بِـمَا اتَّزَنْـ ١ ـتَ وَمَـا يَزِنْـكَ بِـهِ فَزِنْـهُ

مَـنْ جَـا إِلَيْـكَ فَـرُحْ إِلَيْـ ٢ ـهِ وَمَـنْ تَـأَنَّ فَصُـدَّ عَنْـهُ

مَـنْ ظَـنَّ أَنَّـكَ دُونَـهُ ٣ فَـاصْرِفْ هَـوَاهُ إِذًا وَهُنْـهُ

وَارْجِـعْ إِلَى مَلِـكِ الْمُلُـو ٤ كِ فَـكُلُّ مَـا يَأْتِيـكَ مِنْـهُ

1. Examine the one who examined you with [the standards by which] he examined you [and then treat him accordingly].

2. Whoever comes you to then go to him. Whoever stays away,

then avoid him.

3. Whoever thinks that you are beneath him, discard his affection [in your heart] and think little of him.

4. Turn to the King of kings, as everything that comes to you is from Him.

205

مِثْلَمَا تَدِينُ تُدَانُ

As You Sow, So Shall You Reap

Some oppressors are those who are recompensed in the worldly life. But if they do not face anything here, what is waiting for them in the next life is far worse than what their imaginations can fathom.

تَحَكَّمُوا فَاسْتَطَالُوا فِي تَحَكُّمِهِمْ ١ عَمَّا قَلِيلٍ كَأَنَّ الحُكْمَ لَمْ يَكُنِ

لَوْ أَنْصَفُوا أُنْصِفُوا لَكِنْ بَغَوْا فَبَغَى ٢ عَلَيْهِمُ الدَّهْرُ بِالأَحْزَانِ وَالمِحَنِ

فَأَصْبَحُوا وَلِسَانُ الحَالِ يُنْشِدُهُمْ ٣ هَذَا بِذَاكَ وَلَا عَتْبٌ عَلَى الزَّمَنِ

1. They ruled and became oppressive in their rule. Shortly, it was as if the rule did not [even] occur.

2. If they were just, they would have been treated with justice, but they transgressed, so the passage of time transgressed against them with sorrow and tribulations.

3. They became such that [their] condition was singing

to them: "As you reap, so shall you sow.[1] There is no blame on Time."

كُنُوزُكَ

Your Treasures

This worldly life is like a sandcastle. When a child is making a sandcastle, he is either mentally prepared for its eventual fate or will suddenly be hit with the wave of reality. It is thus the duty of the guardians to inform that child about the nature of the sea.

يَا مَنْ تَعَزَّزَ بِالدُّنْيَا وَزِينَتِهَا	١	الدَّهْرُ يَأْتِي عَلَى الْمَبْنِيِّ وَالْبَانِي
وَمَنْ يَكُنْ عِزُّهُ الدُّنْيَا وَزِينَتُهَا	٢	فَعِزُّهُ عَنْ قَلِيلٍ زَائِلٌ فَانِي
وَاعْلَمْ بِأَنَّ كُنُوزَ الْأَرْضِ مِنْ ذَهَبٍ	٣	فَاجْعَلْ كُنُوزَكَ مِنْ بِرٍّ وَإِيمَانِ

1. O the one priding himself over the worldly life and its adornments, Time will eradicate the building [as well as] the builder.

2. Whoever's pride is the world and its adornments, then [he should know that] his pride will shortly vanish and perish.

3. Know that the treasures of the Earth are of gold [and are fleeting], so make your treasures [for the Hereafter] with good deeds and faith.

---

[1] Literally: "This is for that."

إِحْيَاءُ القَنَاعَةِ

Reviving Contentment

It is a characteristic of the lower-self that when it reaches out for more, it forgets what it already has—this is known as greed. Although the ideal would be to kill this greed, it is near impossible. As such, fighting one's greed back is a lifelong struggle.

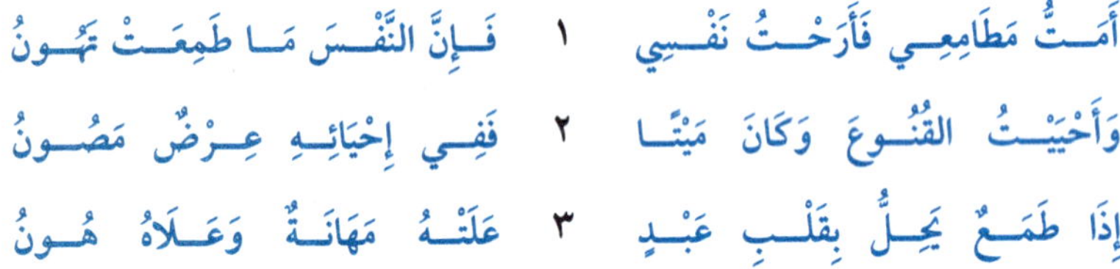
أَمَتُّ مَطَامِعِي فَأَرَحْتُ نَفْسِي ١ فَإِنَّ النَّفْسَ مَا طَمِعَتْ تَهُونُ
وَأَحْيَيْتُ القُنُوعَ وَكَانَ مَيْتًا ٢ فَفِي إِحْيَائِهِ عِرْضٌ مَصُونُ
إِذَا طَمَعٌ يَحِلُّ بِقَلْبِ عَبْدٍ ٣ عَلَتْهُ مَهَانَةٌ وَعَلَاهُ هُونُ

1. I put to death my greed, and thus I gave rest to my lower-self, because the lower-self as it covets, becomes wretched.

2. I have revived contentment that was dead [inside me] as, in doing so, honor is protected.

3. When greed befalls the heart of a slave, humiliation and disgrace overcome him [as well].

قافية الهاء
The End-Rhyme of the Letter *Hā'*

بَينَ السَّفِيهِ والفَقِيهِ
Between a Foolish Person and a Jurist

There are some who are ignorant and know they are ignorant and as a result, they refuse to acknowledge the status of the knowledgeable. Staying away from the evil of such people is the way of caution.

وَمَنْزِلَةُ السَّفِيهِ مِنَ الفَقِيهِ ١ كَمَنْزِلَةِ الفَقِيهِ مِنَ السَّفِيهِ

فَهَذَا زَاهِدٌ فِي قُرْبِ هَذَا ٢ وَهَذَا فِيهِ أَزْهَدُ مِنْهُ فِيهِ

إِذَا غَلَبَ الشَّقَاءُ عَلَى سَفِيهٍ ٣ تَنَطَّعَ فِي مُخَالَفَةِ الفَقِيهِ

1. The status of a foolish person in the eyes of a jurist is like the status of a jurist in the eyes of a foolish person.
2. One is abstinent in coming close to the other, and the other is more abstinent than him in the same.
3. When misfortune seizes a foolish person, he is overly stringent in opposing the jurist.

209

مَرَضُ الحَبِيبِ

Sickness of the Beloved

Even the sight of a beloved can do wonders for a sick person. That may be one of the reasons behind our Prophet's ﷺ great encouragement for the practice of visiting the sick.

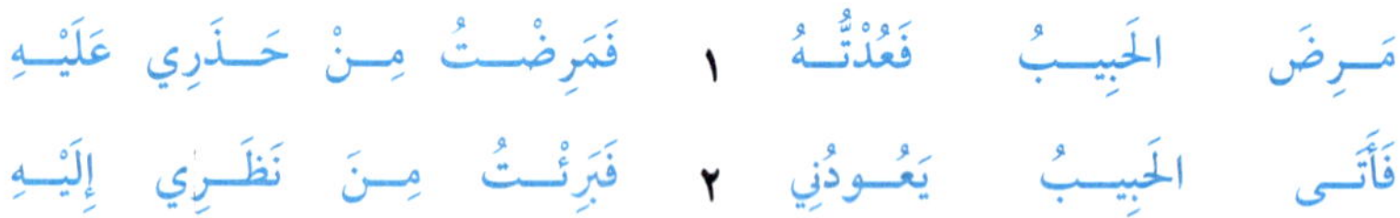

مَرِضَ الحَبِيبُ فَعُدْتُهُ ١ فَمَرِضْتُ مِنْ حَذَرِي عَلَيْهِ

فَأَتَى الحَبِيبُ يَعُودُنِي ٢ فَبَرِئْتُ مِنْ نَظَرِي إِلَيْهِ

1. The beloved was sick, so I visited him then I became sick due to my being wary of it.
2. Then the beloved came to visit me, and so I recovered by my gaze falling on him.

210

عِزَّةٌ وأَنَفَةٌ

Honor and Self-Esteem

When a person surrounds himself with foolish friends—although he himself may be honorable—other respectable people avoid him due to those around him. To gain more noble friends, one must first surround himself with the noble.

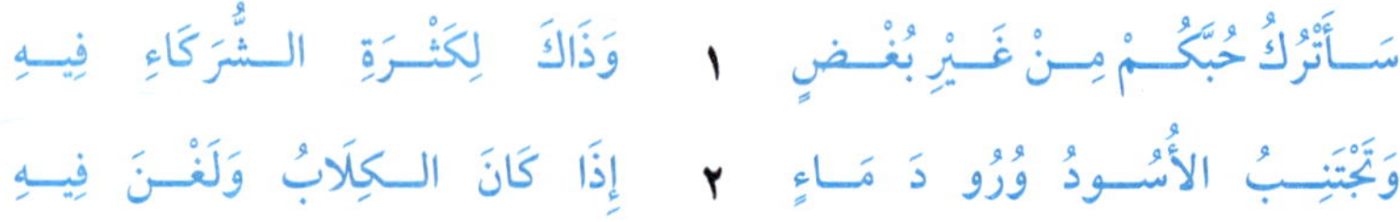

سَأَتْرُكُ حُبَّكُمْ مِنْ غَيْرِ بُغْضٍ ١ وَذَاكَ لِكَثْرَةِ الشُّرَكَاءِ فِيهِ

وَتَجْتَنِبُ الأُسُودُ وُرُودَ مَاءٍ ٢ إِذَا كَانَ الكِلَابُ وَلَغْنَ فِيهِ

إِذَا وَقَعَ الذُّبَابُ عَلَى طَعَامٍ ٣ سَأَتْرُكُهُ وَقَلْبِي يَشْتَهِيهِ
إِذَا شَرِبَ الأَسَدُ مِنْ خَلْفِ كَلْبٍ ٤ فَهَا ذَاكَ الأَسَدُ لَا خَيْرَ فِيهِ
وَيَرْتَجِعُ الكَرِيمُ خَمِيصَ بَطْنٍ ٥ وَلَا يَرْضَى مُسَاهَمَةَ السَّفِيهِ

1. I will stop loving you without any hate, and that is because of the many participants in it.[1]
2. Lions avoid coming to [a source of] water if dogs have sipp from it.
3. When a fly falls in food, I leave it even though my heart [badly] desires it.
4. If a lion drinks after a dog, then there is no good in such a lion.
5. An honorable person will return with an empty stomach but will not be pleased with the participation of the foolish.

211

مَسْأَلَةٌ فِقْهِيَّةٌ

A Legal Matter

Imam al-Shāfi‘ī ﷺ was given a paper in which it was written: “A man died and only left behind one man: the son of the paternal uncle of the son of the brother of the uncle of his father.” So the Imam responded:

صَارَ مَالُ المُتَوَفَّى كَامِلًا ١ بِاحْتِمَالِ القَوْلِ لَا مِرْيَةَ فِيهِ
لِلَّذِي خَبَّرْتَ عَنْهُ أَنَّهُ ٢ ابْنُ عَمٍّ ابْنِ أَخِي عَمِّ أَبِيهِ

[1] Meaning that the person being addressed has many people who love him.

1. All the wealth of the one who passed away—based on what your statement entails—no doubt in it,

2. Will be for the one you informed [me] as being the son of the paternal uncle of the son of the brother of the uncle of his father.[1]

الإعْرَاضُ عَنْ الجَاهِلِ

Avoiding the Ignorant

Noble and righteous people are those who, when the ignorant speak to them, turn away peacefully. The firebrand of the ignorant cannot burn if his fire cannot find fuel.

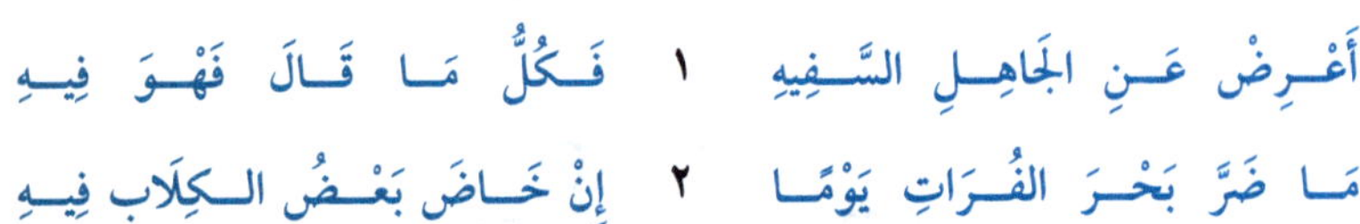

أَعْرِضْ عَنِ الْجَاهِلِ السَّفِيهِ ١ فَكُلُّ مَا قَالَ فَهْوَ فِيهِ

مَا ضَرَّ بَحْرَ الْفُرَاتِ يَوْمًا ٢ إِنْ خَاضَ بَعْضُ الْكِلَابِ فِيهِ

1. Avoid the ignorant, foolish person as everything he says, he himself is [guilty] of it.

2. The Euphrates River is not harmed [in the least] if one day some dogs dive in it.

[1] Referring to the deceased person's father. It seems that the questioner was trying to test the acumen of Imam al-Shāfiʿī ﵀

قافية الواو
The End-Rhyme of the Letter *Wāw*

مِنْ عَجِيبِ القَضَاءِ
A Strange Decree

Divine decree works in ways unfathomable by our weak minds. Although some situations and conditions may seem strange or even wrong to us, it is best that we have faith in the wisdom of Allah ﷻ *and not utter complaints for which we may be taken to task.*

أَرَى حُمُرًا تَرْعَى وَتُعْلَفُ مَا تَهْوَى ١ وَأُسْدًا جِيَاعًا تَظْمَأُ الدَّهْرَ لَا تُرْوَى
وَأَشْرَافَ قَوْمٍ لَا يَنَالُونَ قُوتَهُمْ ٢ وَقَوْمًا لِئَامًا تَأْكُلُ المَنَّ وَالسَّلْوَى
قَضَاءٌ لِدَيَّانِ الخَلَائِقِ سَابِقٍ ٣ وَلَيْسَ عَلَى مُرِّ القَضَا أَحَدٌ يَقْوَى
فَمَنْ عَرَفَ الدَّهْرَ الخَؤُونَ وَصَرْفَهُ ٤ تَصَبَّرَ لِلْبَلْوَى وَلَمْ يُظْهِرِ الشَّكْوَى

1. I see donkeys grazing and being fed what they desire, and [I see] lions hungry and thirsty, not being given [anything] to drink for a long time.

2. [And I see that] the respectable ones of a nation do not get their sustenance, and wicked people eat manna and quail.

3. [It is] a past decree of the Judge of creation, and none have power over the passing of the decree.

4. The one who is aware of Time ever-deceitful and its misfortunes has patience during tribulations and does not make complaints apparent.

214

كِتَابَةُ الدَّين

Writing Down a Debt

There is great wisdom behind the commands of Allah for mankind. One such command is to write out transactions as it safeguards wealth and maintains harmony in society.

أَنِلْنِي بِالَّذِي اسْتَقْرَضْتَ خَطًّا ١ وَأَشْهِدْ مَعْشَرًا قَدْ شَاهَدُوهُ

فَإِنَّ اللهَ خَلَّاقُ البَرَايَا ٢ عَنَتْ لِجَلَالِ هَيْبَتِهِ الوُجُوهُ

يَقُولُ: إِذَا تَدَايَنْتُمْ بِدَيْنٍ ٣ إِلَى أَجَلٍ مُسَمًّى فَاكْتُبُوهُ

1. Let me get what you asked for as a loan in written form and make a group witness it who have witnessed it before,

2. As Allah, the Creator of creation, [to whom] all faces will be humbled due to the splendor of His venerableness,

3. Says, "When you transact a debt payable at a specific time, put it in writing."[1]

---

[1] This is an adaptation (*iqtibās*) of a part of verse 282 of Sūrah Baqarah.

قافية الياء
The End-Rhyme of the Letter *Yā'*

الكِبْرُ على أهْلِ الكِبْرِ فَضِيلَةٌ
Arrogance Before the People of Arrogance is a Virtue

Respect and friendship are two actions that must be mutual. If the other person in a relationship does not reciprocate, then such a relationship is better not kept or pursued.

وَلَسْتُ بِمِهْيَابٍ لِمَنْ لَا يَهَابُنِي	١	وَلَسْتُ أَرَى لِلْمَرْءِ مَا لَمْ يَرَ لِيَا
فَإِنْ تَدْنُ مِنِّي تَدْنُ مِنْكَ مَوَدَّتِي	٢	وَإِنْ تَنْأَ عَنِّي تُلْفِنِي عَنْكَ نَائِيَا
كِلَانَا غَنِيٌّ عَنْ أَخِيهِ حَيَاتَهُ	٣	وَنَحْنُ إِذَا مِتْنَا أَشَدُّ تَغَانِيَا

1. I will not be respectful to the one who does not respect me, and I will not regard a man [as being honorable] so long as he does not regard me [as being honorable].

2. If you come close to me, my friendship will come close to you. And if you keep away from me, you will find me keeping far away from you.

3. We both have no need of each other for our whole lives, and when we have passed away, we will be all the more so free of needing the other.

216

الإسْلَامُ والعَافِيَةُ

Islam and Well-Being

The two greatest favors from Allah ﷻ are Islam and well-being, as the former ensures entry into Paradise, while the latter ensures the possibility of earning a greater reward within Paradise. Anything else is secondary to these two.

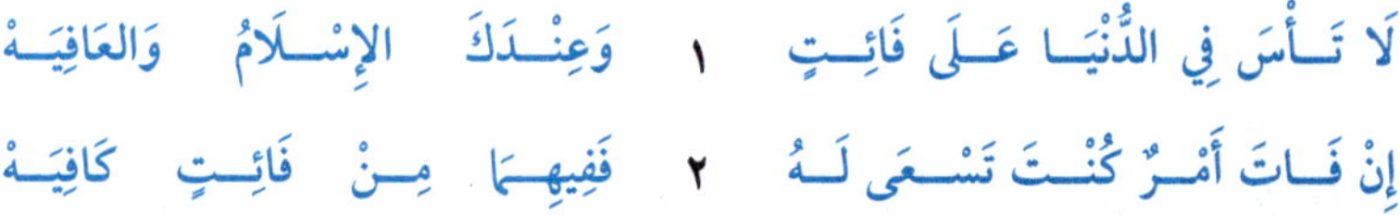

لَا تَـأْسَ فِي الدُّنْيَـا عَـلَى فَائِـتٍ ١ وَعِنْـدَكَ الإِسْـلَامُ وَالعَافِيَـهْ

إِنْ فَـاتَ أَمْـرٌ كُنْـتَ تَسْـعَى لَـهُ ٢ فَفِيهِمَـا مِـنْ فَائِـتٍ كَافِيَـهْ

1. Do not despair at the loss of anything in the worldly life while you possess Islam and well-being.

2. If a matter which you were striving for was lost, then both are sufficient in its place.

217

الجَوهَرُ لا المَظْهَرُ

Essence Not Appearance

It is all too common that people judge based on appearances despite the contrary being proved so often. This often happens with regard to scholars, as some of them look like any other ordinary person, but their hearts contain multitudes of knowledge.

يَـا نَاظِـرِي بِالكِسْـوَةِ البَالِيَـهْ ١ تَحْـتَ ثِيَـابِي هِمَـمٌ عَالِيَـهْ

وَإِنَّـمَا النَّـاسُ بِآدَابِهِـمْ ٢ وَالمَـالُ فِي كَفِّهِـمْ عَارِيَـهْ

1. O the one looking at my shabby clothes, under my clothing are lofty aspirations .[1]

2. People are [known through] their mannerisms, and wealth is [simply something] borrowed in their possession.

كَسَانِي رَبِّي

My Lord Clothed Me

When Allah ﷻ decrees something for us, then we are completely subservient to His decree, whether we are blessed with something sorely needed or bound in some difficult affliction.

كَسَـانِي رَبِّي إِذْ عَرِيـتُ عِمَامَـةً ١ جَدِيـدًا وَكَانَ اللهُ يَخْتَارُهَـا لِيَـا

وَقَيَّـدَنِي رَبِّي بِقَيْـدٍ مُدَاخَـلٍ ٢ فَأَعْيَـتْ يَمِينِـي حَلَّـهُ وَشِـمَالِيَا

1. My Lord covered me with a new turban when I was uncovered, and Allah had chosen such for me.

2. And my Lord shackled me with an entwined shackle which rendered my right and left hands unable to get free.

[1] To show emphasis, he indicates that he himself is lofty aspirations.

219

بطاقة شخصية

Identity Card

It often appears in books of Hadith regarding certain narrators that they were "Shia." In the first few centuries of Islam, this term was used to refer to one who had an intense love for the noble family of the Prophet ﷺ. Later, this term became synonymous with the term "Rāfiḍī," which refers to one who rejects, among other things, the companionship of Abū Bakr and ʿUmar. Thus, we should be careful when coming across this term in earlier sources.

أَنَــا الشِّــيعِيُّ فِي دِينِــي وَأَصْــلِي ١ بِمَكَّــةَ ثُــمَّ دَارِي عَسْــقَلِيَّهْ

1. My religion requires that I be a lover of the Ahl al-Bayt, and in Makkah was my birth, then [current] my abode is Asqalān[1].

220

حُبُّ عَلِيٍّ وسِبْطَيه وفَاطِمَة

Love For ʿAlī, His Two Sons, and Fāṭimah

As the Prophet ﷺ loved his family, we are to do the same. Loving them does not entail giving them a rank higher than all the rest of the Companions, as that would truly be Shiism.

إِذَا فِي مَجْلِـسٍ نَذْكُـرُ عَلِيًّـا ١ وَسِـبْطَيْهِ وَ فَاطِمَـةَ الزَّكِيَّـهْ

يُقَـالُ تَجَـاوَزُوا يَـا قَـوْمُ هَـذَا ٢ فَهَـذَا مِـنْ حَدِيـثِ الرَّافِضِيَّـهْ

بَرِئْـتُ إِلَى المُهَيْمِـنِ مِـنْ أُنَـاسٍ ٣ يَـرَوْنَ الرَّفْـضَ حُـبَّ الفَاطِمِيَّـهْ

[1] A city in Palestine.

1. When in a gathering, we mention ‘Alī, his two sons, and Fāṭimah the pure,

2. It is said, “O people, leave this, for this is the talk of the Shiites.”

3. I absolve myself to al-Muhaymin[1] from a people who consider love for the family of Fāṭimah to be Shiism.

221

العَافِيَةُ أوسَعُ لِي

Well-Being is Greater for Me

To acquire loftiness in society, one must face and overcome those who wish to stop one at all costs. But sometimes, the safety of obscurity may be a better option instead.

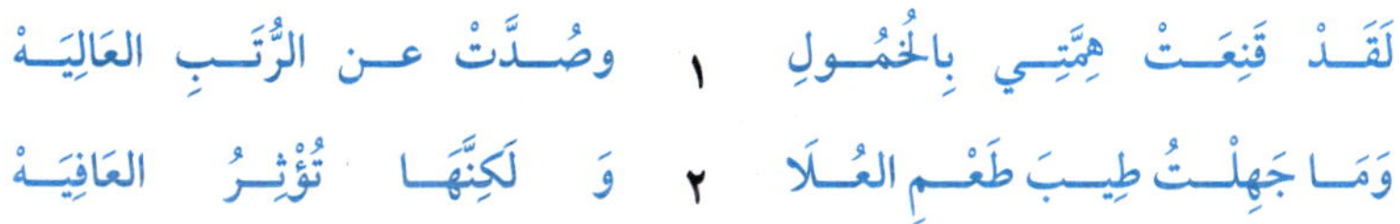

لَقَدْ قَنِعَتْ هِمَّتِي بِالْخُمُولِ ١ وصُدَّتْ عن الرُّتَبِ العَالِيَهْ

وَمَا جَهِلْتُ طِيبَ طَعْمِ العُلَا ٢ وَ لَكِنَّهَا تُؤْثِرُ العَافِيَهْ

1. My ambition has become content with obscurity and has been deterred from lofty ranks.

2. I am not ignorant of the pleasing flavor of loftiness, but [my ambition] prefers well-being.

[1] Name of Allah ﷻ meaning One who is ever watchful and ever protective.

Appendix One: Themes of the Poems

Theme	Poem No.
Abstaining from asking others	22, 42, 85, 95, 140, 156
Accepting apologies	67, 74
Advice	24, 43, 64, 83, 85, 93, 102, 112, 113, 118, 126, 134, 146, 157, 161, 176, 177, 190, 192, 204, 212, 216

Theme	Poem No.
Benefit of travelling	11, 17, 111, 123

Theme	Poem No.
Changing of time and/or conditions	21, 71, 75
Contentment	1, 22, 66, 68, 82, 103, 136, 186, 203, 208

Theme	Poem No.
Dealing with enemies	19, 88, 110, 124
Death	52,63,104,203
Desires	18,65

Theme	Poem No.
Friendship	6,28,56,59,62,89,92,99,119,174
Forgiving others	30, 36, 67
Fulfilling rights	20, 50, 128

Theme	Poem No.

Theme	Poem No.
Generosity	1, 29, 98, 101, 172, 184
Good character	14, 26, 30, 67, 109, 155, 217

Theme	Poem No.
Jealousy	47, 49, 108, 147

Theme	Poem No.
Knowledge	34, 45, 61, 77, 80, 94, 96, 127, 131, 139, 142, 150, 152, 162, 165, 169, 173, 180, 182, 186, 191, 199

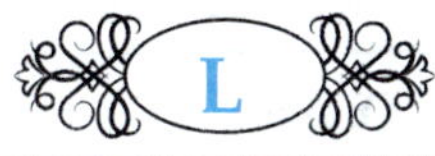

Theme	Poem No.
Light-hearted	23, 53, 72, 138, 143, 185, 194
Love	4, 16, 23, 49, 72, 119, 135, 175, 185, 195, 209
Love for the family of the Prophet ﷺ	32, 33, 100, 141, 220

Theme	Poem No.
Parting with loved ones	2, 5
Patience	2, 37, 73, 200
People's character	13, 27, 35, 122, 170, 208
Placing one's trust in Allah ﷻ	16, 37, 48, 129, 202
Praise for others	116, 149, 144

Theme	Poem No.
Q&A	44, 114, 185, 198

Theme
Poem No.
R

S

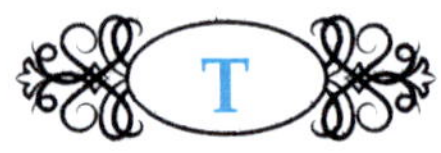
T

W

Appendix Two: Scales of the Poems

ء

١	القَضَاءُ	الوافر
٢	أَحِبَّائِهِ	السريع
٣	الدُّعَاءُ	الوافر
٤	البَلَاءِ	الخفيف
٥	أُوِدَّائِهْ	السريع

٦	مُسَابِبُهُ	الطويل
٧	غَرِيبِ	الطويل
٨	الكَوَاكِبُ	الخفيف
٩	بِالذَّنْبِ	البسيط
١٠	لَبِيبُ	الطويل
١١	غَرِيبَا	الطويل
١٢	رَقِيبُ	الطويل
١٣	كِلَابَا	الوافر
١٤	وَيَخْطُبُ	الطويل
١٥	أَدَبُ	البسيط
١٦	حُبُّ	الخفيف
١٧	واغْتَرِبِ	البسيط
١٨	وَالصَّوَابُ	المتقارب
١٩	جَوَابُ	الخفيف
٢٠	تنوبُ	الطويل
٢١	الكِلَابُ	الوافر
٢٢	إِهَابِهِ	الطويل
٢٣	تُحِبُّهُ	مجزوء الكامل
٢٤	شِهَابُهَا	الطويل
٢٥	يُعَابُ	الوافر

٢٦	وَهَبَّاتُ	البسيط
٢٧	بَيْتَا	الوافر
٢٨	عَثَرَاتِي	الطويل
٢٩	المُرُوءَاتِ	البسيط
٣٠	العَدَاوَاتِ	البسيط
٣١	سُكُوتَا	الوافر
٣٢	يَفُوتُ	الوافر
٣٣	وَسِيلَتِي	مجزوء الكامل
٣٤	نَفَرَاتِهِ	الطويل
٣٥	خَسَارَتُهُمْ	مجزوء الوافر
٣٦	مِلَّتِهِ	الكامل

٣٧	نَجَا	المنسرح
٣٨	وَمَعَاجُهُ	الكامل
٣٩	المَخْرَجُ	الكامل

٤٠	اللَّوْحِ	السريع
٤١	مِفْتَاحُ	البسيط
٤٢	المَالِحَهْ	السريع

٤٣	أَنْصَحُ	الطويل
٤٤	جُنَاحُ	الطويل

د

٤٥	الرَّشَادِ	مخلَّع البسيط
٤٦	وَعِيدَا	الكامل
٤٧	عَدَدَا	البسيط
٤٨	سَعِيدُ	الوافر
٤٩	حَسَدِ	البسيط
٥٠	عَمْدِ	الطويل
٥١	أَرَادَا	الوافر
٥٢	البَلَدِ	البسيط
٥٣	عَمْدِ	الطويل
٥٤	الجَاحِدُ	المتقارب
٥٥	كَالأَعْيَادِ	الكامل
٥٦	الشَّدَائِدِ	الطويل
٥٧	لَبِيدِ	الوافر
٥٨	اعتقَادِي	مخلع البسيط
٥٩	يَدِي	البسيط
٦٠	تَحِيدُ	الطويل

ر

٦١	الفَقْرِ	الطويل
٦٢	وَظُهُورُ	الطويل
٦٣	بَعِيرُ	الوافر
٦٤	وَالأَوَاخِرْ	الوافر
٦٥	ضَرِيرُ	الكامل
٦٦	تِبْرَا	الخفيف
٦٧	مُقِرِّ	الوافر
٦٨	الدَّهْرُ	الطويل
٦٩	أَكْثَرَا	الطويل
٧٠	الجَارِي	البسيط
٧١	قِصَارُ	الطويل
٧٢	لِلْبَصَرِ	البسيط
٧٣	العُسْرِ	الطويل
٧٤	عَارُ	الخفيف
٧٥	أَسْحَارَا	البسيط
٧٦	أُعَاشِرُه	الطويل
٧٧	أَسِيرَا	الوافر
٧٨	سَفَّارَا	البسيط
٧٩	بِخَاسِرِ	الطويل
٨٠	السُّدُورْ	مجزوء الكامل
٨١	وَالقَفْرِ	الطويل
٨٢	ذُخْرَا	الطويل
٨٣	فَجَرَا	البسيط
٨٤	الحَذَرُ	البسيط
٨٥	البَعِيرِ	الخفيف
٨٦	ذِكْرِي	الطويل
٨٧	كَدَرُ	البسيط
٨٨	دَهْرِي	الوافر
٨٩	دَيْرِهِ	الكامل

س

٩٠	يُغْرَسِ	الكامل
٩١	وَالغَلَسِ	البسيط
٩٢	القِيَاسِ	الوافر

٩٣	بِالنَّفَسِ	البسيط
٩٤	المَغْرَسِ	الكامل
٩٥	أَمْسِ	مخلع البسيط

ص

٩٦	المَعَاصِي	الوافر
٩٧	وَأَخْلَصُ	الطويل

ض

٩٨	والقَبْضَا	الطويل
٩٩	عِرْضَا	الخفيف
١٠٠	وَالنَّاهِضِ	الكامل

ع

١٠١	وَأَشْفَعَا	الكامل
١٠٢	نَفَعْ	منهوك الرجز
١٠٣	طَمِعْ	مجزوء الكامل
١٠٤	تَجْزَعُ	الطويل
١٠٥	سُنْعَا	الخفيف
١٠٦	شَفاعَهْ	الوافر
١٠٧	وُقُوعِ	الطويل
١٠٨	أَسْمَعُ	الطويل
١٠٩	وَرَعُهْ	المنسرح
١١٠	يُصَدَّعُ	الطويل
١١١	جَائِعُ	السريع
١١٢	الجَمَاعَهْ	الوافر
١١٣	نَافِعُهْ	الطويل
١١٤	يَصْنَعُ	الطويل

ف

١١٥	حُتُوفُ	الكامل
١١٦	حَنِيفَهْ	الوافر
١١٧	ضَعِيفُ	الكامل
١١٨	خِرَافِ	الكامل
١١٩	التَّأَسُّفَا	الطويل

ق

١٢٠	وَالوَرَقَا	البسيط
١٢١	أَحْمَقُ	الطويل
١٢٢	رَمَقُوا	البسيط
١٢٣	حُرَقِ	البسيط
١٢٤	وِفَاقُ	الكامل
١٢٥	مُوثَقِ	الكامل
١٢٦	الشَّفِيقِ	الوافر
١٢٧	الوَاثِقَهْ	الكامل
١٢٨	الحَقِّ	السريع
١٢٩	رَازِقِي	الطويل
١٣٠	بِمَرْزُوقِ	البسيط
١٣١	صُنْدُوقِ	البسيط
١٣٢	عُقُوقَا	الخفيف
١٣٣	تَخَلُّقِ	الكامل

ك

١٣٤	أَمْرِكْ	مجزوء الكامل
١٣٥	غَيْرَكْ	مجزوء الكامل
١٣٦	مُتَنَسِّكْ	المتقارب
١٣٧	مُتَنَسِّكُ	الطويل

١٣٨	المُبَارَكُ	الطويل

ل

١٣٩	قَابِلِ	الوافر
١٤٠	وَبِيلَا	المتقارب
١٤١	أَنْزَلَهُ	البسيط
١٤٢	جَاهِلُ	البسيط
١٤٣	حَالُ	الكامل
١٤٤	مَنْزِلَهْ	الكامل
١٤٥	يَتَفَضَّلُ	الطويل
١٤٦	جَمِيلُ	الطويل
١٤٧	مَنَالُهَا	الطويل
١٤٨	يَفْعَلِ	الكامل
١٤٩	مِثْلَهُ	مجزوء الرجز
١٥٠	عَقْلِي	مجزوء الرمل
١٥١	مَالِي	الوافر
١٥٢	الأَهْلِ	السريع
١٥٣	الرُّسُلُ	البسيط
١٥٤	طَوَالُهَا	الكامل
١٥٥	أَشَاكِلُهُ	الطويل
١٥٦	ظِلُّ	البسيط
١٥٧	اللَّيَالِي	الوافر
١٥٨	وَمَقَالِهِ	الكامل
١٥٩	الجَهْلِ	الطويل

م

١٦٠	دَمَا	الطويل
١٦١	بِمُسْلِمِ	الكامل
١٦٢	لِئَامُ	الوافر
١٦٣	أَحْلَامِ	البسيط
١٦٤	السَّقَامِ	الوافر
١٦٥	الغَنَمْ	الطويل
١٦٦	وَنَوْمُ	مخلّع البسيط
١٦٧	تَعْلِيمِي	الكامل
١٦٨	فَتَنْدَمَا	الطويل
١٦٩	خَدَمَهْ	الوافر
١٧٠	مُكَرَّمِ	الكامل
١٧١	عِلْمَا	الطويل
١٧٢	يَتَأَلَّمُ	الطويل
١٧٣	عِلْمِي	الطويل
١٧٤	الحَمَامُ	الوافر
١٧٥	لَازِمَهْ	السريع

ن

١٧٦	سُكُونُ	الوافر
١٧٧	ثُعْبَانُ	الكامل
١٧٨	سِوَانَا	الوافر
١٧٩	لِلْمَوَازِينِ	البسيط
١٨٠	سَنَهْ	الرمل
١٨١	لَمْ يَكُنْ	المتقارب
١٨٢	حَلِيمَانِ	البسيط
١٨٣	الدِّينِ	البسيط
١٨٤	بَينِي	البسيط
١٨٥	تِسْعِينَ	البسيط
١٨٦	بِبَيَانِ	الطويل
١٨٧	الهَوَانِ	مخلّع البسيط

١٨٨	كِتْمَانِي	الطويل
١٨٩	تَكْوِينِي	الطويل
١٩٠	صَيِّنُ	الطويل
١٩١	الدِّينِ	البسيط
١٩٢	الفِطَنْ	الرمل
١٩٣	عُيونِهْ	مجزوء الكامل
١٩٤	جُنُونِ	الطويل
١٩٥	البَيْنِ	الكامل
١٩٦	عُيونِهْ	مجزوء الكامل
١٩٧	الفِتَنَا	الرمل
١٩٨	العَيْنِ	السريع
١٩٩	حُسْنَا	الطويل
٢٠٠	مِنَّهْ	مجزوء الكامل
٢٠١	جَبِينِي	الوافر
٢٠٢	لَا تَكُونُ	الخفيف
٢٠٣	بِدُونِهَا	الطويل
٢٠٤	فَزِنْهُ	مجزوء الكامل
٢٠٥	لَمْ يَكُنِ	البسيط
٢٠٦	وَالبَانِي	البسيط
٢٠٧	تَهُونُ	الوافر

ه

٢٠٨	السَّفِيهِ	الوافر
٢٠٩	عَلَيْهِ	مجزوءالكامل
٢١٠	فِيهِ	الوفر
٢١١	فِيهِ	الرمل
٢١٢	فِيهِ	مخلع البسيط

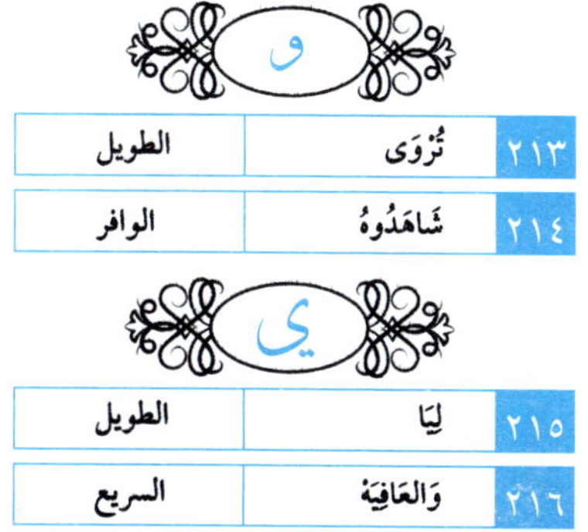

و

٢١٣	تُرْوَى	الطويل
٢١٤	شَاهَدُوهُ	الوافر

ي

٢١٥	لِيَا	الطويل
٢١٦	وَالعَافِيَةْ	السريع
٢١٧	عَالِيَةْ	المتقارب
٢١٨	لِيَا	الطويل
٢١٩	عَسْقَلِيَّهْ	الوافر
٢٢٠	الزَّكِيَّهْ	الوافر
٢٢١	العَالِيَةْ	المتقراب

النادي العربي